International Trade and British Economic Growth

THE NATURE OF INDUSTRIALIZATION

Series editors: *Peter Mathias and John A. Davis*

This is the final volume in the series that is based on the programme of graduate seminars in economic history sponsored by the *Istituto Italiano per gli Studi Filosofici* and held annually between 1986 and 1991 at the Centre for Social History in the University of Warwick

The Nature of Industrialization

Edited by Peter Mathias and John A. Davis

Volume 5

International Trade and British Economic Growth
from the Eighteenth Century to the Present Day

BLACKWELL
Oxford UK & Cambridge USA

Copyright © Blackwell Publishers Ltd 1996
First published 1996
2 4 6 8 10 9 7 5 3 1

Blackwell Publishers Ltd
108 Cowley Road
Oxford OX4 1JF
UK

Blackwell Publishers Inc.
238 Main Street
Cambridge, Massachusetts 02142
USA

British Library Cataloguing in Publication Data
A CIP catalogue record for this book is available from the British Library.

Library of Congress Cataloging in Publication Data

International trade and British economic growth: from the eighteenth century to
  the present day / edited by Peter Mathias and John A. Davis.
    p. cm. – (The nature of industrialization: v. 5)
  Papers originally presented at a seminar.
  Includes bibliographical references and index.
  ISBN 0-631-18116-4
  1. Great Britain – Commerce – History – 18th century. 2. Great Britain –
Colonies – Commerce – History. [1. Great Britain – Commerce – History –
19th century.] I. Mathias, Peter. II. Davis, John Anthony. III. Series.
  HF1533. I655 1996
  382'.0941'009–dc20
                                                                    96-11698
                                                                        CIP

ISBN 0-631-18116-4

Typeset in 10 on 12 pt Garamond
by Pure Tech India Ltd., Pondicherry, India.

Contents

Preface

This volume is based on revised and expanded versions of papers that were first given at the fourth economic history summer school held at the Centre for Social History in the University of Warwick between 1986 and 1991. Those seminars and the publication of this volume have been generously supported by the *Istituto Italiano per gli Studi Filosofici* of Naples, and the editors wish to take this opportunity to express their thanks once again to the President of the Institute, Avvocato Gerado Marotta, its indefatigable General Secretary, Antonio Gargano, and to Professor Luigi De Rosa.

Introduction

Previous volumes in this series on the nature of industrialization have been organized around comparative and thematic topics that have included the nature of the first industrial revolutions, the respective roles of technology, enterprise and labour, and agriculture in modern economic growth. Their aim has been to examine each of these issues and relationships in comparative perspective, and in particular to show how, over the last two decades, economic historians have been moving away from interpretations of industrialization based on the premise that Britain's first industrial revolution provided the model of modern economic growth that all industrializing economies in the nineteenth and twentieth centuries had, in one form or another, to learn to emulate. The shift towards a more pluralistic understanding of the variety of different forms in which modern economic growth has occurred has provided important new opportunities for demonstrating how modern economies have been shaped and determined, not only by their specific mixes of resource endowments, but also by the historical specificities of time and place. It is those contextual specificities that differentiate the craft of the economic historian from that of the economists, and which frequently falsify – and have falsified – the forecasts of economic theory and the intent of public policies derived from those theories.

At a moment when the British path to industrialization has been described as 'the most atypical of all' or even as a myth,[1] it is clear that there is little

---

[1] *See* (in this series) Peter Mathias, 'The Industrial Revolution: Concept and Reality' in *The First Industrial Revolutions* (Oxford, 1989) and Patrick K. O'Brien, 'Modern conceptions of the Industrial Revolution' in P. K. O'Brien and R. Quinault (eds), *The Industrial Revolution and British Society* (Cambridge, 1993) pp. 1–30.

consensus any more on what a 'standard model' of modern economic growth might (never mind should) look like. This means, too, that the focus of comparative economic history has shifted from comparing different paths (since the criteria for comparison have been called into question) to examining forms and processes of interaction within and across different sectors at the level of national economies and between different national economies.

Foreign trade offers obvious and important opportunities for exploring the historical development of these interactions and exchanges within single economies and at an international level. From the time of the classical economists, trade has been described as the great engine of modern economic growth. Yet such a view had its critics from equally early. It was Adam Smith who famously dismissed Britain's Atlantic colonial trade in the eighteenth century as 'mere loss not profit' on the grounds that earnings in trading activities were more than offset by the naval and administrative costs required to protect that trade. Smith's assertion also anticipated how the debates on the gains from trade would criss-cross with those on the profits (or losses) from Empire. Others looked to mercantilist principles to argue that unregulated bilateral trade posed dangers rather than benefits, and many Europeans after 1815 agreed with the German economist, Friedrich List, that unrestricted trade with Britain would inhibit the development of their own industries and reduce the European continent to the status of colonial India.

Thereafter the debate never really let up, making it one of the longest-running issues in economic theory and economic history. After the relatively brief experiments in free trade in the mid-decades of the nineteenth century, the return to tariff protection in continental Europe and the United States in the last quarter of the century brought rival interpretations of the role of foreign trade in domestic economic growth into collision, and the debates have continued more-or-less without interruption down to the present.

In their simplest forms, these debates confront two distinct and generally contrasting models of economic growth: those who favour demand-led interpretations being likely to identify the expansion of trade as a critical 'engine of growth; whereas the protagonists of alternative supply-side models are more likely to argue that 'trade was the child of industry'.[2] The champions of the supply-side model have, in many respects, a strong case. When they call on their opponents to demonstrate first the profitability of

---

[2] For this phrase and a wider discussion of the debates on the role of foreign trade in British industrialization *see:* R. P. Thomas and D. N. McCloskey, 'Overseas Trade and Empire 1700–1860' in R. Floud and Donald McCloskey (eds), *The Economic History of Britain since 1700*, vol. 1, 1700–1860 (1981), p. 102.

foreign trade and secondly the ways in which profits were transferred into domestic capital formation and industrial investment, their demands have proved hard to answer. They have also drawn attention to the critical importance of the changing terms and circumstances in which foreign trade is conducted and to the array of other variables that may affect its profitability. The list of variables is long and, as well as the terms of trade, would most obviously include earnings on foreign investment, shipping, services, insurance, current transactions and other invisibles. On the other hand, demand-side, market-driven gains can come from widening markets, incremental output and economies of scale that bring inducements to innovation, lower costs and so forth.

These variables, however, also indicate that the contrast between demand and supply-side models may be too simple. Many of the essays that follow propose instead models that allow for greater degrees of reciprocity, not least because multilateral or bilateral trading relationships may have had quite different impacts (positive, negative or neutral) on different sectors of the domestic economy. Indeed, one of the weaknesses inherent in the supply-demand dichotomy is a tendency to treat foreign trade as if it were a discrete sector and the metropolitan economy (in its public and in its private forms) as a similarly undifferentiated aggregate. These essays also suggest that, for a better (and hence in most cases quantifiable) understanding of that broader relationship, there is much to be gained by disaggregating foreign trade and the domestic economy into their component parts and specific interrelationships. The integral relationships between foreign trade and the domestic economy are the key to exploring these linkages. For example: home demand encourages imports; imports provide foreign exchange and sterling credits that are potentially advantageous for boosting export demand (and, in the circumstances of the nineteenth century, for increasing liquidity in the international economy).

This also true of the relationship between public policy and foreign trade, another of the central themes of this volume. This can be explored in terms of the effectiveness of specific measures designed to stimulate economic growth through public policy (free trade, protectionism, bilateral trade agreements, systems of exchange rates), but also leads on to a broader consideration of political and institutional contexts of trade. The relationships between trade and colonialism have long been central concerns in the massive bibliography on the economics of imperialism but the tendency, in recent literature on the political economy of imperialism, to draw more careful distinctions between trade and the provision of services, capital investments, financial and credit facilities, and between public policy and private initiative (in the field of investment and services as well as trade) is of much wider significance for the study of the changing role of foreign trade and its linkages with other sectors of the metropolitan economy in quite different institutional and political contexts.

The seven essays in this volume explore the relationship between foreign trade and domestic economic growth in a variety of different perspectives and in different periods. Unlike earlier volumes in this series, all but one focus primarily on the performance of British exports in relation to the development of the British economy over the period from the eighteenth century to the present. Whatever doubts there might be about the universality of Britain's industrial revolution as a paradigm of modern economic growth, there can be no question of Britain's commercial and industrial primacy from the beginning of the nineteenth century. Even if economic historians trace the seeds of Britain's subsequent economic decline back to the last decades of the nineteenth century, this would become visible only very much later – in many respects, not until after World War II.[3] Britain's commercial pre-eminence lasted long after others had outstripped it in terms of industrial productivity and, indeed, despite a steady decline in its (relative) export competitiveness. This means that, for the greater part of the period under consideration, the development of Britain's foreign trade is the key to understanding the changing structures of world trade more generally.

Partly for the same reason, the British case also offers unrivalled opportunities for exploring in broader terms the relationship between foreign trade and domestic growth in a great variety of contrasting situations. In the first half of the period, down to some point in the 1880s, the spectacular rise of British industry seemed to go hand in hand with the no less spectacular expansion of British trade and exports. It would be impossible to argue that there was no connection between the two: but what was the nature of the connection? Was foreign trade the principal engine of growth? Or was trade the child of industry? In the period that followed, the same relationship is posed in inverted form: was the gradual decline in Britain's share in world trade a symptom or a cause of the faltering of momentum in her industrial economy that, for over a century, has resulted in 'uncompetitive exports and the low productivity of industrial labour and capital'?[4]

As well as these two central questions, the British experience in this period also enables us to examine the relationship between external trade and domestic economic growth in a variety of contrasting situations. Starting with foreign trade in the context of *ancien régime* mercantilist regulations, these move sequentially through: the mid-Victorian era of widening industrializa-

---

[3] For an important critique of the idea and chronology of Britain's 'economic decline' *see* P. J. Cain and A. G. Hopkins *British Imperialism: Crisis and Deconstruction 1914–1990* (Longman, 1993), pp. 297–315.

[4] *See* the conclusion to B. R. Tomlinson's essay in this volume: p. 161–3.

tion and more liberal multilateral trade relationships; the nineteenth- and early twentieth-century era of a maturing international economy characterized by the return of protectionism and regulated multilateral and bilateral trade relationships, by systems of formal and informal empire, of fixed and floating exchange rates, and also by the rapid expansion of private business in the fields of international and multinational trade, services and investment; and finally the post-World War II world. To examine the broader relationships between foreign trade and economic growth in the context of Britain's foreign trade in this period is not, therefore, an insular choice.

Kenneth Morgan's opening essay takes us straight to the heart of the oldest of the debates on the role of foreign trade in British economic growth: the role of the eighteenth-century Atlantic colonial trade in financing industrialization. Working from a detailed critique of the classical thesis, advanced most famously by Eric Williams, that Britain's industrial revolution was financed by the slave trade, Morgan shows that there is no evidence that profits from the prosperous but highly risky colonial trade were transferred into industrial investment. Slavery and the slave trade were structural aspects of the dynamics of expansion of the Atlantic economy. Profits from slaves and sugar were conspicuous, but were more likely to be devoted to conspicuous consumption than to industrial enterprise (as Richard Pares puts it, colonial trade produced 'more Fonthills than factories'). Although Morgan discounts the idea that colonial trade contributed to industrial development through capital formation, he acknowledges that the structure and scale of this trade as the century advanced created important new market opportunities for British goods and manufactures (especially for textiles), established the prosperity of Britain's west-country outports (Bristol, Liverpool and Glasgow), increased the taste and the capacity for consumption in the home market and contributed to the rise of a wide range of business institutions and practices (improved systems of settling international payments, insurance, banking, shipping and the organization of merchant firms and operations) that played an indirect but nonetheless important part in British economic growth and commercial competitiveness.

Morgan's emphasis on the complex and often reciprocal relationship between foreign trade, industrialization and economic growth in eighteenth-century Britain is developed in Sidney Pollard's discussion of the impact of British trade on the continental European economies down to the mid-nineteenth century. Firmly adopting the supply-side thesis that Britain's commercial pre-eminence in Europe after 1815 was a direct consequence of Britain's precocious industrialization and capacity for producing cheap manufactured goods, new technologies and capital goods, Pollard argues that the rapid growth of British exports to Europe and the rising demand in Britain for European imports (grain and timber in particular) functioned 'as a trigger, releasing an expanding mass of energy over ever-widening circles in Europe' that accelerated industrialization in other European countries. For this second phase, therefore, Pollard emphasizes the reciprocal, complementary and self-supporting nature of the relationships between trade and industrialization. But he also emphasizes the fundamental importance of context and timing. Although there were some casualties (for example, the Languedoc woollen and the Silesian linen industries) Britain's apparent stronghold over the export of manufactured and industrial goods at the beginning of the century did not have the effect of impeding industrialization in its trade partners as many contemporaries feared. The reason that these fears proved groundless, Pollard argues, lay above all in 'the sequence of industrialization'. Resources and natural endowments were, in reality, remarkably similar over much of Europe but what shaped the process of industrialization was the 'product cycle'. Britain's relatively narrow range of manufactured exports (cheap mass-produced products, most typically cotton yarn) encouraged other economies to specialize in different areas, while Britain was at the same time the source for capital goods and technologies needed for industrial development. Britain's own growing appetite for imports provided its European trade partners with the means to balance their accounts and enter into an increasingly complex web of international exchanges, currency flows and credit transfers.

Pollard's essay effectively highlights how the relationship between foreign trade and domestic growth has to be set within the historical contexts, not only of place and time, but also of the 'sequence of industrialization'. This also leads in to the discussion of the role of foreign trade in the decline of Britain's manufacturing economy because he shows that, on European markets at least, Britain's early lead had in many areas been eroded by the mid-nineteenth century; why did that decline not happen – or at least become visible – at an earlier date? One reason was that British merchants and manufacturers were able to operate on an unparalleled range of old and new markets that were rapidly spreading to embrace the entire globe. One factor that made this possible – or that came into being in response to the geographical dispersion of Britain's markets – was the presence of a merchant navy that was not only the largest but also the most efficient and least costly in the world.

Peter Davies's essay on shipping and Britain's ocean trade in the nineteenth century documents how the greater efficiency and lower cost of British shipping contributed to the competitiveness of British trade in that century. But these advantages were not chance assets. They were linked historically, obviously, to that trading vocation and presence in the Atlantic discussed in Morgan's essay, but they were enhanced in the course of the nineteenth century by a series of technological, organizational and institutional innovations that constantly increased the competitiveness of the British mercantile marine. As the size and cost of ships grew, the British shipping industry succeeded better than any competitors in raising investment and achieving greater efficiency and lower costs so that, even when the volume of British exports declined, the tonnage of cargoes and the number of passengers carried on British vessels continued to increase. Between 1850 and 1910 the total merchant fleet of the world rose from 9 million net tons to 34 million net tons, of which 33 per cent was still British owned in 1910 (and 40 per cent of steam tonnage).

Cheap transport costs for goods and passengers gave British merchants great advantage but, as Davies points out, these opportunities had to be seized. To do that depended on a complex array of factors, in which Britain's ability to keep providing the right mix of export goods was only one. The ability of trading partners to pay for British imports was dependent on their own levels of economic development and on the willingness of industrial nations to offer credit. The complex mix of factors that gave British exports their competitiveness in a wide variety of different world markets down to the 1890s was, Davies concludes, providing the incentive for the development of a highly efficient and effective merchant marine. Through the 'shipping conferences' Britain was able to use its maritime muscle to impose regulations on world navigation and safeguard its mercantile hegemony. In its heyday, the buoyancy of the British shipping industry also clearly made a massive contribution to the development of Britain's industrial base. While efficient and low-cost maritime transport facilitated the expansion of trade, Davies argues that 'the expansion of the British merchant navy came about as a direct result of the extension of British trade'. Trade and shipping 'form a "virtuous circle" in which it is impossible to be sure which is cause and which is effect', but both are driven by the domestic economy. Even before 1914, Britain's supremacy in commercial navigation was being challenged by Germany, Japan and the United States, and in the period between 1913 and 1939 it had largely disappeared. Whereas Britain built about 60 per cent of the world's shipping between 1899 and 1913, by the early 1970s, only 3.9 per cent of new ships came from British yards. Once the buoyancy of the domestic economy weakened, foreign trade and navigation went into decline as well – and the knock-on effects on the shipbuilding industry would, of course, offer one of the starkest indicators of Britain's industrial decline.

The debates on the links between Britain's declining competitiveness in world export markets and the loss of dynamic in the domestic economy in the late nineteenth century are taken up by Charles Feinstein. Industrial output, productivity and exports all fell at roughly the same time, suggesting a series of causal links. Many economic historians have argued that these symptoms of decline were a consequence of the maturation of other industrial economies, which deprived Britain of its earlier monopoly position in many world markets that, with growing rapidity, were relinquished to new and more innovative competitors – and especially to Germany, the United States and Japan. Donald McCloskey famously challenged that thesis in an essay that launched the debate on the failure of the Victorian economy, where he argued that what slowed down the pace of economic growth in Victorian England was lack of resources at home (especially capital and labour) not lack of competitiveness in the foreign market places. Demonstrating that there is no clear evidence to support the claim that the British economy lacked capital or labour, Feinstein argues that the composition and destination of British exports in the second half of the nineteenth century do reveal a steady decline in exports to industrialized European countries and (after the McKinley 1890 and Dingley 1897 tariffs) to the United States, and a growing dependence on developing and underdeveloped countries. The effects of increased competition and the spread of protectionist defences were aggravated by the tendency of export prices to decline in relation to other British goods. On this basis, Feinstein argues that external developments were primarily responsible for Britain's commercial decline, but he also insists that demand-side explanations cannot provide a reason for the third negative indicator in the performance of the late Victorian and Edwardian economy – the decline in productivity. Because not all sectors of the economy exhibited this tendency, no single explanation can be offered – except that the causes were internal to the British economy in that period and did not derive from competition on export markets.

One development that limited the market opportunities for British exports in the final decade of the nineteenth century was the rise of tariff protection in Europe and the United States. Forrest Capie takes a longer view to assess the impact of tariff protection before and after 1914, and argues that tariffs rarely if ever affected the economic objectives they were ostensibly designed to promote. This was largely because pressure for protectionist measures came from interest groups which were inspired more by concepts of nationalist mercantilism than by a close knowledge of the economic impact of imports of different types. But the ways in which protective tariffs functioned could also easily trigger other economic reactions that had not been foreseen and which often frustrated their original objectives, while variables as simple as falling transport costs or exchange rates might easily nullify their impact on prices. For the period before 1914, Capie concludes that 'there is no evidence for the assertion that countries prospered behind high protective walls and that the impact – direct or indirect – of tariffs was small, weak and possibly even perverse'. Their negative impact in reducing and impeding trade flows was, on the other hand, inescapable, and became more damaging after World War I.

Protectionism in the inter-war period was a legacy of the economic and financial chaos that followed World War I, and Capie argues that the adoption of protectionism by the United Kingdom and the United States (with the Hawley-Smoot Act of 1931, the *New York Times* commented, 'war was declared by the Republican Party against the rest of mankind') precipitated a phase of unprecedented upheaval in multilateral world trade. Italy, France and Germany were quick to retaliate and, by 1937, an eighth of world trade was controlled by bilateral trade agreements (although, by 1939, world trade was 60 per cent lower than it had been in 1929). But how can the impact of protectionism be disentangled from the wider impact of the recession in the 1930s? Taking the example of Britain, where the National Government's adoption of protectionism in 1931 was followed by rapid economic growth in 1932–7, Capie concludes that there were no clear links of cause and effect. Because of the recession, British imports had fallen even before the new tariffs came into force (in 1932). More important, Britain's decision to abandon the Gold Standard in 1931 removed fixed exchange rates and thereby effectively undermined the intended function of the tariffs. But, if the tariffs contributed little or nothing to growth in the domestic economy in the years that followed, Capie concludes that the wider impact of Britain's abandonment of free trade had 'reverberations that undoubtedly swept around the world and back to Britain [that] can only have damaged Britain's external trade and hence economic growth'.[5]

The technical difficulties revealed by the repeated failure of attempts to marshal trade and economic growth through legislation and policy offer further indications of the complexity of the relationship and the immense number of variables, political no less than economic or institutional, involved. These points are developed in the context of the two examples of bilateral trade with which this volume concludes.

In the first of these, Rory Miller takes the debate back again to Britain's Atlantic trade and to the changing fortunes of British exports in Latin America from the late nineteenth century down to the period after World War II. Latin America is an important, and for that reason, much-studied context within which to explore and explain the decline in the competitiveness of British exports. Since British capital investment was predominant down to World War I, the region offered important commercial opportunities at a moment when Britain's markets in Europe and in the United States were shrinking. Yet, despite these overwhelming early advantages,

[5] *See also* T. Rooth, *British Protectionism and the International Economy: overseas commercial policy in the 1930s* (Cambridge, 1993), and S. Broadberry and N. F. R. Crafts, *Britain in the International Economy* (Cambridge, 1992).

from the end of World War I, British commerce rapidly lost ground in the key markets of Argentina and Brazil to American interests.

Argentina offers an important example of the complex relationships between foreign investment (i.e. export of capital from the United Kingdom), the export of capital goods and the rise in exports of primary products to the United Kingdom. Even if most capital investment in Argentina came from indigenous savings (as Christopher Platt argued), foreign investments served a critical 'pump-priming' role in the dynamic expansion of the Argentine economy and its integration into the world economy. The equivocal role played by the export of capital in relation to the level of home investment is worth noting, given the vigorous debate to which it has given rise. Miller's focus is the reason for the decline of British commerce in Argentina which has often been blamed on the failure of British manufacturers and merchants to remain innovative and competitive, but Christopher Platt challenged this view when he claimed that the British withdrawal from Latin America was as a rational switch to other and more rewarding markets. Miller argues that both these interpretations fail to take sufficient account of the 'deeper foundations' of the British commercial presence in Latin America (and especially in Argentina and Brazil) before 1914 and the ways in which these foundations subsequently changed or were eroded. Before 1914, Britain was the leading investor in the region, and these investments, combined with British control over credit, capital, services, utilities and business structures more generally, played a leading part in generating demand for British exports. After the war, Latin America remained a major theatre for British companies and economic policy, but the war and the depression 'shattered the structural foundations of Britain's pre-1914 trading relationship with South America'. Britain could no longer supply services (e.g. shipping) or investment capital as it had done before, while US interests were now moving into commercial banking, and the dollar began to challenge sterling. London's return to the Gold Standard in 1925 enabled New York to replace the City as the principal source of investment capital in Latin America. When the Depression destroyed the profitability of Argentine railways (the principal buyers of British exports) and drastic shortages of hard currency encouraged a flight into bilateral trade agreements, Britain was squeezed out even further. The British government's decision to establish a system of bilateral imperial preferences, following the Ottawa Conference of 1932, further weakened the position of British trade and investment in many Latin American countries. By 1939, British companies had been largely squeezed out of Brazil by German competitors and faced growing American competition in Argentina. The shocks caused by two world wars and the Depression 'accelerated the disintegration of Britain's commercial relationship with Latin America because they undermined the bases on which trade had depended before 1914: the dominance of British shipping; the free convertibility of currencies; the role of sterling as the principal medium of international trade; multilateral settlements rather than bilateral trade agreements; and Britain's stock of overseas investments and continued ability to export capital'. British business people and bureaucrats were slow to understand the nature and importance of these changes, with the result that the policies adopted by successive British governments were inadequate, inconsistent and superficial. But, while short-term measures were ineffective, longer-run polices, such as the commercial preferences given to the Empire in the 1930s and to the Commonwealth in the 1950s, proved particularly damaging to the continuation of British trade with Latin America. Miller concludes that Latin America provides a clear illustration of how, in addition to changes in the 'deeper foundations' of trade, the divergent and often contradictory priorities of government, finance and industry have combined to bring about the decline in Britain's competitiveness on world markets.

The performance of British exports in the contexts of 'informal empire' raises the broader question of the international institutional arrangements for trade, investment and economic growth that have been at the centre of the debates on the economic benefits of empire and colonialism. In the final essay, B. R. Tomlinson addresses these issues in the context of Britain's formal empire and her trade relations with India, her most important imperial possession at the turn of the century as well as her single largest export market. But, despite the imperial ties, British exports performed no better in India than they did elsewhere in the world.

Tomlinson's central argument is that the belief that trade necessarily followed the flag or that British economic growth in the nineteenth century was a function of her overseas expansion is based on scant knowledge of the structure of bilateral trading relations. Working from new estimates of the performance of British exports to India from the period of the Raj down to the decades after independence, he shows that there was no clear correlation between export competitiveness and the chronology of the decline of British imperial control in south Asia. From its height before 1914, British power in India was heavily eroded in the inter-war period before ending with independence and the creation of the new states of India, Pakistan and Bangladesh. British exports were more competitive in India than elsewhere in the world, however, in only three periods (1899–1913; 1955–9; 1967–71) while they were least competitive in India in 1929–37 and 1959–63.

The apparent lack of correlation, Tomlinson argues, is explained by the fact that import demand in India was determined by a wide variety of factors. But, in addition to the conventional explanations (increased competition from first Japan and then US imports; growing import substitution as the Indian industrial economy expanded in the inter-war period; the anti-British stance of the nationalist movement), import demand in India was shaped by private business as well as by public policy: 'India's capacity to import was linked closely to capital formation, a large part of which consisted of foreign investment or the use of capital controlled by expatriate firms'. Reflecting many of the developments in Latin America discussed by Rory Miller, Tomlinson shows how the decline in British investments in India after World War I triggered a series of chain reactions that weakened the demand for British exports. British merchant houses remained tied to traditional staples (jute, coal and tea) and missed out on new commodity markets. As in Latin America, the decline of British capital in public utilities and services (especially electricity and railways) resulted in a heavy fall in demand for British goods while, for political reasons, the public sector looked to alternative suppliers for stores purchases. 'By the 1940s the institutional links that had previously bound the Indian economy tightly to British exports of capital, equipment and expertise, had been severely weakened.'

British government attempts to reverse these trends were remarkably ineffective. Neither imperial preferences in the 1930s nor the post-war Commonwealth trade preferences had measurable success (although, as Miller points out for Latin America, the impact on British exports in other parts of the world was very negative) while the brief booms in British exports after independence were linked to short-term opportunities (the first resulting from the Aid for India programme after 1957 and the second from the 1967 devaluation of sterling). This leads Tomlinson to conclude that the performance of British exports in India was shaped less by public policy or by the political relationship between the two countries than by patterns of private investment and private capital flows from Britain to India and the operations of international firms. The stark lesson to be learned from the history of Britain's bilateral trade relationship with India is, therefore, that even imperial controls offered no solution to the longer-run problem of Britain's 'uncompetitive exports and low productivity of industrial labour and capital'.

The essays in this volume provide an extended, although obviously not comprehensive, critical commentary on the issues set out at the start of this Introduction. They provide little indication that foreign trade was ever an engine of growth, but they offer a wealth of examples of the ways in which foreign trade was a key element in the complex mix of foreign investment and the provision of credit, services and utilities that gave British capitalism its capacity for global expansion in the nineteenth and twentieth centuries. Because of the strength of these accompanists, foreign trade could even figure as an indispensable but unprofitable partner in a highly profitable partnership. They also suggest that the older search for links between foreign trade and manufactured or industrial exports often missed the more important connections with capital flows and services. Finally, they provide important examples of the ways in which private enterprise has generally proved more successful in establishing profitable contexts for foreign trade than public intervention and political controls.

If there are broader methodological conclusions to be drawn from these essays, the first would be that the mechanisms linking foreign trade and domestic growth are complex and extremely difficult to measure, which may explain why public policy has rarely been able to draw on a sufficiently informed knowledge of economic realities to achieve its intended goals. Secondly, any macro-economic model of the relationship between foreign trade and domestic growth that fails to take proper account of the ways in which this relationship is shaped by specific contexts of time and place, of the terms and conditions of trade, is likely to be inadequate and, indeed, misleading. And finally, historically the profitability or otherwise of foreign trade has been inseparable from what Sidney Pollard terms the 'sequence of industrialization' and from what Rory Miller terms the 'deeper foundations' of foreign trade, because foreign trade cannot be separated from the networks of foreign investment, capital flows, credit transfers, foreign-exchange mechanisms and services that develop around it. Ultimately, the advantage of any single-sector analysis – including the one attempted here – is to demonstrate that in economic history, at any rate, single sectors are no more than heuristically indispensable abstractions that help us understand better the interconnectedness of economic phenomena and the political and human environments in which they occur.

1

Atlantic Trade and British Economic Growth in the Eighteenth Century

Kenneth Morgan

The contribution of Atlantic trade to eighteenth-century British economic growth is an appropriate subject for this volume, for the years between 1700 and 1800 witnessed not only the 'Americanization' of British overseas trade but also the birth of the first industrial nation.[1] English domestic exports and retained imports both quadrupled in value over the course of the century. But this growth was accompanied by a marked shift in the pattern of trade: the transatlantic sector expanded while trade with Europe experienced relative decline. In 1700–1, English colonies in the New World accounted for 11 per cent of the value of English exports and for 20 per cent of imports. By 1772–3, they took 38 per cent of exports and provided 39 per cent of the imports. By 1797–8, North America and the West Indies received 57 per cent of British exports and supplied 32 per cent of imports. Many re-exported goods also consisted of colonial commodities.[2] British exports sent across the Atlantic were mainly finished manufactured wares, while imports from the Americas were

---

[1] Previous studies of Atlantic trade and eighteenth-century British economic growth include W. E. Minchinton (ed.), *The Growth of English Overseas Trade in the Seventeenth and Eighteenth Centuries* (London, 1969), pp. 36–52; Jacob M. Price, 'Colonial Trade and British Economic Development, 1660–1775' in *La Révolution Américaine et l'Europe*, Colloques internationaux du Centre Nationale de la Recherche Scientifique, no. 577 (Paris, 1979), pp. 221–42; *idem*, 'What Did Merchants Do? Reflections on British Overseas Trade, 1660–1790', *JEcH*, XLIX (1989), pp. 267–84; and Pat Hudson, *The Industrial Revolution* (London, 1992), pp. 181–200.

[2] For overviews of these changing trade patterns *see* Ralph Davis, 'English Foreign Trade, 1700–1774', *Economic History Review*, 2nd series, XV (1962–3), pp. 285–303; *idem*, *The Industrial Revolution and British Overseas Trade* (Leicester, 1979; and Phyllis Deane and W. A. Cole, *British Economic Growth, 1688–1959*, 2nd edn. (Cambridge, 1967), p–87. On re-exports *see* David Ormrod, 'English Re-Exports and the Dutch Staple Market in the Eighteenth Century' in D. C. Coleman and Peter Mathias (eds), *Enterprise and History: Essays in honour of Charles Wilson* (Cambridge, 1984), pp. 89–115.

dominated by sugar, tobacco, rice, coffee, naval stores, dyestuffs and other products increasingly in demand with British and European consumers. The most lucrative of these products were staple commodities grown in the tropical or semi-tropical colonies rather than in temperate zones.

The degree to which burgeoning international trade accelerated economic growth in eighteenth-century Britain has long divided opinion. As early as the 1770s, Adam Smith pointed to the colonies as a drain on the resources of the mother country whereas Edmund Burke regarded the preservation of the Empire as of paramount economic importance.[3] Historians have similarly failed to reach consensus. Some depict foreign trade as an 'engine of growth' that enabled merchants to exploit productivity advances in widening markets abroad, and suggest that rising demand for imports stimulated the expansion of the export industries and overall economic growth.[4] These arguments draw support from the dynamic performance of overseas trade in a British economy that experienced gradual growth for most of the eighteenth century. The annual level of trade rose by 0.8 per cent between 1700 and 1740, by 1.7 per cent between 1740 and 1770, and by 2.6 per cent between 1770 and 1800 – a faster rate of growth than total output.[5] Overseas trade also contributed significantly to national income in the period 1780–1801, when an export boom, largely directed to transatlantic markets, led to a 19.3 per cent increase in the incremental ratio of exports to gross national product.[6]

Other historians place more emphasis on the home market as the mainspring of growth. They regard the progressive cheapening of food between 1730 and 1750, the rise in middle range incomes, and the changing tastes of a swiftly rising population as stimuli for the production of manufactured goods mainly for domestic rather than foreign markets from the 1740s onwards.[7] It has been

---

[3] Adam Smith, *An Enquiry into the Nature and Causes of the Wealth of Nations* (London, 1776), pp. 899–900, and Edmund Burke, 'On Conciliation with the Colonies', 22 March 1775, in Ernest Rhys (ed.), *Speeches and Letters on American Affairs* (London, 1945), pp. 84–6, plus the discussion in Richard B. Sheridan, *Sugar and Slavery: An Economic History of the British West Indies 1623–1775* (Baltimore, 1973), pp. 5–7.

[4] For example, K. Berrill, 'International Trade and the Rate of Economic Growth', *EcHR*, 2nd series, XII (1960), pp. 351–9; H. J. Habbakuk and Phyllis Deane, 'The Take-Off in Britain' in W. W. Rostow (ed.), *The Economics of Take-Off into Sustained Growth* (London, 1963), pp. 77–80; E. J. Hobsbawm, *Industry and Empire: An Economic History of Britain since 1750* (London, 1968), pp. 32–3; C. H. Lee, *The British Economy since 1700: A Macroeconomic Perspective* (Cambridge, 1986), pp. 107–24; and Deane and Cole, *British Economic Growth*, pp. 83, 86–9.

[5] Deane and Cole, *British Economic Growth 1688–1959*, p. 46.

[6] N. F. R. Crafts, 'British Economic Growth, 1700–1831: A Review of the Evidence', *EcHR*, 2nd series, XXXVI (1983), table 8, p. 197.

[7] For example, A. H. John, 'Agricultural Productivity and Economic Growth in England, 1700–1760', *JEcH*, XXV (1965), pp. 19–34; D. E. C. Eversley, 'The Home Market and

argued that lack of evidence for variations in British retained imports systematically preceding variations in exports supports an emphasis on the home market as the impetus for growth.[8] Clearly, however, there are widely divergent views on the links between foreign trade and the economy as a whole. These are difficult to assess in the absence of convincing indices on the terms of trade in the eighteenth century.[9] Yet, by offering a critical appraisal of the main approaches pursued by historians on this topic, one can outline the distinctive ways in which colonial trade was significant for eighteenth-century British economic growth. Perhaps the most influential discussion of this theme has been Eric Williams's *Capitalism and Slavery* (1944), which was much concerned with the economic impact of the Atlantic empire on Britain, and specifically the role of the slave–sugar nexus, at the onset of industrialization. By examining the connections between transatlantic trade and British economic growth, one can place Williams's treatment of this topic in *Capitalism and Slavery* within the context of the scholarship of the past fifty years.[10]

The first approach to explore is the proposition that the profits of the slave trade played an important part in capital investment at the onset of the Industrial Revolution in Britain. This well-known thesis was first given wide currency in *Capitalism and Slavery*. Eric Williams perceived that, by the late eighteenth century, Liverpool was booming on the back of the slave trade at the same time that industrialization, notably factory-based cotton spinning, was becoming firmly established in south Lancashire. Williams considered that there must surely be an economic link between these two phenomena, and that the connection lay in channelling profits from the slave trade into industry. As he put it in a characteristically pithy phrase, the 'profits obtained' from the triangular trade

---

Economic Growth in England, 1750–1780' in E. L. Jones and G. E. Mingay (eds), *Land, Labour and Population in the Industrial Revolution: Essays presented to J. D. Chambers* (London, 1967), pp. 206–59; Neil McKendrick, John Brewer and J. H. Plumb, *The Birth of a Consumer Society: The Commercialisation of Eighteenth-Century England* (London, 1983), pp. 1–33.

[8] T. J. Hatton, John S. Lyons, and S. E. Satchell, 'Eighteenth Century British Trade: Homespun or Empire Made?' *Explorations in Economic History*, XX (1983), pp. 163–82.

[9] P. K. O'Brien and S. L. Engerman, 'Exports and the Growth of the British Economy from the Glorious Revolution to the Peace of Amiens' in Barbara L. Solow (ed.), *Slavery and the Rise of the Atlantic System* (Cambridge, 1991), p. 191.

[10] Eric Williams, *Capitalism and Slavery* (Chapel Hill, NC, 1944) has spawned many assessments: *see*, for example, Roger Anstey, '*Capitalism and Slavery*: A Critique', *EcHR*, 2nd series, XXI (1968), pp. 307–20; Hilary Beckles, 'Capitalism and Slavery: the Debate over the Williams Thesis', *Social and Economic Studies*, XXXIII (1984), pp. 171–90; Barbara L. Solow and Stanley L. Engerman (eds), *British Capitalism and Caribbean Slavery: The Legacy of Eric Williams* (Cambridge, 1987); Seymour Drescher, *Econocide: British Slavery in the Era of Abolition* (Pittsburgh, 1977); *idem*, 'Eric Williams: British Capitalism and British Slavery,' *History and Theory*, XXVI (1987), pp. 180–96.

'provided one of the main streams of that accumulation of capital in England which financed the Industrial Revolution'.[11] At the time he was writing, however, it was virtually impossible to substantiate this hypothesis with systematic data. A few historians had investigated surviving accounts of a handful of slave traders, with the general conclusion that handsome profits accrued from the trade.[12] But it was not until after the Second World War that more slave trading firms' records became available, allowing historians to test the strength of this conclusion.

Modern research has now questioned the notion that slave trading profits were an Eldorado. Potential bonanzas could of course be made when export cargoes of rum, beads, textiles and guns sold well in west Africa, when full complements of healthy slaves arrived at American markets, and when the arrival of ships in the plantation colonies coincided with the harvest of staple crops. But the slave trade was a very risky affair that rarely achieved these optimum targets. The need to time voyages lasting more than a calendar year to secure three sets of returns in an internationally competitive trade; changing social, economic and epidemiological conditions in west Africa; the frequent high mortality rates of crew and slaves on the Middle Passage; the rise in average unit costs for provisions and for management of black cargoes – these are among the reasons why slave trade profits fluctuated widely and why annual net returns in the trade averaged less than 10 per cent on capital outlay in the period 1740–1807.[13] The most comprehensive study of the late British slave trade shows that in the period 1785–1807 profits of between 5 and 10 per cent were the norm.[14]

[11] Williams, *Capitalism and Slavery*, esp. pp. 52 (the source of the quotation), 68, 98, 105.

[12] For example, Gomer Williams, *History of the Liverpool Privateers and Letters of Marque with an account of the Liverpool Slave Trade* (London, 1897), pp. 594–608, modified and corrected by Stanley Dumbell as 'The Profits of the Guinea Trade', *Economic History*, II (1931), pp. 254–7.

[13] For example, Roger Anstey, *The Atlantic Slave Trade and British Abolition 1760–1810* (London, 1975), pp. 38–57; David Richardson, 'Profits in the Liverpool Slave Trade: The Accounts of William Davenport, 1757–1784' in Roger Anstey and P. E. H. Hair (eds), *Liverpool, the African Slave Trade, and Abolition* (Historic Society of Lancashire and Cheshire, Occasional series, vol. 2, 1976), pp. 60–90; *idem*, 'The Costs of Survival: The Transport of Slaves in the Middle Passage and the Profitability of the 18th-Century British Slave Trade', *EEH*, XXIV (1987), pp. 178–96. Cf. David Hancock, *Citizens of the World: London Merchants and the Integration of the British Atlantic Community, 1735–1785* (Cambridge, 1995), pp. 419–24.

[14] Stephen D. Behrendt, 'The British Slave Trade, 1785–1807: Volume, Profitability, and Mortality' (University of Wisconsin Ph.D., 1993), ch. 2. This study effectively rebuts recent articles claiming that higher venture profits were made in the late British slave trade. For that argument, based on a greater volume of slaves fetching higher sale prices, *see* Joseph E. Inikori, 'Market Structure and the Profits of the British African Trade in the late Eighteenth Century', *JEcH*, XLI (1981), pp. 745–76, and his rejoinder in ibid., XLIII

It is a moot point whether these average profits should be characterized as modest or competitive returns. More important, however, even though these funds were ploughed back into the trade and other commercial and industrial activities, slave trade profits seem to have played only a minor role in capital formation. Stanley L. Engerman's analysis of this issue estimated the number of slaves carried by the British from Africa to the Americas, the profits per slave, and the ratio of slave trading investment to national income, and found that slave trade profits amounted to over 0.5 per cent of British national income in only one period between 1688 and 1800.[15] A recalculation of this 'small ratios' argument suggested that, in relative terms, this proportion was quite large for one industry.[16] Yet there remains the problem of formulating and testing a theoretical model that would explain the significance of these numbers: the models used so far by economic historians all have limitations.[17]

A second line of analysis emphasizes the flow of capital from slavery and the Atlantic trading system into industry in Britain. This linkage underpins many passages in *Capitalism and Slavery*. A central concern here is the argument that capital accumulation in Britain was boosted by the wealth produced by the Caribbean plantations, wealth based on the productivity of slaves and the profits of the sugar trade. This seems an obvious mode of enquiry, for the West Indian islands were the richest part of the first British Empire. By 1776 the valuation of sugar estates in Jamaica alone, which accounted for half of British investment in the Caribbean, amounted to some £18 million sterling (about £9 billion in today's money), with an annual net income to the mother country of £1.5 million.[18] Contemporaries were well aware of the wealth of the West Indies and

---

(1983), pp. 723–8, and William A. Darity, Jr, 'The Numbers Game and the Profitability of the British Trade in Slaves,' ibid., XLV (1985), pp. 693–703, and 'Profitability of the British Trade in Slaves Once Again,' *EEH*, XXVI (1989), pp. 380–4. Critiques of Inikori and Darity can be found in B. L. Anderson and David Richardson's rejoinders in *JEcH*, XLIII (1983), pp. 716–17, and ibid., XLV (1985), pp. 705–7, and in David Richardson, 'Accounting for Profits in the British Trade in Slaves: Reply to William Darity', Explorations in *EEH*, XXVI (1989), pp. 492–9.

[15] S. L. Engerman, 'The Slave Trade and British Capital Formation in the Eighteenth Century: A Comment on the Williams thesis', *Business History Review*, XLVI (1972), pp. 430–43.

[16] Barbara L. Solow, 'Caribbean Slavery and British Growth: the Eric Williams hypothesis', *Journal of Development Economics*, XVII (1985), pp. 105–6.

[17] William Darity, Jr, 'A Model of "Original Sin": Rise of the West and Lag of the Rest', *American Economic Review*, LXXXII (1992), pp. 162–3.

[18] R. B. Sheridan, 'The Wealth of Jamaica in the Eighteenth Century', *EcHR*, 2nd series, XVIII (1965), pp. 303, 305. The estimate of the modern value of the Jamaican plantations is based on John J. McCusker, 'How Much is that in Real Money? A Historical Price Index for use as a Deflator of Money Values in the Economy of the United States', *Proceedings of the American Antiquarian Society*, CI (1991), pp. 342, 350.

offered valuations, probably exaggerated, that exceeded this figure.[19] They acknowledged the economic status of the West India plantocracy. No less a personage than George III, when visiting Weymouth, came across a splendid equipage with outriders belonging to an absentee Jamaican planter, and exclaimed to his companion, the prime minister, 'Sugar, sugar, hey? all *that* sugar! How are the duties, hey, Pitt, how are the duties?'[20]

The extent to which the wealth of the British Caribbean was still substantial by *c.*1800, however, is a matter of historical controversy. Taking his cue from Lowell Joseph Ragatz's argument that the planter class began to decline after 1763, Williams insisted in *Capitalism and Slavery* that, by the late eighteenth century, by many older West Indian sugar estates suffered from soil exhaustion, overproduction, debt, and the waste of absentee ownership they therefore represented relatively poor investments for British merchants and planters.[21] Certainly, difficulties occurred in the American War of Independence when shipping lanes were interrupted in Caribbean waters, sugar prices and plantation profits declined, and commercial depression hit the West Indies.[22] But most historians consider these problems were overcome by *c.*1790 and that the plantation economy did not experience permanent difficulties until after 1815 when it faced worldwide competition in sugar production, falling sugar prices and rising duties.[23]

Recent research has discounted the notion of general economic decline in the British Caribbean by the time the English slave trade was abolished. Though there is no space here for a technical discussion, the following points have been demonstrated. Soil exhaustion is a red herring as sugar is not a staple crop that particularly depletes the fertility of the land. Technical improvements were made by a number of planters. Profits were still being made on plantation accounts even in hard times during the French revolutionary and Napoleonic wars. The productivity of slaves in planting sugar increased, allowing owners to achieve

---

[19] *See* the contemporary estimates cited in Drescher, *Econocide*, pp. 22–3.

[20] Quoted in Richard Pares, *Merchants and Planters*, *EcHR*, Supplement no. 4 (Cambridge, 1960), p. 38.

[21] Lowell Joseph Ragatz, *The Fall of the Planter Class in the British West Indies, 1763–1833* (New York, 1928); Williams, *Capitalism and Slavery*, pp. 145, 149–52.

[22] Selwyn H. H. Carrington, 'The American Revolution and the British West Indies' Economy' in Solow and Engerman (eds), *British Capitalism and Caribbean Slavery*, pp. 135–62, and *idem*, *The British West Indies during the American Revolution* (Dordrecht, 1988).

[23] John J. McCusker, 'Growth, Stagnation or Decline? The Economy of the British West Indies, 1763–1790' in Ronald Hoffman et al. (eds), *The Economy of Early America: The Revolutionary Period, 1763–1790* (Charlottesville, VA, 1988), pp. 275–302; J. R. Ward, *Poverty and Progress in the Caribbean 1800–1960* (London, 1985), pp. 17–22; William A. Green, *British Slave Emancipation: The Sugar Colonies and the Great Experiment 1830–1865* (Oxford, 1976), ch. 2.

economies of scale. Overproduction of sugar was a temporary phenomenon.[24] Examining the period 1783–1807, Drescher established in *Econocide* that West Indian slavery had an expanding frontier; that the British Caribbean retained its share of world sugar production; and that West India trade remained an important segment of total British overseas commerce.[25] There are, to be sure, detailed critiques of these views,[26] but the historical consensus discounts any overall case for serious economic decline in the British Caribbean by 1807. The most recent summation of the plantation economy accepts Drescher's positive appraisal of the economic health of the British West Indies, implying that substantial wealth was still generated in that sector of the British Empire by the turn of the nineteenth century.[27]

Yet, despite the wealth created by sugar and slaves, the contribution of plantation profits to industrial investment is not clearcut. In some cases a direct connection existed. Among the families that transferred funds from their Jamaican sugar estates to domestic industrial enterprise were the Pennants (who invested in slate quarries in north Wales) and the Fullers (who owned ironworks and gun foundries in Sussex).[28] But in other cases the link was tenuous. Two substantial families that amassed West India fortunes, the Pinneys and the Beckfords, both invested in government funds and land in England but did not

---

[24] *See* three studies by J. R. Ward: 'The Profitability of Sugar Planting in the British West Indies, 1650–1834', *EcHR*, XXXI (1978), pp. 197–213; *Poverty and Progress*, pp. *17–23; and British West Indian Slavery, 1750–1834: The Process of Amelioration* (Oxford, 1988).

[25] Drescher, *Econocide*, esp. ch. 1–6. Cf. David Eltis, *Economic Growth and the Ending of the Transatlantic Slave Trade* (Oxford, 1987), pp. 5–6.

[26] For example, W. E. Minchinton, 'Williams and Drescher: Abolition and Emancipation,' *Slavery and Abolition*, IV (1983), pp. 81–105, and *idem*, 'Abolition and Emancipation: Williams, Drescher and the Continuing Debate' in Roderick A. McDonald (ed.), *West Indies Accounts: Essays on the History of the British Caribbean and the Atlantic Economy in honour of Richard Sheridan* (Mona, Jamaica, 1996); Selwyn H. H. Carrington, "Econocide" – Myth or Reality – The Question of West Indian Decline, 1783–1806', with a reply by Seymour Drescher, *Boletin de Estudios Latinoamericanos y del Caribe*, XXXVI (1984), pp. 13–67; *idem*, 'The State of the Debate on the Role of Capitalism in the Ending of the Slave System,' *Journal of Caribbean History*, XXII (1988), pp. 20–41. For Drescher's response to his critics *see* his article 'The Decline Thesis of British Slavery since *Econocide*', *Slavery and Abolition*, VII (1986), pp. 3–24.

[27] B. W. Higman, 'Economic and Social Development of the British West Indies, from Settlement to ca. 1850' in Stanley L. Engerman and Robert E. Gallman (eds), *The Cambridge Economic History of the United States, vol. 1: The Colonial Era* (Cambridge, 1996), pp. 330–1.

[28] Sheridan, 'The Wealth of Jamaica,' p. 307, and *idem, Sugar and Slavery*, pp. 478–9; D. W. Crossley and Richard Saville (eds), *The Fuller Letters: Guns, Slaves and Finance, 1728–1755* (Sussex Record Society's Publications, LXXVI, 1991).

put much of their wealth into domestic industry.[29] It seems likely that they were more typical of absentee proprietors in this respect than the Pennants and the Fullers. The lure of land, government stocks, annuities and conspicuous consumption appear to have been higher priorities for West India planters than industrial investments, or, as Richard Pares put it, 'there seem to have been more Fonthills than factories';[30] but this still meant that Caribbean-based wealth raised aggregate demand in the British economy.

One assumes that absentee proprietors extracted their money invested in the Caribbean, but the degree to which their wealth was repatriated is by no means easy to establish. Richard B. Sheridan has presented data showing that between 8 and 10 per cent of British income in the late eighteenth century consisted of funds flowing via this route, and that the percentage was larger in the period before the American War of Independence. But Robert P. Thomas, emphasizing the costs of imperial defence and the inflation of sugar prices by preferential tariffs, has argued contrariwise that the colonies were a net drain on British resources and that they absorbed finance that would have been better deployed elsewhere.[31] This debate failed to reach a consensus, perhaps because of inherent flaws in both approaches. Thomas's analysis applied more to specific commercial and imperial policies followed by British governments than to the value of the West Indies themselves. His interpretation failed to note the positive effect of colonial expansion on British incomes in the first place and the necessity, whether or not colonies were involved, for the British to maintain a costly naval presence in the Caribbean to counteract French maritime rivalry. Sheridan, for his part, probably overestimated the ease of extracting money tied up in mortgage and plantation debts in the West Indies.[32] For these reasons, as

---

[29] Richard Pares, *A West-India Fortune* (London, 1950); Richard B. Sheridan, 'Planter and Historian: The Career of William Beckford of Jamaica and England, 1744–1799', *Jamaican Historical Review*, IV (1964), pp. 36–58.

[30] Richard Pares, 'The Economic Factors in the History of the Empire', *EcHR*, VII (1936–7), p. 130.

[31] Sheridan, 'The Wealth of Jamaica,' p. 306; Robert Paul Thomas, 'The Sugar Colonies of the Old Empire: Profit or Loss for Great Britain?' *EcHR*, 2nd series, XXI (1968), pp. 30–45; R. B. Sheridan, 'The Wealth of Jamaica in the Eighteenth Century: A Rejoinder', ibid., pp. 46–61. For another study that argues in favour of negative returns from the Empire for the mother country *see* Philip R. P. Coelho, 'The Profitability of Imperialism: The British Experience in the West Indies, 1768–1772', *EEH*, X (1973), pp. 253–80.

[32] Solow, 'Caribbean Slavery and British Growth,' pp. 106–9; Michael Duffy, *Soldiers, Sugar, and Seapower: The British Expeditions to the West Indies and the War against Revolutionary France* (Oxford, 1987), p. 20 n. 23; William A. Darity, Jr, 'A General Equilibrium Model of the Eighteenth- Century Atlantic Slave Trade: A Least-Likely Test for the Caribbean School' in Paul Uselding (ed.), *Research in Economic History*, VII (1982), pp. 292, 322 n. 14; Pares, *Merchants and Planters*, pp. 44–6. Jacob M. Price has noted our lack of good

Barry Higman notes, 'a definitive answer to the question of whether the colonies were a source of profit or loss remains elusive.'[33]

Immanuel Wallerstein has revived the debate on a broader scale by depicting a 'world system' of trade that emerged in the early modern era, a system in which wealth generated in the 'periphery' (i.e. the colonies) became a vital source of capital accumulation in the 'core' (i.e. the metropolitan centre of empire). These grand themes, however, are almost certainly overstated. Patrick O'Brien, in a re-examination of this topic, has constructed careful estimates to show that commerce with the 'periphery' generated funds sufficient to finance only 15 per cent of gross investment expenditures during the Industrial Revolution.[34] Future studies of this 'small ratios' argument will need fuller investigation of the composition of trade, links between industries and various multiplier effects, but current scholarship has not vindicated Wallerstein's expansive claims.[35]

It is equally difficult to prove that merchant capital amassed from colonial commerce was decisive for industrial investment in Britain. Profits earned in the Atlantic trades were undoubtedly put into shipbuilding, snuff mills, sugar refineries, glassworks, ironworks, textiles, leather manufactories, coal mines and other industrial enterprises in London, Liverpool, Bristol, Glasgow, Whitehaven and their hinterlands.[36] From surviving records, however, it is impossible to establish what proportion of merchants' investment in industry originated from overseas trade rather than from sources such as banking, insurance, land and

---

estimates of the plantation mortgage debt in the British West Indies: *see* his 'Credit in the Slave Trade and Plantation Economies' in Solow (ed.), *Slavery and the Rise of the Atlantic System*, p. 325.

[33] Higman, 'Economic and Social Development,' p. 321.

[34] Immanuel Wallerstein, *The Modern World System, vol. 2: Mercantilism and the Consolidation of the European World Economy 1600–1750* (New York, 1980); P. K. O'Brien, 'European Economic Development: The Contribution of the Periphery,' *EcHR*, 2nd series, XXXV (1982), pp. 1–18. Cf. the exchange of comments between O'Brien and Wallerstein in ibid., pp. 580–5.

[35] William Darity, Jr, 'British Industry and the West Indies Plantations' in Joseph E. Inikori and Stanley L. Engerman (eds), *The Atlantic Slave Trade: Effects on Economies, Societies, and Peoples in Africa, the Americas, and Europe* (Durham, NC, 1992), pp. 252–5.

[36] W. E. Minchinton, 'Bristol – Metropolis of the West in the Eighteenth Century,' *Transactions of the Royal Historical Society*, 5th series, IV (1954), pp. 82–5; Kenneth Morgan, 'The Economic Development of Bristol, 1700–1850' in Madge Dresser and Philip Ollerenshaw (eds), *The Making of Modern Bristol* (Tiverton, 1996), pp. 54–63; J. V. Beckett, *Coal and Tobacco: The Lowthers and the Economic Development of West Cumberland, 1660–1760* (Cambridge, 1981), pp. 114–15; T. M. Devine, 'The Colonial Trades and Industrial Investment in Scotland, c.1700–1815', *EcHR*, 2nd series, XXIX (1976), pp. 1–13; F. E. Hyde, *Liverpool and the Mersey: An Economic History of a Port 1700–1970* (Newton Abbot, 1971), pp. 19–21.

government stock. The case of Glasgow is instructive, for it is the one British port where this matter has received full attention. In the forty years before the American Revolution, Glasgow thrived on the success of the Chesapeake tobacco trade. But though merchant industrial investment was significant on the Clyde, no substantial transfer of capital from the tobacco trade to the cotton industry occurred in Scotland: by *c.*1795 only about 17 per cent of the value of cotton firms north of the border was financed by colonial traders. There was also no straightforward flow of trading profits generally into the Scottish domestic economy. Glasgow's position as an entrepôt in the tobacco trade probably accounts for such a limited multiplier effect, but these findings also fit our knowledge of the modest fixed capital requirements of the early stages of industrialization.[37]

A third way of looking at the connection between Atlantic trade and eighteenth-century British economic growth is to emphasize demand both in the Americas and within Britain as a major spur to exports from England and Scotland – a theme hinted at, though not fully discussed, in sections of *Capitalism and Slavery* that deal with connections between British industry and the triangular trade.[38] The outcome of the American demand for British export wares can be seen in the rapid growth of such trade from about 1740 onwards. The annual average value of English exports and reexports to American markets more than doubled from £1,490,000 in 1741–5 to £3,009,000 in 1766–70, and then nearly trebled from £3,540,000 in 1781–5 to £11,164,000 in 1796–1800.[39] Such growth points to an Atlantic extension of the consumer revolution of eighteenth-century England.[40] It was achieved despite the boom-and-bust charac-ter of the dry goods trade, temporary boycotts of British goods for part of the

---

[37] Devine, 'The Colonial Trades and Industrial Investment', pp. 12–13; T. M. Devine, *The Tobacco Lords: A Study of the Tobacco Merchants of Glasgow and their Trading Activities, c. 1740–90* (Edinburgh, 1975), pp. 43–6; R. H. Campbell, *Scotland since 1707: The Rise of an Industrial Society*, 2nd edn (Edinburgh, 1985), pp. 41–3; Peter Mathias, 'Capital, Credit and Enterprise in the Industrial Revolution' in his *The Transformation of England: Essays in the Economic and Social History of England in the Eighteenth Century* (London, 1979), pp. 88–94.

[38] Williams, *Capitalism and Slavery*, pp. 51–5, 65–73, 81–4.

[39] E. B. Schumpeter, *English Overseas Trade Statistics, 1697–1808* (Oxford, 1960), table V, p. 17.

[40] For elaboration of this theme *see* T. H. Breen, 'An Empire of Goods: The Angliciza-tion of Colonial America, 1690–1776', *Journal of British Studies*, XXV (1986), pp. 467–99; *idem*, ' "Baubles of Britain": The American and Consumer Revolutions of the Eighteenth Century', *Past and Present*, no. 119 (1988), pp. 73–104; Thomas M. Doerflinger, 'Farmers and Dry Goods in the Philadelphia Market Area, 1750–1800', in Hoffman et al. (eds), *Economy of Early America*, pp. 166–95. S. D. Smith, 'British Exports to Colonial North America and the Mercantilist Fallacy', *Business History*, XXXVII (1995), pp. 45–63, and idem, S. D. Smith, 'British Exports to Continental North America, 1690–1776' (Univer-sity of Cambridge Ph.D., 1992).

1760s and 1770s, and major interruptions through war, especially the closing of markets in the thirteen American mainland colonies during the War of Independence. In the quarter century before the American Revolution, the range of exports widened to include not only textiles – the dominant wares in export cargoes until 1750 – but a variety of manufactures that were probably concentrated at the top and bottom ends of the price range.[41] By 1770 about half of all English exports of ironware, copperware, earthenware, glassware, window glass, printed cotton and linen goods, silk goods and flannels were sent to the colonies plus two-thirds or more of all exports of cordage, sailcloth, iron nails, beaver hats, wrought leather, linen, and Spanish cloth woollen goods. The chief characteristic of the second phase of growth after 1783 was the renewed dominance of textiles, for by 1801 cottons and woollens comprised 39 per cent of total exports to American markets and 56 per cent of British exports as a whole.[42]

The substantial increase in commodities shipped across the Atlantic was fuelled by rapid population growth, rising living standards, and changing tastes in America and the West Indies. The population of those parts of North America that became the United States multiplied twenty-fold from 275,000 people in 1700 to 5.3 million in 1800, an incredible upsurge that Malthus referred to as 'a rapidity of increase almost without parallel in history.'[43] During the eighteenth century, the per capita income of white settlers rose at an annual rate of between 0.3 and 0.6 per cent – not spectacular by modern standards but comparable to growth rates in Britain and France at that time.[44] Between 1700 and 1790 the predominantly black population of the British Caribbean quadrupled from 148,000 to 570,000 people, while by the 1770s the net worth of white settlers in Jamaica amounted to £1,200 per person.[45] Rising prosperity enabled white colonists to buy a wide array of consumer goods.

Several advantages helped Britain to tap these funds. The Navigation Acts provided a large protected market for British manufactures within the Empire. Competition from homespun industry was reduced by high labour costs in the colonies and by government restrictions on the American manufacture of

[41] Ralph Davis, *A Commercial Revolution* (London, 1967), pp. 4, 18–20; Jacob M. Price, 'The Transatlantic Economy' in Jack P. Greene and J. R. Pole (eds), *Colonial British America: Essays in the New History of the Early Modern Era* (Baltimore, MD, 1984), p. 35.

[42] John J. McCusker and Russell R. Menard, *The Economy of British America, 1607–1789* (Chapel Hill, 1985) table 13.2, p.284; Customs 3170, Public Record Office, London; N. F. R. Crafts, *British Economic Growth during the Industrial Revolution* (Oxford, 1985), p. 143.

[43] U. S. Department of Commerce, Bureau of the Census, *Historical Statistics of the United States: Colonial Times to 1970*, 2 vols (Washington, DC, 1975), I, series A 6–8, p. 8, II, series Z 1–19, p. 1168; T. R. Malthus, *An Essay on the Principle of Population*, 6th edn (London, 1826), I, p. 517.

[44] McCusker and Menard, *Economy of British America*, pp. 55–60, 268.

[45] Ibid., table 7.2, p. 154; McCusker, 'Growth, Stagnation or Decline?', table 1, pp. 277–9, 301 n. 29.

products such as cloth, hats, nails, earthenware and refined iron. British merchants also offered attractive terms to American customers. They allowed a credit period of 9–12 months before payment for goods was required, became familiar over time with the varied tastes of colonial consumers, and generally sold cheaper, better quality textiles and other wares than similar goods produced in America. Great attention was paid to different figures, colours and patterns among textiles to suit changing fashions. It is not surprising, therefore, that some American merchants maintained contacts with British firms during the War of Independence and that British manufactured products were so much in demand in the United States after 1783, when European firms were trying to capture that market.[46]

The interplay between external and internal factors underlying the growth of British exports is difficult to separate out.[47] Clearly, though, the demand for British manufactured goods was not entirely an exogenous affair, for exports sent to American markets were stimulated by increased purchasing power in both Britain and the Caribbean. David Richardson has emphasized the growth of the slave trade and sugar consumption in meeting this demand. Sugar and its by-products, rum and molasses, were the most valuable British imports from anywhere in the world in the eighteenth century. Between 1748 and 1776 sugar imports doubled from 900,000 to 1.8 million cwt.; sugar consumption doubled to reach a per capita level of 25 lb.; and average gross revenues from sugar sales also doubled, from £1.6 to £3.2 million. Such extensive demand from British consumers acquiring a sweet tooth through drinking sugar with tea, cocoa and chocolate was probably aided by rising wages in the industrializing areas of the country and by constraints on the production of other beverages such as beer. Incomes accruing from expanding sugar sales in Britain provided the impetus to expand the slave trade to maintain the output of the plantations (given the heavy mortality rate among slaves in the West Indies). The annual number of slaves shipped in English vessels rose from around 25,800 between 1749 and 1755 to reach a peak of 43,500 in the period 1763–75. Booming sugar sales also

---

[46] Thomas M. Doerflinger, *A Vigorous Spirit of Enterprise: Merchants and Economic Development in Revolutionary Philadelphia* (Chapel Hill, NC, 1986), pp. 54, 68–9, 86, 96–7, 138, 172–3, 222–3, 244, 333; Jacob M. Price, *Capital and Credit in British Overseas Trade: The View from the Chesapeake, 1700–1776* (Cambridge, Mass., 1980); Kenneth Morgan, *Bristol and the Atlantic Trade in the Eighteenth Century* (Cambridge, 1993), pp. 89–127; Michael M. Edwards, *The Growth of the British Cotton Trade, 1780–1815* (Manchester, 1967), pp. 64–5; Pat Hudson, *The Genesis of Industrial Capital: A Study of the West Riding Wool Textile Industry c.1750–1850* (Cambridge, 1986), pp. 160, 163–5; Kenneth Morgan (ed.), *An American Quaker in the British Isles: The Travel Journals of Jabez Maud Fisher, 1775–1779* (Oxford, 1992), pp. 282–327; Alfred P. Wadsworth and Julia de Lacy Mann, *The Cotton Trade and Industrial Lancashire, 1600–1780* (Manchester, 1931), pp. 148–67.

[47] O'Brien and Engerman, 'Exports and the Growth of the British Economy,' p. 207.

induced a demand for exports of clothing (mainly linen at this stage) and plantation equipment destined for the West Indies. In addition, surpluses derived from trade between mainland America and the Caribbean paid for about one quarter of the goods that North Americans bought from Britain between 1750 and 1770. It has been argued, therefore, that Caribbean-based demand may have accounted for about 35 per cent of the growth of total British exports between 1748 and 1776, and for about 12 per cent of the increase in English industrial output in the quarter century before the American Revolution.[48]

To evaluate whether this varied demand acted as a trigger for British economic growth, one needs data on the proportion of industrial output that was exported and, in particular, dispatched across the Atlantic. This is a tricky matter because we lack accurate production estimates for most branches of British industry in the eighteenth century. It seems that the proportion of industrial output exported rose from about one- fifth in 1700 to about one-third in 1800.[49] But there was considerable variation among individual industries. Exports of copper and brass – both comparatively small industries at this time – accounted for around 40 per cent of production on the eve of the American Revolution, while the nailmaking trades in Birmingham and the Black Country were said to export three- quarters of their product to British America by the 1760s.[50] Two branches of textiles were also very reliant on exports. The woollen industry sold 45 per cent of its product abroad in 1772 and about 55 per cent in 1799. Indeed the Yorkshire woollen industry exported some 72 per cent of its production in 1772, when Yorkshire was supplying approximately half of Britain's cloth exports and when nearly one-third of all woollen exports were sent to the colonies. The woollens in demand overseas included broad cloths, blankets, bays and Rochdale goods, worsteds, kerseys and half thicks. By 1800, America took 40 per cent of British wool textile exports, including well over half of the woollens and worsteds produced in Yorkshire.[51] The most significant industry with a high ratio of exports to production was cotton, which sold 50

[48] David Richardson, 'The Slave Trade, Sugar, and British Economic Growth, 1748–1776', in Solow and Engerman, eds, *British Capitalism and Caribbean Slavery*, pp. 103–33. For a broader statement that supports Richardson's arguments *see* Barbara L. Solow, 'Capitalism and Slavery in the Exceedingly Long Run' in ibid., pp. 69–77.

[49] W. A. Cole, 'Factors in Demand, 1700–80' in R. C. Floud and D. N. McCloskey (eds), *The Economic History of Britain since 1700, vol.1:1700–1860* (Cambridge, 1981), I, table 3.1, p. 40.

[50] J. R. Harris, *The Copper King: A Biography of Thomas Williams of Llanidan* (Liverpool, 1964), p. 12; 'The Humble Petition of the Merchants & Manufacturers of Birmingham . . .', Jan. 1766, Miscellaneous correspondence, bundle 10 (1765–6), Society of Merchant Venturers, Bristol.

[51] Crouzet, 'Toward an Export Economy,' pp. 87–9; Hudson, *Genesis of Industrial Capital*, table 3.4, p. 66, and pp. 156, 163; R. G. Wilson, 'The Supremacy of the Yorkshire Cloth Industry in the Eighteenth Century' in N. B. Harte and K. G. Ponting (eds), *Textile*

per cent of its manufacture abroad in 1760 and 62 per cent in 1801. American consumers particularly bought cotton and linen printed cloths and plain calicoes.[52] Other industries present a less striking picture. Scottish and English linen exports accounted for, at most, 20 per cent of production by the 1770s, while the iron trades – important suppliers of colonial markets at mid-century – depended on exports for 20 per cent of their gross product by the 1770s and for 24 per cent in 1801.[53]

This analysis reveals the complex relationship between exports and economic growth and brings us to the heart of the debate on the respective roles of home and foreign demand at the beginnings of industrialization. Historians who see the home market as the main source of growth can argue that only one industry (cotton) ever had more than half of its product exported in the eighteenth century – and then only in certain years in the period 1760–1801. A good case could be made, in fact, for cotton being the one British industry that was essentially nourished by transatlantic trade. Estimates of sectoral growth rates in eighteenth-century British industry show a steady rise in the output of various industries, including many that did not provide significant exports (soap, coal, brewing, building and construction are examples).[54] This broadly-based industrial output for the domestic market underscores the significance of home demand for economic growth.

A strong case can nevertheless be made for exports as a generator of growth. The increase in the quantity and variety of manufactured exports encouraged the development of the non- agricultural sector of the British economy and diversified Atlantic trade so that it was no longer 'import-led.' British merchants vended goods to America at a critical period in the mid-eighteenth century when long-standing European markets for woollens and worsteds were in decline and when exports, rather than agricultural incomes, were becoming a major stimulus to manufacturing.[55] Without markets in the colonies, English industries would not have had the incentive for rapid expansion at that time. Thus the large

---

History and Economic History: Essays in honour of Miss Julia de Lacy Mann (Manchester, 1973), pp. 230, 243–4; Phyllis Deane, 'The Output of the British Woollen Industry in the Eighteenth Century', *JEcH*, XVII (1957), p. 215.

[52] Edwards, *The Growth of the British Cotton Trade*, pp. 72–3 and table B-3, p. 246; Crafts, *British Economic Growth*, p. 143.

[53] Price, 'Colonial Trade and British Economic Development', pp. 229–32, 239; Crafts, *British Economic Growth*, p. 143; Alastair J. Durie, *The Scottish Linen Industry in the Eighteenth Century* (Edinburgh, 1979), pp. 145, 147–8, 152. Price notes that 90 per cent of English, Irish and German linen exports in the 1770s went to the Americas.

[54] Crafts, 'British Economic Growth, 1700–1831,' table 2, p. 181.

[55] Davis, 'English Foreign Trade, 1700–1774', pp. 102–3; Lee, *The British Economy since 1700*, pp. 115–16; Patrick O'Brien, 'Agriculture and the Home Market for English Industry, 1660–1820', *English Historical Review*, C (1985), pp. 773–800. Crafts calculates that manufac-

trading bowl of the British Empire became vital after 1750 for industrializing areas in Britain because it gave added incentive for manufacturers in Yorkshire, Lancashire and the Midlands to quicken the productivity of textiles, metalware and hardware through extra employment, the division of labour, and improved commercial organization.[56] If the labour force had produced mainly for the home market without the stimulus of expanding exports, lower levels of labour productivity would have been achieved because of prevailing unemployment, underemployment and cheap labour.[57] The rapid growth of cotton exports from mid-century onwards may have stimulated technological improvements on the spinning side of the industry by creating a larger market for finished cotton goods. Certainly, the diffusion of the technological breakthrough accelerated during the export boom of the last twenty years of the century.[58] By 1800, British industrial output was not circumscribed by home demand and the domestic market had also probably increased partly through productivity induced by overseas trade. Integration of the export sector into an economy with increased manufacturing may well have been crucial in giving Britain a comparative advantage over other regions of western Europe poised for industrialization in the late eighteenth century.[59]

A fourth connection between Atlantic trade and eighteenth-century British economic growth lay in developments in business institutions. Although these aspects of trade are not quantifiable, they contributed much to the commercial dynamism of the British economy. *Capitalism and Slavery* drew attention to the links between slave trading and the worlds of insurance and banking.[60] More recent research has enabled us to identify more fully the connections between Atlantic trade and business developments. Three main institutional improvements deserve mention. First of all, increased sophistication in the finance of commerce accompanied the growing scale and intricacy of Atlantic trade. An international payments mechanism involving bills of exchange enabled transfers

---

tured exports accounted for 75 per cent of British exports in 1750 and for 88 per cent in 1801 (*British Economic Growth*, p. 143).

[56] Ralph Davis, *The Rise of the English Shipping Industry in the Seventeenth and Eighteenth Centuries* (London, 1962), pp. 391–4; Joseph E. Inikori, 'Slavery and the Development of Industrial Capitalism in England' in Solow and Engerman (eds), *British Capitalism and Caribbean Slavery*, pp. 79–101.

[57] O'Brien and Engerman, 'Exports and the Growth of the British Economy', pp. 200–2; John Rule, *The Vital Century: England's Developing Economy 1714–1815* (London, 1992), p. 272.

[58] Joseph E. Inikori, 'Slavery and the Revolution in Cotton Textile Production in England' in Inikori and Engerman (eds), *The Atlantic Slave Trade*, pp. 145–81; Crouzet, 'Toward an Export Economy', p. 92.

[59] Cf. Cole, 'Factors in Demand', p. 41, and Jan de Vries, *Economy of Europe in an Age of Crisis, 1600–1750* (Cambridge, 1976), pp. 144–5.

[60] Williams, *Capitalism and Slavery*, pp. 98–102, 104–5.

to be made on either a bilateral or multilateral basis between British, North American, West Indian and European port cities. This was particularly important since specie was often in short supply and commercial banks non-existent in British America. Marine insurance also benefited from the growth of Atlantic commerce; indeed, the two were mutually reinforcing. The livelihood of underwriters at the London Assurance Company, the Royal Exchange Assurance and Lloyd's Coffee House – the three early centres of British marine insurance – was closely linked to the higher premiums charged for hazardous long-distance voyages during eighteenth-century wars.[61]

Atlantic trade also helped to foster what Jacob M. Price has called 'a miniature banking revolution' in the outports. Between 1750 and 1775, colonial merchants became prominent partners in the first banks established in Bristol, Glasgow and Liverpool, for the availability of deposit and transfer facilities suited the needs of substantial businessmen.[62] The provision of credit was a further way in which international trade was connected with more sophisticated financial transactions. The chain of credit linking suppliers of goods in provincial Britain, merchants at various ports, and customers in the Americas affected many commercial decisions in transatlantic trade, and offered flexible options in payment for goods. The slave trade played a significant role in the deployment of credit over long distances.[63]

New commercial strategies employed during the post-1783 export boom were a second business development associated with Atlantic trade. After 1790 English woollen manufacturers often sent out agents or partners to the United States, something which helped to quicken the pace of sales and to provide closer supervision of the composition of woollen shipments for different markets.[64] At the same time close links were forged between American merchants and British businessmen, with personnel sent to and fro across the

---

[61] Charles Wright and C. Ernest Fayle, *A History of Lloyd's* (London, 1928); Barry Supple, *The Royal Exchange Assurance: A History of British Insurance 1720–1970* (Cambridge, 1970), esp. pp. 3–4, 53, 187; A. H. John, 'The London Assurance Company and the Marine Insurance Market in the Eighteenth Century', *Economica*, new series, XXV (1958), pp. 126–41.

[62] Price, *Capital and Credit*, pp. 67–9, 94 (quotation on p. 67); Devine, *Tobacco Lords*, p. 93; John Hughes, *Liverpool Banks and Bankers* (Liverpool, 1906); C. H. Cave, *A History of Banking in Bristol from 1750 to 1899* (Bristol, 1899); S. G. Checkland, *Scottish Banking: A History, 1695–1973* (Glasgow, 1975), pp. 106–7, 168; Hyde, *Liverpool and the Mersey*, pp. 18–19.

[63] Price, 'Credit in the Slave Trade and Plantation Economies', pp. 298–323; Joseph E. Inikori, 'The Credit needs of the African Trade and the Development of the Credit Economy in England', *EEH*, XXVII (1990), pp. 197–231.

[64] Herbert Heaton, 'Yorkshire Cloth Traders in the United States, 1770–1840', *The Thoresby Miscellany*, vol. II, *Publications of the Thoresby Society*, XXXVII, 1941 (Leeds, 1945), pp. 241–3.

Atlantic to gain knowledge of the varied export wares on offer and to see, on the spot, the best ways of gauging price and quality in relation to diverse consumer tastes. The shift towards more aggressive marketing strategies has been examined for trade in the 1780s between British ports and Philadelphia, the largest city and biggest port in the new United States. Instead of allowing their American correspondents to assume title to the goods they exported, many British firms began to ship off large cargoes on their own account, and often dispatched young partners to Philadelphia to solicit business. Moreover some British adventurers purchased goods on credit, took them to Philadelphia, rented a store, and sold the goods on their own account.[65] These innovations in business practice were a response by merchants to widening economic opportunities and increased competition – though the obverse of this situation was that textiles and trade were the most prominent sectors of the economy for English bankrupts during early industrialization.[66]

The growth and complexity of Atlantic trade led to a third significant business development, namely, an increase in the size and style of British merchant houses. Between 1675 and 1775 – and especially in the latter half of that period – there was a considerable increase in the concentration of tobacco and sugar imports among large firms in Bristol and Glasgow, and a squeezing out of marginal competitors; and this also occurred to a lesser degree in London and Liverpool. By the 1780s and 1790s, a similar concentration was apparent among slave traders at London, Liverpool and Bristol.[67] The increase in concentration ratios was assisted by the availability of marine insurance and credit to large, seemingly secure firms. This transformation of the size and style of firms led to higher levels of capitalization and to greater economic efficiency in the conduct of business, with large turnovers of goods speeded up by the concentration of resources.

Finally, Atlantic trade can be seen as having various additional effects on economic growth in Britain. As *Capitalism and Slavery* suggested, and as modern research has amplified, it was crucial for the development of the west coast outports and had a significant impact on the metropolis.[68] Glasgow rose from being a small port in 1700 to become one of the great commercial cities of eighteenth- century Europe; and this was achieved largely by generating new

---

[65] Doerflinger, *Vigorous Spirit of Enterprise*, p. 245.

[66] Julian Hoppit, *Risk and Failure in English Business, 1700–1800* (Cambridge, 1987), esp. ch. 5.

[67] Jacob M. Price and Paul G. E. Clemens, 'A Revolution of Scale in British Overseas Trade: British Firms in the Chesapeake Trade, 1675–1775', *JEcH*, XLVII (1987), pp. 1–43; Morgan, *Bristol and the Atlantic Trade*, pp. 143, 158–60, 189, 191–2; Inikori, 'Market Structure and the Profits of the British African Trade', pp. 749–52.

[68] Williams, *Capitalism and Slavery*, pp. 60–4, 73–5.

marketing strategies and productivity advances in the shipment of tobacco.[69] Liverpool prospered by the growth of oceanic trade to become the most important slave-trading port in the world by 1800. The increase in the volume of Liverpool's trade was sustained after 1720 by the construction of five wet and two dry docks, which protected ships against damage and allowed for more efficient loading and unloading of cargoes.[70]

At Bristol, where dock expansion was more sluggish, merchants profited from broadly-based Atlantic commercial interests. Continuing influxes of sugar by a cohesive mercantile elite helped to moderate Bristol's relative commercial decline.[71] The slave trade strengthened the merchant community of Lancaster and enhanced the town's potential to participate in colonial trade.[72] The impact of Atlantic trade on Whitehaven was more muted because the only colonial trade to flourish there was tobacco importation, and then only for a brief period in the 1740s.[73] The indirect effects of Atlantic trade on the west-coast outports were most beneficial at Liverpool where an extensive hinterland developed and home and foreign demand could therefore intertwine; they were less significant for Whitehaven and, to a lesser extent, Bristol where hinterlands showed fewer signs of expansion.[74] The sheer size of London meant that it was always a large market for the products of colonial trade and for distribution and re-export.

[69] Jacob M. Price, 'The Rise of Glasgow in the Chesapeake Tobacco Trade, 1707–1775', *William and Mary Quarterly*, 3rd series, XI (1954), pp. 179–99; *idem, France and the Chesapeake: A History of the French Tobacco Monopoly, 1674–1791, and of its relationship with British and American Tobacco Trades*, 2 vols (Ann Arbor, 1973), esp. I, ch. 23; Devine, *Tobacco Lords*; T. M. Devine, 'The Golden Age of Tobacco' in T. M. Devine and Gordon Jackson (eds), *Glasgow: Volume 1: Beginnings to 1830* (Manchester, 1995), pp. 139–83; Richard F. Dell, 'The Operational Record of the Clyde Tobacco Fleet, 1747–1775', *Scottish Economic and Social History*, II (1982), pp. 1–16.

[70] Hyde, *Liverpool and the Mersey*, pp. 10–15, 31–4, 72–7; Paul G. E. Clemens, 'The Rise of Liverpool, 1665–1750', *EcHR*, 2nd series, XXIX (1976), pp. 211–25; David Richardson, 'The Eighteenth-Century British Slave Trade: Estimates of its Volume and Coastal Distribution in Africa' in Uselding (ed.), *Research in Economic History*, XII (1989), app, pp. 184–95; Gordon Jackson, 'The Ports' in Derek H. Aldcroft and Michael J. Freeman (eds), *Transport in the Industrial Revolution* (Manchester, 1983), pp. 200–1.

[71] W. E. Minchinton, *The Port of Bristol in the Eighteenth Century* (Bristol, 1962); Kenneth Morgan, 'Bristol West India Merchants in the Eighteenth Century', *TRHS*, 6th series, III, (1993), pp. 185–208; *idem, Bristol and the Atlantic Trade*; *idem*, 'Sugar Refining in Bristol' in Kristine Bruland and Patrick O'Brien (eds), *From Family Firms to Corporate Capitalism: Essays in Business and Industrial History in honour of Peter Mathias* (Oxford, 1997).

[72] Melinda Elder, *The Slave Trade and the Economic Development of Eighteenth-Century Lancaster* (Halifax, 1992).

[73] Beckett, *Coal and Tobacco*, pp. xii, 104, 106–8.

[74] P. J. Corfield, *The Impact of English Towns 1700–1800* (Oxford, 1982), pp. 42–3; John Langton, 'Liverpool and its Hinterland in the late Eighteenth Century' in B. L. Anderson

London had many consumer-oriented industries derived from the wealth produced by overseas trade and government expenditure. Its colonial merchants coordinated people, products and capital and thereby helped to integrate the economy of the British Empire.[75]

Many other significant, though not immediately obvious, indirect ways in which Atlantic trade impinged on the eighteenth-century British economy reveal the increasingly interdependent nature of seaborne commerce. Large imports of hemp, flax, timber and naval stores from the Baltic region, for instance, were partly fuelled by the growth of demand for shipbuilding materials for vessels plying oceanic shipping routes.[76] Multilateral trading links 'enabled a system of compensating balances to function long before the better-known settlements of the nineteenth century came into being.'[77] Invisible and clandestine earnings from trade were also important even though, for obvious reasons, their precise statistical significance cannot be calculated. British coffers were swelled by the capture of prize goods during wartime, the supply of slaves and contraband via Jamaica to the French West Indies and the Spanish Main, the remittance of bullion from the Caribbean to England, the smuggling of tobacco into Britain, and profits from sales of Newfoundland cod and American grain in the Iberian peninsula. For example, some £2,368,484 worth of bullion alone was sent to England from the West Indies in the period 1748–65.[78] It is likely that the receipts from the sale of these invisibles expanded more rapidly than visible exports during the eighteenth century.[79]

Atlantic trade also gave impetus to the circulation of business news at coffee houses, in newspapers, and via the transatlantic postal system. It contributed to the growth of large-scale warehousing in ports, with warehousemen acting as important intermediaries between merchants and manufacturers. It assisted employment in urban and rural areas that supplied export goods; provided work

---

and P. J. M. Stoney (eds), *Commerce, Industry and Transport: Studies in Economic Change on Merseyside* (Liverpool, 1983), pp. 1–25.

[75] Christopher J. French, 'The Trade and Shipping of the Port of London, 1700–1776' (University of Exeter Ph.D., 1980); *idem*, ' "Crowded with Traders and a Great Commerce": London's Dominion of English Overseas Trade, 1700–1775', *The London Journal*, XVII (1992), pp. 27–35; P. J. Cain and A. G. Hopkins, *British Imperialism: Innovation and Expansion 1688–1914* (London, 1993), p. 62; Hancock, *Citizens of the World*.

[76] D. A. Farnie, 'The Commercial Empire of the Atlantic, 1607–1783', *EcHR*, 2nd series, XV (1962–3), p. 213.

[77] Cain and Hopkins, *British Imperialism*, p. 88.

[78] Sheridan, *Sugar and Slavery*, pp. 318–19, 426–7, 451–2 and appendix XI, p. 506; Allan Christelow, 'Contraband Trade between Jamaica and the Spanish Main, and the Free Port Act of 1766', *Hispanic American Historical Review*, XXII (1942), pp. 309–43; H. E. S. Fisher, *The Portugal Trade: A Study of Anglo-Portuguese Commerce 1700–1770* (London, 1971), pp. 128–9, 138–9; Robert C. Nash, 'The English and Scottish Tobacco Trades in the Seventeenth and Eighteenth Centuries: Legal and Illegal Trade,' *EcHR*, 2nd series, XXXV (1982), pp. 354–72.

[79] O'Brien and Engerman, 'Exports and the Growth of the British Economy,' p. 184.

for merchants, shipowners, shipbuilders, customs officials, packers, hauliers, dock labourers and seamen; helped to develop the commercial sectors of ports and their hinterlands; and raised the level of aggregate demand in the economy. Less tangibly, it stimulated the development of commercial education, entrepreneurship, and attitudes towards accumulation and investment.[80]

Throughout this essay the suggested links between the slave–sugar complex, Atlantic trade and the eighteenth-century British economy have been delineated, with particular reference to the pioneer work represented in *Capitalism and Slavery* and subsequent scholarship. Advances in quantitative techniques and extra primary material gathered since the time when Eric Williams was writing suggest that it is no longer accurate to state that the profits of the slave trade directly fuelled British industry in the late eighteenth century: annual net returns in the trade were relatively modest. Plenty of capital was amassed from slave plantations but the various arguments for slavery and sugar's role in metropolitan capital accumulation need further examination: more thorough wealth estimates of the British Caribbean are needed, firmer evidence that West India fortunes were repatriated, and better analysis of the multiplier effects created by colonial capital in Britain. Whether or not the colonies were a net gain or net loss to Britain has not been proven definitively.

Nevertheless, there were significant links between Atlantic trade and eighteenth-century British economic development. The intricate connections between consumer demand and British exports, aided by population growth in the Americas and income from the slave–sugar nexus, helped to boost manufactured exports at a time when transatlantic markets were capturing an increasing portion of British overseas trade. The growth of business institutions such as long-term credit, banks and marine insurance in London and the expansion of west-coast outports were vital for the long-term development of the British economy. Atlantic trade also had a considerable impact on shipping, ports and their hinterlands, and employment. *Capitalism and Slavery* hinted at many of these issues without analysing them fully. My own emphasis on increasing commercial sophistication and business efficiency in the British Atlantic economy underlines the burden of this essay: that Atlantic trade was indeed significant for eighteenth-century British economic growth, but as much for its stimulus to manufacturing production in textiles, metalware and hardware, receipts from the sale of invisibles, and business improvements than for its direct impact on capital investment and national income.

[80] I. K. Steele, *The English Atlantic, 1675–1740: An Exploration of Communication and Community* (Oxford, 1986); Price, *Capital and Credit*; Davis, *Rise of the English Shipping Industry*; Marcus Rediker, *Between the Devil and the Deep Blue Sea: Merchant Seamen, Pirates, and the Anglo-American Maritime World, 1700–1750* (Cambridge, 1987), esp. ch. 1; Corfield, *The Impact of English Towns*, pp. 34, 42–3, 50; Minchinton (ed.), The Growth of English Overseas Trade, pp. 45–8; Peter Mathias, *The First Industrial Nation: An Economic History of Modern Britain, 1700–1914*, 2nd edn (London, 1983), p. 96.

2

British Trade and European Economic Development (1750–1850)

Sidney Pollard

During the century covered by this chapter, the industrial revolution in Great Britain ran its complete course. On the continent of Europe, several countries had set out upon a vigorous course of industrialization before our period came to an end, and others, which were not yet so involved, were undoubtedly influenced by what happened in the industrial regions of Europe. How far did developments in the pioneer country affect the changes in the remainder of the European economies? Assuming that their growth and structural transformation were desirable things in themselves, may the course of British change be said to have had a positive or a negative impact on them?

This chapter, which sets out to find answers to these questions, is divided into five sections. The first attempts a quantitative summary of the trading activities between Britain and the continent, in absolute terms and as a share of general incomes and output. The second traces the changes in the nature and direction of British trade over different phases of our period, with some reference to the effects of the war against France and the economic blockade imposed in its course. The third section will concern itself with some consequences of British exports to the continent, and with some continental manufactured exports, while the fourth will deal with the food and raw material imports from the continent into Britain. The final section will attempt to summarize the evidence in answer to the questions posed at the beginning.

A Quantitative Summary of Trade between Britain and Europe

It will not be necessary, presumably, to emphasize the problems of translating the official British statistics of overseas trade, particularly for the eighteenth century, into usable terms, even with the aid of the excellent work of Ralph Davis and of Mrs Schumpeter.[1] Continental statistics are, on the whole, even less reliable; so much so, that many continental historians, attempting to study the trade of their own countries, begin with the British series as their fixed base.

Throughout our period, trade showed a vigorous rate of expansion. For England and Wales, in 1750–80, this has been calculated at 1.1 per cent a year (counting exports and retained imports), rising for Great Britain to 2.3 per cent in 1770–1800, and further to 2.7 per cent in 1800–20 and to 4.4 per cent in 1820–50 for the United Kingdom. Exports alone, using 'official values' which tend to measure volume, grew faster still.[2] As a proportion of the rapidly rising national income, however, the change was less dramatic. Exports fluctuated between 7 per cent and 11 per cent of national income in 1770 to 1841, starting to rise only in the 1840s, to 12 per cent of national income by one calculation, to 14 per cent and even to over 15 per cent, at constant prices, according to others. As a proportion of industrial output, a somewhat vague category, exports rose to 42 per cent in 1851.[3] Retained imports have been calculated as 8 per cent of gross national income in *c.* 1770, and then to have remained unchanged at around 15 to 16 per cent in 1804–50.[4]

The larger continental countries remained well below the British ratio of total trade (retained imports plus domestic exports, leaving out re-exports) at 21 to 27 per cent of national income. In other words, trade played a smaller part in their economic lives. In France, trade thus defined fluctuated at, or just below, 14 per cent between 1780 and the 1840s, rising a little thereafter; for Germany it was 13 per cent in 1840 and for Italy, 10 per cent

---

[1] Ralph Davis, 'English Foreign Trade, 1700–1774', *Economic History Review* (henceforth, *Ec.H.R.*) 15 (1962–3), pp. 285–303; *idem, The Industrial Revolution and British Overseas Trade* (Leicester, 1979); Elizabeth Boody Schumpeter, *English Overseas Trade Statistics 1697–1808* (Oxford, 1960).

[2] Phyllis Deane and W. A. Cole, *British Economic Growth 1688–1959* (Cambridge, 1967), p. 29; François Crouzet, 'Toward an Export Economy: British Exports during the Industrial Revolution', *Explorations in Economic History* 17 (1980), pp. 51–3.

[3] Paul Bairoch, *Révolution industrielle et sous-développement* (Paris/Hague, 1974), p. 259; Crouzet, 'Export economy', pp. 79, 86; Joel Mokyr, 'Demand vs. Supply in the Industrial Revolution', in his *The Economics of the Industrial Revolution* (Totowa, 1985), p. 100; Simon Kuznets, 'Quantitative Aspects of the Economic Growth of Nations: X. Level and Structure of Foreign Trade: Long-term Trends', *Economic Development and Cultural Change* 15 (1967), Part II, p. 96.

[4] Davis, *Industrial Revolution*, p. 51.

in 1830, in each case on a rising trend. For some smaller countries, the ratio was necessarily higher but, in the European periphery, including Russia, it was considerably lower.[5] For Europe as a whole, the role of trade was much smaller than in Britain. (*see* Table 2.1).

Table 2.1 Exports as a proportion of gross national product, 1830–50.

	1830	*1850*
United Kingdom	7.8 per cent	11.4 per cent
Continental Europe	3.9 per cent	6.0 per cent
All Europe	4.4 per cent	7.0 per cent
(Years are the middle values of three years)		

Source: Paul Bairoch, *Commerce extérieur et développement économique de l'Europe au XIXe siècle* (Paris/Hague, 1976) p.79.

Calculated on a different basis, while British trade per head amounted to 8 current dollars in 1830 (and 22 in 1860), the French figure was but 3 (11), the German 3 (11) and the Russian 1 (2); against this the Belgian was 5 (19), the Dutch 5 (10), and the Swiss even exceeded the British at 12 (31).[6] Though it started from a low level, European trade as a whole was expanding vigorously. The volume of world trade tripled in the eighteenth century, and rose by 29 per cent per decade in 1800–30, and by 50 per cent per decade in 1820–50, the European share of it remaining constant at around 60 per cent. Exports of continental Europe's own produce are estimated to have risen from 157 million dollars (of 1899–1901) in 1800, to 309 million dollars in 1830 and 604 million dollars in 1850.[7] It may therefore be said that, even in countries in which foreign trade played a relatively minor part, it formed a dynamic element. At the same time, in some of the larger countries with a low foreign trade ratio, notably France, the Habsburg Monarchy and Russia, imports were kept down deliberately by high tariffs or prohibitions.[8]

---

[5] Kuznets, 'Aspects', pp. 22, 98, 102, 106; Bairoch, *Révolution industrielle*, p. 333; I. T. Berend and G. Ránki, *The European Periphery and Industrialization 1780–1914* (Cambridge, 1982), p. 112.

[6] Paul Bairoch, 'European Foreign Trade in the XIXth Century: The Development of the Value and Volume of Exports (Preliminary Results), *Journal of European Economic History* (henceforth: *J.E.Ec.H.*) 2 (1973), p. 17.

[7] Angus Maddison, *Phases of Capitalist Development* (Oxford, 1982), p. 254; Kuznets, 'Aspects', pp. 4, 11; Bairoch, *Commerce extérieur*, p. 73.

[8] *See*, in general, Judith Blow Williams, *British Commercial Policy and Trade Expansion 1750–1850* (Oxford, 1972).

Changes in the Nature and Direction of British Trade

It would be wrong to assume that in the run-up to the industrial revolution, British foreign trade had been stagnant or 'traditional'. On the contrary, it had been subject to considerable change, reflecting, as well as itself initiating, significant economic developments in Europe as much as overseas, particularly in the colonies.

Among the changes, the links with Europe were being reduced significantly as a proportion of British trade between *c.* 1700 and 1770, partly because continental countries were able to substitute their own textiles for their former imports from Britain. This development was aided by mercantilist policies on the part of the more developed countries of Europe, while growing British home production of linens trenched into what had formerly been a major European export commodity to Britain. The re-export of colonial goods to Europe, however, remained buoyant. Southern Europe still formed an important market for British home produce. At the same time, the overall British export surplus of grain to Europe in the first half of the eighteenth century had disappeared by the 1760s and 1770s, as the rising population, and its rising consumption, absorbed the former British output surplus.

The main items of trade on the eve of industrialization are listed in Table 2.2, and the distribution by countries, including the distortions of the war years, is shown in Table 2.3.

Thus, of the countries on the continent that were to industrialize early, the Netherlands and Germany, plus Switzerland which obtained many of her goods through their territory, had a large trade with Britain, while France, despite her size and proximity, kept her trade down largely because of restrictions, as indeed did Russia. The high levels of English exports to Spain and Portugal are notable, as are the imports from the northern countries, in which iron and naval stores figure largely. The distortions caused by the Napoleonic wars, and the relative decline of European trade altogether in the war years, are equally evident.

The major effect of the industrial revolution on British exports was the meteoric rise of the export of cotton manufactures: whether or not the cotton industry was indeed the 'leading' industry in Britain, there is no doubt that it quickly overwhelmed the export statistics. Other textile exports, notably woollens, also expanded very fast, though they could not compare with cotton. By the 1830s and 1840s, iron as well as iron goods and other metal goods were added as important items.

British exports consisted to an even larger extent than before of manufactures, while the small proportion of her imports made up of manufactures shrank further to about 6 per cent of the total and even down to 2 to 4 per

Table 2.2 Selected items of English trade to Europe, as a proportion of total English trade to Europe, 1752–74

	1752–4	1772–4
English imports from Europe::		
Manufactures	22.2	16.9
(of which linens)	(14.4)	(9.9)
Food and drink	41.4	50.9
(of which wines)	(4.6)	(3.2)
(of which corn)	–	(3.1)
Raw materials	36.3	32.2
(of which raw and thrown silk)	(8.2)	(5.9)
English exports to Europe:		
Manufactures	53.3	54.2
(of which woollens)	(33.0)	(26.7)
Food and drink	11.9	3.7
(of which grain)	(7.5)	–
Raw materials	5.4	5.1
All home-produced exports	70.7	62.9
Re-exported manufacturers	9.6	10.0
Re-exported food and tobacco	16.2	22.6
(of which tobacco)	(8.0)	(5.8)
Re-exported raw materials	3.5	4.6
All re-exported exports	29.3	37.1

Source: Ralph Davis, 'English Foreign Trade', pp. 300–3. Ireland excluded throughout. *See also* C. P. Kindleberger, 'Commercial Expansion and the Industrial Revolution' *Journal of European Economic History* 4 (1975) pp. 632 and throughout.

cent according to Crafts. The share of food in imports remained high, and the share of raw materials, dominated by raw cotton, rose from about one-half to almost two-thirds by 1850. It has to be remembered that the remarkable increase in British manufactured exports to Europe occurred despite the rapid fall in their costs of production and their prices. Thus, between 1814 and 1846, while the values of exports to northern Europe rose by 0.9 per cent a year, and to southern Europe by 1.0 per cent a year, their volume rose by 4.1 per cent and 4.2 per cent a year respectively.[9] By the

[9] Crouzet, 'Toward an Export Economy', p. 73; Kuznets, 'Aspects', pp. 121, 123; N. F. R. Crafts, *British Economic Growth during the Industrial Revolution* (Oxford, 1985), p. 143.

Table 2.3 English trading partners in Europe, percentage of total trade of England and Wales, 1751–1800.

	Exports to Europe			Imports from Europe		
	1751–5	*1776–8*	*1796–1800*	*1751–5*	*1776–80*	*1796–1800*
Flanders	3.8	8.9	0.6	1.1	3.1	0.1
France	3.9	0.6	1.2	0.7	0.3	0.2
Germany	11.4	9.9	28.9	8.3	5.8	8.6
Netherlands	23.5	10.0	3.6	3.7	4.5	1.7
Denmark, Norway, Sweden	0.9	2.1	1.8	3.3	2.8	0.6
Russia, Poland	2.3	2.3	3.8	9.4	12.7	12.3
Portugal	9.3	4.2	2.5	3.3	3.4	2.9
Spain	8.8	5.7	0.3	4.9	3.3	2.2
Italy	2.2	4.8	1.2	7.6	4.6	1.0
Others (Turkey, Straits)	6.3	0.6	1.0	3.4	1.2	0.6
All Europe	72.4	49.1	44.9	45.7	41.7	30.2

Source: Elizabeth Boody Schumpeter, *English Overseas Trade Statistics 1697–1808* (Oxford, 1960).

Table 2.4 Share of certain manufacturers in British exports, 1784–1846.

	1784/6 1794/6	*1794/6 1804/6*	*1814/16 1844/6*
Woollen fabrics and yarns	18.1%	6.0%	10.8%
Cotton fabrics and yarns	28.8	72.8	45.9
Other textiles	10.4	3.3	9.8
Iron and iron wares	9.6	3.6	16.9
Non-ferrous metals and Manufactures	10.0	3.8	16.9
All other	23.1	10.5	–

Source: François Crouzet, 'Toward an Export Economy: British Exports during the Industrial Revolution', *Explorations in Economic History* 17 (1980), p. 63; also Phyllis Deane and W. A. Cole, *British Economic Growth 1688–1959* (Cambridge, 1967), p. 31; Ralph Davis. *The Industrial Revolution in British Overseas Trade* (Leicester, 1979), throught.

early 1840s, Germany and the Netherlands between them took about 18 per cent of total British home-produced exports, France and Italy about 5 per cent each, and Belgium and Portugal about 2 per cent each. Altogether, Europe accounted for 39.3 per cent of British domestic exports in 1842–4.[10]

[10] G. Porter, *Progress of the Nation* (1847 ed.), pp. 364–7.

As a large, rich country, with a high trading ratio to national income, Britain necessarily captured a large share of European trade. This has been calculated as 27.5 per cent in 1830, rising to 29.8 per cent in 1860, compared with 15.9 per cent (19.2 per cent) for France, 4.7 per cent (5.8 per cent) for Austria, 7.9 per cent (5.6 per cent) for Russia and 18.4 per cent in 1860 for Germany.[11] More significant for our purpose is the share that trade with Britain played in the trade of other countries, in other words, how important the British trading partner was for them. Towards the end of our period, the share of British trade was as follows:

Table 2.5 Share of the United Kingdom in the trade of some European countries, 1832–52 (in per cent)

	1832–4		1845–9		1850–2	
	Imports	*Exports*	*Imports*	*Exports*	*Imports*	*Exports*
Belgium			16.2	12.9	17.6	15.1
France	12.9*	16.3*	8.2	18.3	8.8	21.6
Netherlands			21.5†	24.2†	19.7	26.9
Russia	30.0	42.3	27.1**	38.6**	25.8	39.9
Spain			17.0††	33.3††	19.5	27.6
Sweden	10.8	23.2	15.1	32.4	14.7	36.7

* 1842–4
† 1846–9
** 1847–9
†† 1849

Source: B. R. Mitchell, *European Historical Statistics 1750–1975* (Cambridge, 1981). Also see Paul Bairoch, *Révolution industrielle et sous-développement* (Paris/Hague, 1974), p. 338. According to E. Levasseur, *Histoire du commerce de la France*, 2 vols (Paris, 1911), vol. II, pp. 148–9, Britain furnished 15 per cent of French 'general' imports in 1821, falling to 3 per cent in 1829, and took 6 per cent, rising to 11 per cent, of her 'general' exports in those years. Of 'special' trade, Great Britain provided 10 per cent of imports in 1825 and 6 per cent in 1829, taking 18 per cent and 19 per cent respectively of French exports.

For Germany the ratio is difficult to establish because, on the one hand, much British trade to the lands which later became Germany went through Holland and Belgium while, on the other, some of the goods exported to the free cities of Hamburg and Bremen might be destined

[11] Bairoch, 'European Foreign Trade', p. 14.

for countries beyond Germany. According to the data collected by Bodo von Borries, and including all the traffic via the Netherlands, Britain supplied 22 per cent of German imports in 1841 and 45 per cent in 1851, while taking 33 per cent and 28 per cent of German exports respectively on those dates. Kutz, making similar calculations for 1830, came to 31 per cent of German imports and 54 per cent of exports, not including the traffic through Holland. More significant still was the distribution between types of goods:

	Finished goods	Food and raw materials
British share in:		
German imports	72.5 per cent	0 per cent
German exports	0.9 per cent	78.2 per cent

While this would be modified a little by the Dutch Rhine trade, it would justify the description of Germany as a dependent economy.[12]

Leaving out the re-export of colonial goods from Britain to the continent, 'the most consistently dynamic sector of foreign trade throughout the

Table 2.6 Europe's share of certain British imports and exports, 1831–50, per cent.

		1831	1850
UK imports:	Grain	86	90
	Flax and hemp	99	84
	Wines	91	
	Timber		36
	Wool		28
UK exports:	Coal		73
	Cotton yarns and fabrics	47	39
	Woollen yarns and fabrics	25	32
	Linens	32	26
	Cutlery, hardware	14	27

Source: William Woodruff, 'The Emergence of an International Economy 1700–1914', *Fontana Economic History of Europe*, vol. 4, Part II (1973), pp. 718, 724. Also Ralph Davis. *The Industrial Revolution and British Overseas Trade* (Leicester, 1979) pp. 15, 22, 29.

---

[12] Bodo von Borries, *Deutschlands Außenhandel 1836 bis 1856* (Stuttgart 1970), p. 186; Martin Kutz, *Deutschlands Außenhandel von der französischen Revolution bis zur Gründung des Zollvereins* (Wiesbaden, 1974), pp. 257, 363–6.

[eighteenth] century',[13] and leaving aside the interesting thought that British manufactured cotton exports might be considered a substitution of a domestic export for a colonial re-export[14] from the British point of view, Europe took the share of Britain's imports and exports of important commodities shown in Table 2.6.

From the European point of view, as we have seen, imports and exports each tended to be around 7 per cent of national income, and the British share in it seldom higher than one-third, or a little over 2 per cent of national income of these countries. Could this kind of quantity have made any noticeable difference to their development?

On the face of it, the share of Britain as a supplier of commodities, or her role as an ultimate purchaser of their output, seem too insignificant to have made a noticeable impact. Yet even quantities of that order of magnitude might make a difference if they are of a strategic or dynamic kind. As an example, we might note the impact of the Napoleonic blockade and counter-blockade, over which there is a broad consensus in the literature.

The British entry into the war against France in 1793 occurred at the end of a long period of expansion of colonial trade, particularly on the part of France, and in the midst of the rapid technical transformation of certain British key industries, particularly cotton spinning, iron making and engineering. The loss of access to her colonies suffered by France as a result of the dominance of British naval power, clearly had important effects on the French economy, especially in the maritime provinces. But equally significant was the impact of the war on European industries competing with British industries in process of transformation. At least three major effects have been noted. First, the cutting off of British exports permitted some continental centres to develop rapidly, even feverishly, in the years of the strict blockade. Examples are Belgium, the Rhineland and Alsace. Secondly, areas in which the blockade was not effective, as for example Sweden, were overwhelmed by the inrush of British manufactures. But thirdly and most importantly, by the end of hostilities, the continent, by being cut off from acquiring the latest British technology for so long, was wholly unable to stand up to the cheaper imports as soon as these became possible in 1814–15. The devastation these imports caused among the European industrial centres, and the policy measures and political attitudes directly traceable

[13] A. Milward and S. B. Saul, *The Economic Development of Continental Europe 1780–1870* (London 1973), p. 109.

[14] D. A. Farnie, *The English Cotton Industry and the World Market 1815–1896* (Oxford, 1979), p. 81.

to this, were by common consent among major factors in the economic development of Europe after 1815.[15]

It follows that trade, even if small in volume, can have significant effects on a country's economic development, if it has a dynamic impact on certain key sectors. How far may British trade be said to have had such effects on Europe in our period?

Some Consequences of British Exports to Europe

The significance of the transfer of British technology, in the form of the migration of skilled workers, managers and technicians, of blueprints, models and prototype machines, has often been described[16] and need not detain us here. Clearly, without them, the industrialization on the continent would have occurred much later, and would have been much costlier in terms of false starts and worthless experiments. But the goods involved, even if they were not smuggled out and were bought legally, would hardly be numerous enough to show up in the export statistics.

More in the nature of trade was the export of machinery and other commodities in larger quantities from Britain to continental countries because they could not yet be produced there to meet all of the demand. A well-known example was the opportunity provided for Germany in her first two decades of railway building, at least to 1850. Because railways there have themselves often been considered to have been a 'leading sector' of the country's industrialization, the British contribution was doubly important.

[15] F. Crouzet, 'War, Blockade and Economic Change in Europe, 1792–1815', *Journal of Economic History* (henceforth *J.Ec.H.*) 24 (1964), pp. 567–89; Clive Trebilcock, *The Industrialization of the Continental Powers 1780–1914* (London 1981), pp. 30–2, 130–1; Eli F. Heckscher, *The Continental System. An Economic Interpretation* (Oxford, 1922), p. 265; Milward and Saul, *Economic Development*, pp. 268, 294–6, 302; Kutz, *Außenhandel*, pp. 12, 39; Gerhard Bondi, *Deutschlands Außenhandel 1815–1870* [Berlin (East), 1958], pp. 31–2, 46, 49; J. Holland Rose, 'The Continental System, 1809–14', *Cambridge Modern History* IX (repr. Cambridge, 1969), pp. 361–89; Joel Mokyr and N. Eugene Savin, 'Stagflation in Historical Perspective: The Napoleonic Wars Revisited', *Research in Economic History* 1 (1976), pp. 224–8, 250.

[16] See esp. W. O. Henderson, *Britain and Industrial Europe 1750–1870* (Liverpool, 1954); A. Klima, 'The Beginnings of the Machine-Building Industry in the Czech Lands in the First Half of the 19th Century', *J.E.Ec.H.* 4 (1975), pp. 49–78; Werner Kroker, *Wege zur Verbreitung technologischer Kenntnisse zwischen England und Deutschland in der zweiten Hälfte des 18. Jahrhunderts* (Berlin, 1971); H.-J. Braun, *Technologische Beziehungen zwischen Deutschland und England von der Mitte des 17, bis zum Ausgang des 18. Jahrhunderts* (Düsseldorf, 1974); Martin Schumacher, *Auslandsreisen deutscher Unternehmer 1750–1851* (Cologne, 1968), pp. 132 ff.

Without British locomotives, and above all the British bar and rail iron, the construction of the first German railway network would have been much delayed. Some 88 per cent of the rail stock in Germany in 1843, and 51 per cent still in 1853, were of British origin. At that time also, 153 of the 729 locomotives came from Britain. Other countries in which British rails played a significant part up to 1850 included Spain, Italy, Austria and Denmark.[17] Coal was another key commodity in this context: in 1846, all of the coal used in Berlin came from Britain, and, even in 1860, it was still 57 per cent. There was, besides, the demonstration effect in the development of markets by British exports of various kinds which were later to be supplied by native German suppliers.[18] Even in France, despite the virtually prohibitive tariff, some British imports of bar iron, at least until 1821, of chemicals and of machinery, were of significance.[19]

More generally, all reductions in costs and/or the expansion of output in Britain benefited her trading partners in Europe, because their real national income gained by buying cheap British coal or cheap British textiles.[20] These benefits can be measured for the first half of the nineteenth century by the dramatic fall in the prices of British manufactured exports compared with import prices, in other words, by the sharply deteriorating net barter terms of trade for Britain. In addition to the falling costs of production, the reduction, and later repeal, of export duties for coal in 1831 and 1845 and for wool in 1823 and 1845, also played a part. In the case of cotton fabrics, the quality of exports to the more advanced area of Europe actually rose, so that the price reductions were more remarkable still.[21]

[17] Rainer Fremdling, '*Britische Exporte und die Modernisierung der deutschen Eisenindustrie während der Frühindustrialisierung*', *Vierteljahrschrift für Sozial- und Wirtschaftsgeschichte* 68 (1981), pp. 307, 318–20; *idem, Eisenbahnen und das deutsche Wirtschaftswachstum 1840–1879* (Dortmund, 1985), p. 74; *idem, Technologischer Wandel und internationaler Handel im 18. und 19. Jahrhundert. Die Eisenindustrie in Großbritannien, Belgien, Frankreich und Deutschland* (Berlin, 1985), pp. 225–7; *idem*, 'Foreign Trade Patterns, Technical Change, Cost and Productivity in the West European Iron Industries, 1820–1870', in *idem* and Patrick K. O'Brien (eds), *Productivity in the Economies of Europe* (Stuttgart, 1983), p. 157.

[18] Fremdling, *Eisenbahnen*, p. 62; *idem*, '*Britische Exporte*', p. 307; Richard Tilly, '*Los von England: Probleme des Nationalismus in der deutschen Wirtschaftsgeschichte*', *Zeitschrift für die gesamte Staatswissenschaft* 124 (1968), p. 190.

[19] Fremdling, *Technologischer Wandel*, p. 55; Patrick O'Brien and Caglar Keyder, *Economic Growth in Britain and France 1782–1914* (1978), pp. 161–2.

[20] Davis, *Industrial Revolution*, pp. 20, 30; Werner Schlote, *British Overseas Trade from 1700 to the 1930's* (Oxford, 1952), p. 147.

[21] F. E. Hyde, *Mr. Gladstone at the Board of Trade* (London 1934), pp. 87, 95; C. P. Kindleberger, 'The Rise of Free Trade in Western Europe, 1820–1875', *J.Ec.H.* 35 (1975), p. 24; Lars Sandberg, 'Movements in the Quality of British Cotton Textile Exports, 1815–1913', *J.Ec.H.* 28 (1968), pp. 7–8.

Net barter terms of trade (export prices divided by import prices), and the export price index, move as follows:

Table 2.7 British Terms of Trade, 1798–1850 (Index 1880 = 100)

		Net barter terms of trade	*Export price index*
Average	1798–1800	210.0	419.0
	1814–16	157.9	316.4
	1828–30	148.9	166.7
	1848–50	115.8	100.8

Source: Albert H. Imlah, 'Terms of Trade of the United Kingdom, 1798–1913', *Journal of Economic History*, 10 (1950), pp. 176–8. Also see I. A. Glazier, V. N. Bandera, R. B. Berner, 'Terms of Trade between Italy and the United Kingdom 1815–1913', *Journal of European Economic History*, 4 (1975), pp. 5–48.

Compared with the drastically falling export prices, import prices changed relatively little: a measure using real values over 'official' (constant) values averaged 155 for 1784–6, 179 in 1824–6, 174 1834–6 and 172 in 1854–6.[22] Inasmuch as half the cotton exports and large proportions of other products went abroad, much of the ingenuity and overwork that were expended in British factories benefited, in fact, the foreign buyers rather than the British population.

Yet even these data do not measure to the full extent the impact of British trade on the European economies. The most significant effects – and it forms a major argument of this chapter – are to be found in the dynamic consequences of the trading relations as they developed between the fully industrialized country and its industrializing partners. The new, cheapened, mass-production methods in Britain were not uniformly found in all industrial sectors. On the contrary, they were highly concentrated in a few industries, notably in the spinning and preparation of cotton yarn as well as other textile yarns, including woollen and linen yarns, and in the production of pig iron and puddled bar iron. On the basis of these greatly cheapened semi-finished manufactures, imported from Britain, other advanced countries in Europe were able actually to expand the later stages of production, such as the weaving of textiles and the manufacture of iron goods, in which Britain had not yet a technical lead and in which, therefore, their lower wage costs, and often the high skill of their craftsmen and craftswomen, could undersell British producers. At the least, they could keep and develop their own home market, and the markets of the more

---

[22] Davis, *Industrial Revolution*, pp. 69, 71; Schlote, *Trade*, p. 21.

backward parts of Europe in the east and south. They were also in a good position to copy, and ultimately equal, the technical innovations pioneered by Britain even in the mass-production sectors. In the words of Ralph Davis:

> West European countries soon learned to import British semi-finished products and to concentrate their own labour on the hand process in which British industry had no substantial advantages... (British) trade with western Europe... tended to be the export, not of the finished products of British industry, but of the semi-finished output of its most advanced industrial processes, cotton and worsted yarn, iron billets, bars and girders, and the spin-offs from its own vast markets in such raw materials as wool, cotton and hides.[23]

This temporary international division of labour, in which expanding British semi-manufactured exports boosted first the traditional, and ultimately the modern, industrial sectors of the advanced regions of Europe had, because of its concentrated effect in a few key sectors, consequences on the industrialization of Europe far beyond the measure of the relatively limited quantities of trade goods that were involved. Given the preceding favourable developments of those regions, this trade functioned as a trigger, releasing an expanding mass of energy over ever-widening circles in Europe.

The effect is probably seen most clearly in the case of Germany. Here a drastic reduction in German imports of finished cotton and woollen goods in the decades after 1815 was accompanied by a steady expansion in the quantities of yarn imported. By 1836–8, imports as a percentage of output stood at 200 in the case of cotton *yarn* and were still 88 in 1854–6; by contrast, the proportions for cotton *goods* were only 3 and 1. Similarly, in the case of iron, British sales of pig iron to the German states and the Netherlands combined rose from 200 tons in 1821–5 to 44,000 tons in 1846–50, or more than two-hundred fold, while bar iron and rail imports rose in the same period from 5500 tons to 10,500 tons, or only double. Put differently, by 1849 the Zollverein still imported 17 per cent of its needs of pig iron, while imports of bar had shrunk to 5 per cent. The ratio in British exports to Germany of bar iron over pig iron, that is to say, of the later stage

---

[23] Davis, *Industrial Revolution*, pp. 33–4. Also *see* S. Pollard, *Peaceful Conquest: The Industrialization of Europe 1760–1970* (Oxford, 1981), pp. 170–84; *idem*, 'Industrialization and the European Economy', *Ec.H.R.* 24 (1975) 638–48; P. J. Cain and A. G. Hopkins, 'The Political Economy of British Expansion Overseas, 1750–1914', *Ec.H.R.* 33 (1980), p. 475.

in production over the semi-product, fell from 43.4 in 1821 to 4.8 in 1830, 1.4 in 1840 and 0.7 in 1850.[24]

As far as France was concerned, 'British industry sent machinery and intermediate goods to French industry which returned finished manufactured goods to British consumers'.[25] The tendency for the exports of finished cloth from Britain to decline, and yarn exports to expand, applied, in fact, to the whole of Europe, and similar developments took place in relation to iron. Whatever part continental tariffs[26] may be have played in this tendency, its main driving force was the relative position of the leading industrial nation against the others, and the nature of the diffusion of the new processes itself.

The dominant trading pattern, with Britain specializing in sending manufactures to Europe, and later very specific types of manufactures, did not depend, as so much economic theory tends to stress, on differences in natural endowments: these were remarkably similar over much of Europe.[27] They depended rather on the sequence of industrialization, in a manner well captured by the modern theorem of the 'product cycle'. According to this, international specialization may depend to a considerable extent on the fact that new products or processes are developed first in the leading country; their production is, in due course, transferred to less-developed countries able to accept the technology but paying lower wages, and may ultimately be found in even less-advanced countries, as soon as the techniques have been simplified to enable these to work them, as they have lower labour costs still.[28] The temporary position of the years 1800–50 in which Britain exported mass-produced, semi-finished goods to the more advanced nations of Europe was thus part of a process of transfer of technology in which the countries of the continent, one after the other, were enabled to start on a path of industrialization.

---

[24] Borries, *Außenhandel*, p. 200; Fremdling, 'Britische Exporte', pp. 309–11; *idem*, 'Foreign Trade Pattern', p. 161; *idem*, *Technologischer Wandel*, pp. 48–9, 220; John Bowring, *Report on the Prussian Commercial Union*, Parl. P. 1840, XXI, p. 435; J. R. McCulloch, *Statistical Abstract of the British Empire* (2 vols, 1837), II, p. 74; Rolf Horst Dumke, 'Anglo-deutscher Handel und Frühindustrialisierung in Deutschland', *Geschichte und Gesellschaft* 5 (1979), pp. 179, 189–90; Tilly, '*Los von England*', p. 187; W. O. Henderson, *The Zollverein* (Ambkidge 1938), p. 183; Kutz, *Außenhandel*, pp. 61–5, 294.
[25] O'Brien and Keyder, *Growth*, p. 162.
[26] Crouzet, 'Toward an Export Economy', p. 66; also D. A. Farnie, *The English Cotton Industry and the World Market 1815–1896* (Oxford, 1979), pp. 37, 88, 91; Michael M. Edwards, *The Growth of the British Cotton Trade 1780–1815* (Manchester, 1967), pp. 62–3; Davis, *Industrial Revolution*, p. 18.
[27] Davis, *Industrial Revolution*, pp. 72–3.
[28] On the product cycle, *see* Raymond Vernon, 'International Investment and International Trade in the Product Cycle', *Quarterly Journal of Economics* 80 (1966); *idem*,

Meanwhile, these continental countries were well able to compete internationally in the case of industries in which their own traditional manual skills were superior to those of the less-developed areas in the European periphery, while their lower wages undercut the prices of British goods. It was, above all, in textile weaving and finishing that their output and exports were expanding, but also in the working of metals as well as in traditional sectors, such as making musical instruments or the production of fashion goods – items which, for Germany, McCulloch summarized condescendingly as 'wooden clocks and other inferior articles'. Thus, in Prussia in 1828, 56.9 per cent of exports were manufactures (of which 49.9 per cent of the total were textiles); for the Zollverein as a whole, in 1836–8 the figures were 53 per cent and 39.5 per cent respectively, not counting re-exports, and in 1848–50 they were 53.1 per cent and 36.4 per cent. In France, 31 per cent of the export to Britain in 1854 consisted of finished industrial goods, mainly silk, leather and cotton manufactures.[29]

Ultimately, the manufacture of these articles would also be mechanized, not least because of the enlarged market created by the cheap semi-manufactures as input. Meanwhile, Britain also aided that process by forming a rich, expanding market unhampered by high tariff barriers.

Against this, the cheap mass-produced imports from Britain were bound to harm those areas which had hitherto supplied the same commodities by traditional methods. In the case of cotton spinning, those areas lay in India, while the industry was expanding so fast that capacity was added rather than replaced. This was also true of ironmaking, in which some minor charcoal iron areas declined but, on the whole, because of the rising demand, coke and charcoal blast furnaces could exist side by side for half-a-century or so. In the case of the woollen industry, however, some traditional regions were driven out by competition, and some were wholly de-industrialized, the most notable being the Languedoc. Worst of all affected were the traditional linen

---

'The product Cycle Hypothesis', *Oxford Bulletin of Economics and Statistics* 41 (1979); Seev Hirsch, 'The Product Cycle Model of International Trade', ibid. 37 (1975); *idem, Location of Industrial and International Competitiveness* (Oxford, 1967); Paul Krugman, 'A Model of Innovation, Technology Transfer and World Distribution of Income', *Journal of Political Economy* 67 (1979). Also cf. Alfred Marshall, 'Memorandum on Fiscal Policy of International Trade' (1903), in *Official Papers* (1926), pp. 403–5.

[29] Borries, *Außenhandel*, pp. 60–1; Bondi, *Außenhandel*, pp. 83, 91; McCulloch, *Statistical Account*, II, p. 150; O'Brien and Keyder, *Growth*, pp. 161–2. Also *see* Lucy Brown, *The Board of Trade and the Free Trade Movement, 1830–42* (Oxford, 1958), pp. 114, 159; Lennart Schön, 'British Competition and Domestic Change: Textiles in Sweden', *Economy and History* 23 (1980), pp. 72–4; John Bowring, *Report*, pp. 55–6; Dumke, *'Anglo-deutscher Handel'*, pp. 186, 190; Tilly, *'Los von England'*, p. 187; Davis, *Industrial Revolution*, pp. 17, 24, 36.

areas of Europe for, in their case, not only did they suffer competition from the mechanized spindle capacity, and soon after also the power looms, of Great Britain, linen as a whole lost part of its market to the cotton upstart. The sufferings of the linen regions, such as Flanders and Silesia, were among the gravest social costs of the European trading connection with the British economy.[30]

Imports from the Continent into Britain

As a market, Britain's main significance for the countries of continental Europe lay above all in her demand for food and raw materials. In the later decades of eighteenth century, as she ceased to be a net exporter, and later even ceased to be self-sufficient in grain in view of the growth and structural changes in the population, the supplies to meet the relatively limited deficits came largely from Ireland. With the rise and decline of the Baltic grain trade, and the encouragement of a 'second feudalism' which this was alleged to have brought about in the sixteenth to eighteenth centuries, Britain had very little to do. In the war years, Baltic, mainly German, grain became of increasing importance. For those suppliers, certainly in the short run, the Corn Law of 1815 had disastrous consequences.[31]

[30] G. Jacquemins, *Historie de la crise économique des Flandres 1845–50* (Brussels, 1929); C. Vandenbroeke, 'The Regional Economy of Flanders and Industrial Modernization in the XVIIIth Century', *J.E.Ec.H.* 16 (1987), pp. 149 ff and literature cited there; *idem*, *'Mutations économiques en Flandre au cours de la phase proto-industrielle, 1650–1850'*, *Revue du Nord* 63 (1981), pp. 85–94; *idem*, *'Le cas flamand: évolution sociale et comportements démographiques aux XVIIIe–XIXe siècles'*, *Annales E.S.C.* 39 (1984), pp. 915–38; H. Blumberg, *'Ein Beitrag zur Geschichte der deutschen Leinenindustrie von 1834–1879'*, in Hans Mottek et al., *Studien zur Geschichte der industriellen Revolution in Deutschland* [Berlin (East) 1960], pp. 65–143; Herbert Kisch, 'The Textile Industries in Silesia and the Rhineland: A Comparative Study in Industrialization', *J.Ec.H.* 19 (1959); Elizabeth Harder-Gersdorff, *'Leinen-Regionen im Vorfeld und im Verlauf der Industrialisierung (1780–1914)'*, in Hans Pohl (ed.), *Gewerbe-und Industrielandschaften vom Spätmittelalter bis ins 20. Jahrhundert* (Stuttgart 1986); M. Bergman, 'The Potato Blight in the Netherlands and its Social Consequences', *International Review of Social History* 12 (1967); C. Lis and H. Soly, *Poverty and Capitalism in Pre-Industrial Europe* (Brighton 1979), pp. 141–4, 178–86.

[31] Maria Bogucka, 'The Role of Baltic Trade in European Development from the XVIth to the XVIIIth Centuries', *J.E.Ec.H.*, 9 (1980), p. 14; Jerzy Topolski, 'Economic Decline in Poland from the Sixteenth to the Eighteenth Centuries', in Peter Earle (ed.), *Essays in European Economic History* (Oxford, 1974), pp. 127–42; Deane and Cole, *British Economic Growth*, p. 65; Brinley Thomas, 'Food Supply in the United Kingdom During the Industrial Revolution', in Mokyr, *Economics*, p. 141; C. R. Fay, *The Corn Laws and Social England* (Cambridge, 1932), pp. 28 ff.; D.G.

An enormous literature exists on the history of the Corn Laws and of corn imports 1815–46, but most of it is written from the British point of view, and it need not detain us for long. For some of the British free traders, the unhindered imports of corn were desirable to get foreign countries to specialize in grain production and keep them from entering the industrial field: that, indeed, was the gist of Bowring's official report.[32] In reality, the position was more complex than that.

Much of the debate has turned on the question whether there was sufficient surplus on the continent in the period of the Corn Laws to flood the British market with grain – at least to the extent of lowering prices substantially and driving some marginal British farmers out of business. The answer must lie in the time-scale adopted. No matter what the actual position in the short term, there can be no doubt that, had an open and lucrative market existed in Britain in the decades after 1815, European output could have been enlarged in the long term to meet it. As it was, continental suppliers suffered from the extraordinary instability of the British grain market, which was completely closed in some years, only to absorb large quantities of grain in others – a factor that also played havoc with the annual balances of payments. But they gained by selling their grain, when they did sell it, at a very high price, so that some suppliers were, in fact, in favour of retaining the Corn Laws in Britain.[33]

The main supplying region was the hinterland of Danzig, the eastern Prussian and Polish provinces. For Prussia as a whole, grain exports accounted for 8.1 per cent of exports in 1828, 11.5 per cent in 1837 for the Zollverein as a whole, and 15.2 per cent in 1850.[34] This is not insignificant, but still limited. The quantities were rising, however, especially in the last years.

Barnes, *A History of the English Corn Laws from 1660–1864* (1930), pp. 30 ff.; Wilhelm Abel, *Agrarkrisen und Agrarkonjunktur* (Hamburg/Berlin, 1966), p. 196; W. F. Galpin, *The Grain Supply of England During the Napoleonic Period* (New York, 1925); Mancur Olson, *The Economics of the Wartime Shortage* (Durham, N.C., 1963), pp. 51–5; L.M. Cullen, *An Economic History of Ireland Since 1660* (revd ed., 1987), pp. 59, 103, 109.

[32] Bowring, *Report*; Kindleberger, 'Free Trade', p. 33; Alexander Brady, *William Huskisson and Liberal Reform* (1928, repr. N.Y., 1967), pp. 44–5, 50, 64, 70–1.

[33] Kutz, *Außenhandel*, pp. 257–9; Barnes, *Corn Laws*, pp. 208–10; S. Fairlie, 'The Nineteenth- Century Corn Laws Reconsidered', *Ec.H.R.* 18 (1965) pp. 262–75; *idem*, 'The Corn Laws and British Wheat Production 1829–76', ibid. 22 (1969), pp. 102–3, 114; Boyd Hilton, *Corn, Cash, Commerce. The Economic Policies of the Tory Governments 1815–1830* (Oxford, 1977), pp. 273, 292–9; Fay, *Corn Laws*, p. 116; Schlote, *Overseas Trade*, p. 61; Davis, *Industrial Revolution*, p. 42; R.C.O. Matthews, *A Study in Trade Cycle History. Economic Fluctuations in Britain 1833–1842* (Cambridge, 1954), pp. 30, 37–41.

[34] Bondi, *Außenhandel*, pp. 55, 83, 91.

Table 2.8 British corn imports, 1784–1856, yearly averages, £000

Imports from	Ireland	Rest of world	Northern Europe*	North-western Europe*	Southern Europe
1784–6	224	534	275	233	–
1794–6	399	2013	1058	774	29
1804–6	678	2227	1714	361	2
1814–6	1799	1359	385	912	1
1824–6	2914	1244	543	569	6
1834–6		805	207	512	2
1844–6		5685	1144	1985	436
1854–6		18,240	3418	4696	1644

*'Northern Europe': all the Baltic States except Germany, Iceland.
'North-western Europe': Germany, France, Low Countries.
Source: Ralph Davis, *The Industrial Revolution and British Overseas Trade*, (Leicester, 1979), pp. 110–24.

This trade my have had larger significance still if we accept Dumke's thesis that it helped to connect the economies of eastern and western Germany, which otherwise had very few links, via the triangular trade with Britain: the east selling grain which paid for the industrial imports of the west from Britain.[35]

Other areas also developed grain exports to Britain, among them Denmark and what was later to become Romania.[36] In both cases, these exports tended to confirm the economies in their role as suppliers of food; yet their later history shows that it is not so much the composition of exports that determines the economic fate of a country, as its manner of reacting to it. While Denmark used its growing food exports as a means of rapid rise in incomes and ultimately also of industrialization, Romania stayed among the poorest and most backward regions of Europe.

Among other primary imports from Europe, timber played the most important part. Much of it came from the Baltic coasts of Prussia and Poland, where these exports had at times an importance comparable to that of grain exports. Timber exports had greater significance still for Sweden and Norway. In the eighteenth century, most British timber needs had been met from the Baltic but, because this supply was threatened during the Napoleonic wars, production in North America was encouraged and later, from

[35] Dumke, *'Anglo-deutscher Handel'*.

[36] Paul Cernovudeanu and Beatrice Marinescu, 'British Trade in the Danubian Ports of Galatz and Braila between 1837 and 1853', *J.E.Ec.H.* 8 (1979), pp. 707–42; Farnie, *Cotton Industry*, p. 42; Milward and Saul, *Economic Development*, p. 502.

1809, supported by preferential tariffs. Only from 1842 on were import duties on timber reduced, finally to be abolished in 1860.[37] The timber sales to Britain which followed that relaxation were a major factor in the economic spurt and ultimate industrialization of Sweden, Norway and, somewhat later, Finland.[38]

Yet a third significant imported commodity was iron, supplied by Sweden and Russia in the eighteenth century largely in the form of bar iron. Between 1750 and 1800, British imports from Sweden were kept at around 18,000 tons a year by the Swedish sales cartel, while Russian supplies grew from an average of 3600 tons a year in the 1750s to 26,000 tons in the 1790s. Thereafter, Britain, using new methods, was able to provide most of its own supplies, but continued to import the high-grade bars for special purposes, such as the making of steel. While British purchases of Swedish iron formed a major part of the country's export earnings (far less so in the case of Russia), the iron industry which was fostered thereby formed only a small sector of the economy: in 1760, iron workers and miners made up only 3.2 per cent of the population in Sweden, and 1 per cent in Finland.[39]

Other European imports of some significance to the regions of supply included tar, hemp and flax, mainly from the Baltic lands and from Russia; wool from Germany; and wines and spirits from France, Portugal and Spain.[40] With rising incomes in Britain, the quantities of these items continued to grow, except in the case of wool, in which Australian deliveries began to encroach on those of European origins in the 1840s.

[37] Hyde, *Gladstone*, pp. 90–3; Berend and Ránki, 'Foreign Trade', p. 576; H. S. K. Kent, *War and Trade in the Northern Seas* (Cambridge, 1973); Bowring, *Report*, p. 64; Bondi, *Außenhandel*, pp. 45, 86; Brinley Thomas, 'Towards an Energy Interpretation of the Industrial Revolution', *Atlantic Economic Journal* 8 (1980), pp. 3–6, 9; Kutz, *Außenhandel*, pp. 49–53; Davis, *Industrial Revolution*, pp. 47–8; S.-E. Aström, 'English Timber Imports from Northern Europe in the Eighteenth Century', *Scandinavian Economic History Review* 18 (1970).

[38] E. Jutikkala, 'Industrialization as a Factor in Economic Growth in Finland; Edvard Bull, 'Industrialisation as a Factor in Economic Growth'; Karl Gustaf Hildebrand, 'Sweden', all in: First International Conference of Economic History, *Contributions* (Paris/Hague, 1960).

[39] Eli F. Heckscher, *An Economic History of Sweden* (Cambridge, Mass., 1954), pp. 141, 174–82; Svante Lindqvist, 'National Resource and Technology. The Debate about Energy Technology in Eighteenth-Century Sweden', *Scandinavian Journal of History* 8 (1983) pp. 85–6; Artur Attman, 'The Russian Market and World Trade', *Scandinavian Economic History Review* 29 (1981), pp. 188–91; Paul Bairoch, '*Commerce international et genèse de la révolution industrielle anglaise*', *Annales, E.S.C.* 28 (1973) pp. 559–60; Fremdling, *Technologischer Wandel*, pp. 39–40.

[40] Davis, *Industrial Revolution*, pp. 49–50; Attman, 'Russian Market', *passim*; McCulloch, *Statistical Account*, p. 47; Kutz, *Außenhandel*, pp. 47–55.

A Summary of the Evidence

We may now attempt a brief summary of the ways in which trade with Britain affected the economic development of Europe in the hundred years 1750–1850. Possibly the most significant contribution of Britain lay in fostering the industrial development and, indeed, the industrialization of the more advanced continental countries by the export of advanced machinery, by the supply of key materials which would otherwise have been lacking and, above all, by the supply of cheap semi-manufactures which became the basis of an expansion of the later stages of production. Thus, in 1843, at a critical stage of German railway building, Britain supplied 55 per cent of the total pig iron consumption, and its bar iron exports to Germany in 1844 were the equivalent of 85 per cent of the Prussian bar iron output. British exporters opened up markets and stimulated the taste for industrial products which could later be supplied by native makers. At the same time, Britain offered a large, rich and open market for such industrial and manufactured goods as the continent could supply.[41]

Some of the products imported from Britain, such as cotton and iron, were either new or grew to such an extent that the losses were limited. In other cases, the penalty for contact with British exports was the decline or de-industrialization of a whole formerly active industrial area before the onslaught of cheap machine-produced goods. The woollen industry in Languedoc, and the linen industries in Flanders and in Silesia were among the worst sufferers.[42]

Britain also became a wealthy market for agrarian and other primary products from the continent. Those who saw the future of their own countries in terms of a developing agrarian society greatly welcomed this development.

'The commercial revolution which is now taking place in England', Cavour enthused in 1845, '... will have a mighty impact on the Continent. By opening up the richest market in the world to foodstuffs, it will encourage their production, the principal aim, that is, of all agricultural industry which everywhere is the most important. The need to provide for regular foreign demand will arouse the energy of these agricultural industries ... Trade will then become an essential element in the prosperity of the agrarian classes.'[43]

[41] Fremdling, 'Britische Exporte', p. 320; *idem, Technologischer Wandel*, pp. 136–7; Tilly, '*Los von England*', p. 195; O'Brien and Keyder, *Growth*, pp. 162–3.

[42] David S. Landes, *The Unbound Prometheus* (Cambridge, 1969), pp. 138–9; P. K. O'Brien, 'Do We Have a Typology for the Study of European Industrialization in the XIXth Century?', *J.E.Ec.H.* 15 (1986), pp. 300–2.

[43] Quoted in Giorgio Mori, 'The Genesis of Italian Industrialization', *J.E.Ec.H.*, 4 (1975), pp. 91–2.

The new industrial regions with their overcrowded slums, their poor and riotous labouring population, and their newly rich dominant middle classes, were by no means the ideal for everyone who had observed the developments in Great Britain. Some hoped to gain prosperity and social peace by developing the agrarian sector as an efficient producer in complementarity with the industrial regions elsewhere. Some countries in the European 'periphery' managed to achieve this; others failed and stayed poor and backward. For countries that were totally dependent on an advanced market, as was Portugal on Britain, progress was particularly difficult.[44]

There is a further problem, that of the general balance of payments. Although this depends on more than the trade figures, being affected also by payments for services and other invisibles and by capital transactions, trade in our period still played the leading part. Earlier in the eighteenth century, a great deal of money had been lent by Dutch capitalists to Britain, mainly invested in government loans and in shares in the East India Company and similar organizations. Much of this was paid back by the end of the century, and, as far as the available statistics may be trusted, Britain developed a surplus, and with it a net stream of capital investments abroad, thereafter. This surplus, however, was deposited largely with overseas territories. As far as trade with Europe was concerned, Britain had a negative balance with 'northern' Europe, a positive balance with 'north-western' Europe, for which it advanced mostly short-term capital. Much of this trade therefore became possible only because of the mercantile capital available in London – though, in turn, some of the London merchant bankers had continental European origins and sources of finance.[45]

The evidence shows that contact with the British economy through trade in our period could have positive and negative effects on the continental economies.[46] The existing literature stresses almost exclusively the negative effects, being concerned largely to defend one or other protective or restrictive measure.[47] This chapter has therefore deliberately tended to err on

[44] Berend and Ránki, *European Periphery*, esp. p. 113; Milward and Saul, *Economic Development*, p. 108.

[45] Tilly, '*Los von England*', pp. 191–3; Deane and Cole, *British Economic Growth*, pp. 34–6, 87; S. D. Chapman, 'The International Houses: The Continental Contribution to British Commerce 1800–1860', *J.E.Ec.H.* 6 (1977); Kutz, *Außenhandel*, pp. 14 ff., 79–82; Davis, *Industrial Revolution*, pp. 54–8.

[46] Berend and Ránki, *European Periphery*, pp. 7–8; *idem*, 'Foreign Trade', p. 552; C. P. Kindleberger, 'Foreign Trade and Economic Growth: Lessons from Britain and France, 1850–1913', *Ec.H.R.* 14 (1961–2), pp. 289–90; Trebilcock, *Continental Powers*, pp. 392–4; Paul Bairoch, 'Free Trade and European Economic Development in the 19th Century', *European Economic Review* 3 (1972), pp. 216–18.

[47] Tilly, '*Los von England*', pp. 179–86.

the side of emphasizing the positive influence exerted on the countries of Europe by their commerce with Britain. No corner of the continent remained unaffected by the transformation of the British economy. To all it provided opportunities – but only some were able to make use of them to their own benefit.

3

Nineteenth-century Ocean Trade and Transport*

Peter Davies

The economic history of Great Britain was little different from that of the other countries of western Europe until towards the end of the seventeenth century. At that time, the majority of the population, estimated at approximately 5½ million,[1] was employed primarily in rural activities or in agriculturally based industries. The country had already enjoyed, however, a long tradition of naval success, and its geographic position was gradually encouraging a greater emphasis on overseas trade. Thus, at the beginning of the eighteenth century, it has been estimated that: '... Imports totalled, perhaps, 10 per cent of a net national product of £50 million, with exports about the same level, an unusually high figure for any country, at the time...'[2]

Over the ensuing century, this situation was change dramatically to for, while other nations made relatively moderate progress, a series of fortuitous, though interconnected, events was to double the size of Britain's population and to see the country emerge as 'The Workshop of the World'. As a result, Britain quickly developed into the cheapest producer of many manufactures and, indeed, as the only source of a number of the newer items.

* An earlier version of this paper was presented at the Fuji Conference held in Japan in 1984 under the title 'British Shipping and World Trade: Rise and Decline, 1820–1939.' *See*: T. Yui and K. Kakagawa (eds), Business History of Shipping – Strategy and Structure (Tokyo, 1985) pp. 39–85.

[1] Peter Mathias, *The First Industrial Nation* (London, 1980), p. 186.

[2] Ibid., p. 30.

Economic historians have never been able to decide precisely why this so-called 'industrial revolution' should have happened at this time in England and Wales, nor as to the exact weight that should be given to the numerous factors which first initiated, and then nurtured, this rapid technological growth. It is customary, however, to give a high priority to certain innovations in the textile and iron and steel industries, while the reduction in transport costs has always been regarded as extremely significant. Indeed, the transformation of the British economy was foreshadowed by Adam Smith when he stressed the importance of water carriage as a means of reducing the costs of production and distribution. This meant that,

> ... a more extensive market is opened to every sort of industry than what land carriage alone can afford, so it is upon the sea coast and along the banks of navigable rivers that industry of every kind naturally begins to sub-divide and improve itself, and it is frequently not till a long time after that those improvements extend themselves to the inland parts of the country...[3]

Thus, it will come as no surprise to learn that the development of the British canal network virtually coincided with the traditional dates (1760 to 1820) which have usually been given to the Industrial Revolution. This extended the benefits of cheap transport to large parts of inland England and, as a result, the cost of moving: '... bulky or heavy commodities such as coal, iron, timber, stone, salt and clay was greatly reduced...' so that, '... agricultural regions which had been remote from the market were brought within the widening circle of exchange...'[4]

Without these developments in water transport, it is difficult to see how economic growth could have occurred on any real scale for, in spite of the work of the Turnpike Trusts and the activities of such men as John Metcalf, Thomas Telford and John Macadam, the country's roads were in a deplorable condition. Even after some improvements had been undertaken, roads were able to operate only feeder services to support the canals in many areas, and it was not until the building of the railway system after 1829 that the internal revolution in transport could be regarded as complete.

According to the eminent economist, Alfred Marshall, the reduction in transport costs was by far the most important, single factor in promoting industrialization,[5] and it seems certain that the pace and growth of output owed at least as much to these savings as to innovations in productive

---

[3] Adam Smith, *The Wealth of Nations* (London, 1776), p. 14.

[4] T. S. Ashton, *The Industrial Revolution* (London, 1961), p. 84.

[5] Alfred Marshall, *Principles of Economics*, MacMillan, London, 8th Edition, 1938, pp. 674–5.

techniques. This was essentially because of their impact on the size of the market for:

> ... a vital condition for industrial growth – according to the degree that goods are bulky relative to their value, becomes a function of transport costs. The cheaper transport costs become the larger the area over which such cheap and bulky goods can get marketed. Areas with special advantages in processing costs – cheap coal, cheap power, cheap raw materials, good local labour supplies – can thus expand their markets as 'transfer costs' decline. And this chance of expanding markets makes possible and encourages more division of labour, innovation, all the economies of larger-scale production. Rising output and productivity will lower the average costs of the commodity – but only if the goods can be cleared to a widening market. Cheap transport thus becomes economically important according to the degree of its effects upon total costs.[6]

These theoretical considerations were to be demonstrated fully by the growth of the British economy in the nineteenth century. The increasing efficiency of production, supplemented and encouraged by improvements in inland transport, resulted in lower unit costs to the consumer, and a wider internal market was created. The reduction in unit costs also made British goods more attractive in foreign countries and, by the end of the century, its overseas trade had increased dramatically: imports rising approximately fivefold and exports growing roughly sixfold in value.[7] While much of this growth in external trade was directly linked to the comparative advantage then enjoyed by Britain's goods, a further factor was the favourable facilities that were developed by the British shipping industry. As these also became superior to the services available to their competitors, Britain's manufacturing advantage was to be effectively reinforced.

For this potential to be fully realized, it was clear that ocean carriage would have to be developed in such a manner as to enable it to cope with bulk cargoes for the first time. This, of course, was a far cry from the traditional demands that had been made upon the shipping industry in the eighteenth century when scale and distance were quite small. Thus, a series of technical and commercial problems needed to be solved, and it was fortunate for the British shipowners that the early lead in industrialization enabled them to have ready access to the necessary technology. The development of a large-scale industrial base had, in turn, encouraged the emergence of a commercial and financial structure which, with all its imperfections, was far in advance of comparable institutions elsewhere.

[6] Mathias, *First Industrial Nation*, p. 106.
[7] T. S. Ashton, *An Economic History of England, The 18th Century*, (London, 1961), p. 151.

The obvious technical answer was to construct larger and larger ships but this apparently simple solution conceals the many constraints that had to be overcome for it to be implemented. For a start, it was not feasible to build wooden vessels over a certain size – 300 feet (90 metres) was regarded as the maximum – so the nineteenth century was to see the gradual adoption of iron and, later, steel for the construction of hulls. Furthermore, while the uncertainties of the wind could be accepted when trade was of an *ad hoc* nature, the need to provide regular, uninterrupted services led inevitably to the use of steam propulsion. Early engines, however, were extremely wasteful of fuel and, apart from the cost of the coal, this had the unfortunate effect of requiring that a high proportion of carrying capacity was filled with non-paying bunkers. The latter part of the nineteenth century was then to witness a whole series of innovations that steadily reduced this cost so that steam was eventually to replace sail on virtually every route.

Of course, the larger the vessel and the more sophisticated its design and construction, the more substantial was its capital cost. The financing of what became large, 'lumpy', long-lasting investments required a new approach so that changes in the law – particularly in respect of 'limited liability' – became essential. Once expensive ships had been constructed, it was then necessary to devise systems so that they could be operated on a profitable basis, and this, in turn, demanded a complete reorganization of the commercial institutions. These considerations led to the formation of new forms of company structures and, in time, to the regulation of many routes via shipping conferences and 'deferred rebate systems' in many trades.

In practice, it proved to be quite possible for British shipbuilders to construct the appropriate amounts of tonnage to cope with the changing demands of world trade, and the limiting factors tended to be the ability to supply cargoes and the expansion of port facilities. These do not appear to have been major constraints, however, for Britain's overseas commerce grew rapidly throughout the nineteenth century. The cargoes themselves consisted principally of manufactured goods being exported and raw materials and foodstuffs being imported, and, although the population grew rapidly in the nineteenth century – England and Wales rose from nine to 32½ million – the volume of trade per head grew twenty-fivefold.

The advances in maritime technology mentioned above had many direct consequences in other areas. These developments can best be illustrated by the cargo and passenger capacities of three vessels of the Cunard Line. In 1840, *Britannia*, built of wood, with a simple side-lever engine, had a gross tonnage of 1139 and could carry only 225 tons of cargo and 90 passengers. The *Persia*, an iron paddle steamer of 3300 tons gross, constructed in 1855, had a capacity for 1100 tons of cargo and 180 passengers, while *Bothnia*, an iron screw vessel fitted with compound engines, which went into service in

1874, had a gross tonnage of 4556, could carry 3000 tons of cargo together with 340 cabin and 800 third-class passengers. In addition, the increase in speed from the 8.3 knots of *Britannia* to the 13 knots of *Bothnia* meant that annual capacity was even greater because of the larger number of voyages that could be completed in a year.[8]

From a commercial point of view, the provision of such vast quantities of cargo, and the arrangements that had to be made to deal with such enormous numbers of passengers meant that it was necessary to evolve an entirely new form of business organization. In the seventeenth and eighteenth centuries, a ship would spend a very low proportion of its life at sea.[9] This was partly because of the need to repair and re-equip after just about every voyage and also the difficulty in arranging for substantial quantities of cargo to coincide with the arrival of a vessel destined for an appropriate port. The advent of steam did little, at first, to reduce the time spent on repairs but, by the 1870s, a very high degree of reliability had been achieved, and systems of planned maintenance could be used to ensure a rapid turn-round during normal operations.

The corollary of this was the development of an effective management structure that could undertake the organization of the business so that the provision of the service and the demands of the shippers and passengers would be effectively matched. In the course of time, this meant that big shore staffs were necessary, for the work done in the offices and at the docks became as important to profitability as the efficiency of the ships themselves.[10] An example of the way in which it became essential to organize the new style of shipping services can be seen by reference to the returns which had to be completed by the officers of the early vessels of the African Steam Ship Company – nearly 50 separate items had to be submitted to the firm's office after each voyage when sailings began in 1853.(*See* Table 3.1)

As a typical sailing ship of the early nineteenth century would carry only a log and a manifest which would be supplemented by a customary, verbal report when its captain reached his home port, it will be seen that the vessels of the African Steam Ship Company produced very sophisticated returns. Indeed, with the exceptions of items concerned with taxation, they were virtually equal to the information provided by a modern cargo liner.

Another consequence of the increase in the size and complexity of ships was on their capital cost. When Samuel Cunard negotiated with Robert

---

[8] C. Ernest Fayle, *A Short History of the World's Shipping Industry,* (London, 1933), p. 241.

[9] R. Davis, Merchant Shipping in the Economy of the late Seventeenth Century, *Economic History Review,* Second Series, Vol. IX, No. 1, August 1956, p. 67.

[10] Fayle, *World's Shipping Industry,* p. 266.

Table 3.1 Documentation of the African Steam Ship Company

Three Manifests of Cargo	Vouchers for Stores purchased on Coast
Three Epitomes of Cargo	Passenger Lists, with amounts extended
Three Passenger Lists	
Three Specie Lists	Cash Book
Three Parcel Lists	Wine Book
Bills of Lading – cargo	Towage Account
Bills of Lading – specie	List of Stores supplied to other vessels
Report on Conduct of Servants	
Surplus Stores List	Government Passengers' Wine Accounts
Manifest Book	
Report on Conduct of Officers	Accounts of Wines, etc.
Admiralty Log	Visitors, Cooking, Medicine, Breakage
Ship's Log Book	
Bills of Lading for Outward Cargo	Agents' Accounts
Cargo Receipt Book	Kroomen's Wages Accounts
Parcel Receipt Book	Kroomen's Victualling Accounts
Admiralty Returns, viz. Journal	List of Draughts and what taken for Ship's Disbursement Account and Vouchers
Abstract of Journal	
Average Speed	
List of Mails	Account Current
List of Vessels Spoken	Government Requisitions and Dinner Certificates to be handed in within 3 days of Arrival
List of Admiralty Packages	
Cash Keeper's Department	
Victualling Account of Passengers	Indent for Next Voyage
Victualling Account of Captain-Officers and Crew	Inventory and Expenditure Book
Portage Bill	
Wine Account – Captain, Officers and Engineers	
Abstract Wine Account	
Abstract Intercolonial Freight out home	

Source: Documents recovered by the author from Messrs J. T. Fletcher (Shipping) Ltd – formerly Liverpool Agents of the African Steam Ship Company.

Napier in 1839 for the construction of vessels for his proposed Atlantic service, the price quoted for a ship of 960 tons with a motive power of 375 horsepower was £32,000.[11] Less than 30 years later, Cunard purchased the *Oregon*, of 7375 tons, for the sum of £220,000.[12] In these circumstances, demurrage (the cost of operating a ship for a 24-hour period), which had been of little account with smaller and less expensive sailing vessels, assumed great significance, so that speed of turn-round in port became a critical factor in determining profitability. Furthermore, the high capital cost of large steamships meant that, in many cases, it was beyond the resources of a single individual, or even a partnership, to finance the purchase of enough vessels to create a viable line. Consequently, the principal mail and passenger firms were set up as chartered companies, and were substantial organizations from their inception.[13]

The general public was prepared to invest in these because of the protection provided by the 'limited liability' status that this type of enterprise enjoyed long before it could be claimed by other forms of business organization. By the 1860s, however, a series of new companies acts made this form of protection widely available and, from then onwards, the potential risk was restricted to the amount of the original investment. This change then ensured that large amounts of additional capital were forthcoming on reasonable terms, but the development of liner services for passengers and for cargo created such enormous demands for long-term funds that it became necessary to introduce further control mechanisms which effectively regulated the majority of ocean routes. These consisted of the establishment of 'shipping conferences' and/or the encouragement of substantial mergers.

A 'shipping conference' is a combination of shipping lines that has been formed to regulate and restrict competition in the carrying trade of a particular route. It has two main aims. The first is to modify rivalry between the regular companies themselves so as to obtain and maintain what they regard as reasonable rates of freight. This can be achieved by charging unified rates, and the trade may then be divided by fixing the number of sailings for each line during a specific period, or by allotting certain ports to each company, or by pooling an agreed proportion of freight receipts. The second aim is to restrict the entry of other shipping lines, or individual vessels, and this is normally undertaken by the use of some form of deferred rebate system.[14]

Many shippers were discontented with the monopoly powers possessed by the shipping conferences, or 'rings', for they alleged that these were

---

[11] F. E. Hyde, *Cunard and the North Atlantic, 1840–1973*, (London, 1975) p. 7.

[12] Ibid., p. 124.

[13] A. W. Kirkaldy, *British Shipping*, (Newton Abbot, 1970) p. 170.

[14] P. N. Davies, *The Trade Makers: Elder Dempster in West Africa, 1852–1972*, [London, 1973 (Reprinted 1980)] p. 107.

frequently abused.[15] This belief led, in time, to a number of investigations, of which the first was the most important – this was the Royal Commission on Shipping Rings which sat from 1906 to 1909.[16] After due consideration, the majority of the Commission recommended that an association be formed in each trade so that the merchants could present a solid front to the shipowners and thus make bargaining a more realistic feature of the system. They also suggested the compulsory publication of tariff rates that would include every item. A minority of members wanted the Board of Trade to establish a system of limited supervision over individual conferences.[17] They also concluded that a comprehensive tariff should be published and circulated regularly to the shippers, but neither the majority nor minority reports made any proposal for ending the deferred rebate system or the conference structure itself.[18] A similar enquiry was made by the Alexander Committee in the United States. This issued its findings in 1914, and its conclusions were broadly in line with its British predecessor.[19]

A second method adopted by shipowners concerned about the protection of their capital involved a move towards larger units either by growth or by amalgamation. With few exceptions, the liner services that covered the world's shipping routes in 1875 were British owned, and used British-built steamships. The Hamburg-America Line, the North German Lloyd of Bremen and the Netherlands Steamship Company of Amsterdam had all been founded in the mid-1850s but their activities were still relatively small, and they continued to employ the products of British shipyards.[20] The Americans possessed the Pacific Mail Steamship Company which successfully used American-built ships on the San Francisco to Yokohama route, and their Guion Line operated on the North Atlantic with vessels constructed in the United Kingdom. The only other rival at this time was the Austrian Lloyd which provided a number of services using steamers built in Trieste.[21]

This position remained virtually unchanged in 1880 but ten years later the German challenge was becoming more obvious. In that period, the tonnage of German steamships had increased from 215,758 to 723,656 tons – a significant development that pointed the way to the near 2½ million tons

---

[15] P. N. Davies, *Henry Tyrer: A Liverpool Shipping Agent and his Enterprise*, (London, 1979) pp. 39–43.

[16] Royal Commission on Shipping Rings, H.M.S.O., Cd. 4668–70 and 4685, (London, 1909).

[17] Davies, *The Trade Makers*, p. 141.

[18] R.C.S.R., Vol. I, *The Report*.

[19] Daniel Marx Jn., *International Shipping Cartels*, (Princeton, New Jersey, 1953), p. 4.

[20] R. H. Thornton, *British Shipping*, (Newton Abbot, 1970) p. 58.

[21] Ibid., p. 59.

owned by 1910.[22] Compared with Britain withnearly 42 per cent, Germany still lagged far behind with only 9 per cent of world tonnage. But the effect of German competition cannot be adequately quantified in this way for, while many British vessels were concerned with the bulk and tramp trades, the Hamburg-Amerika and the North German Lloyd concentrated almost exclusively on the liner trades.[23]

It was during this period that the Meiji regime, which was established in Japan in 1868, decided to give high priority to the development of modern shipping and ship-construction industries.[24] At first, ships were purchased from abroad, mainly from Britain,[25] but from very small beginnings, both activities grew significantly up to 1914.[26] Japan's progress at that stage was not sufficient effectively to challenge the established lines in the Far East but some British firms, including Alfred Holt and Company, were already becoming apprehensive about the future.[27]

The conference system was essentially a British device inaugurated at a time when British shipping was the undoubted world leader in this area. When foreign competitors appeared, they were sometimes admitted into these organizations but, such were the terms and conditions, that the conference structure usually tended to perpetuate British superiority. One alternative method of assailing this position was to be the drawing together of numbers of companies – mainly with similar interests – so as to form powerful combinations that could take advantage of the optimum economies of scale and, perhaps, acquire quasi-monopolies of their own in some areas. In the 1880s, the British India Steam Navigation Company and the (British) Peninsular and Oriental Company were the largest single firms but, although they continued to grow, by 1914 they had both been easily overtaken by a number of 'groups' which had evolved by amalgamation. Before World War I, one of the biggest was undoubtedly the Hamburg-Amerika Line which possessed a fleet of 408 vessels totalling nearly a million-and-a-quarter tons.[28]

Another very large combine was that formed by Mr J. Pierpont Morgan, the American merchant banker, under the title of the International Mercantile Marine Company. By 1900, this included the American Line, the British

---

[22] *See* Table 3.5 in the Appendix to this chapter.

[23] Thornton, *British Shipping*, p. 77.

[24] T. Chida and P. N. Davies, *The Japanese Shipping & Shipbuilding Industries: A History of their Modern Growth*, (London, 1990) p. 5.

[25] *Commercial Reports from H. M. Consuls in China, Japan and Siam*, (London, 1866). Vessels sold to Japan in 1865, p. 22.

[26] *See* Table 3.5 in the Appendix to this chapter.

[27] S. Marriner and F. E. Hyde, *The Senior John Samuel Swire*, (Liverpool, 1967) p. 94 and p. 198.

[28] Kirkaldy, *British Shipping*, pp. 171–2.

Inman Line, the Belgian 'Red Star' Line and, in that year, it acquired two more British firms – the 'Leyland' and the 'National'. At a later stage, it also took over the 'White Star Line' and was responsible for the construction and operation of the ill-fated *Titanic*. It was, however, the (British) Royal Mail Shipping Group that became the largest of these combines. At one stage, it was able to control no less than 13 per cent of the entire sea going fleet of the British mercantile marine but, as this was essentially a development of the twentieth century, it cannot be discussed in this chapter.[29]

Although, in practice, conferences may have worked against the interests of foreign shipping firms, they were primarily concerned with preserving the rights and positions of all existing lines against *any* 'interlopers', whether domestic or alien. Consequently, British owners felt some resentment towards what they regarded as the 'unfair' competition from Germany in the liner trades. The German government used combined rail-and-sea rates,[30] offered visible subsidies and secret bounties,[31] and diverted all emigrants who wished to cross its territory to Hamburg[32] in a sustained effort to help its growing shipbuilding and ship-operating companies. This aid was conditional upon firms agreeing to combine into bigger and more efficient units so that German lines did not compete with one another – only with foreign services. So far as Britain was concerned this was, in effect, an attack, for the United Kingdom was the main operator of liner shipping, and 80 per cent of German tonnage fell into this category. The success of the policy of the German government will be seen by the fact that only two companies, the Hamburg-Amerika and the North German Lloyd included no less that 40 per cent of the entire German mercantile marine, and that, before the outbreak of war, the first of these operated 68 lines which covered the whole world.[33]

In the period from 1850 to 1910, the total merchant fleet of the world rose from just over 9 million net tons to over 34 million net tons.[34] Within this expansion the British mercantile marine was able to more than maintain its dominant position – *see* Table 3.2.

It is also clear that, after the British advantage had peaked *c.* 1890, other nations – however, particularly Germany and to a lesser extent the United States and Japan – were beginning to catch up.[35] The world freight market was, and remains, near perfect for commercial transactions so the conclusion

---

[29] P. N. Davies and A. M. Bourn, 'Lord Kylsant and the Royal Mail', *Business History*, Vol. XIV, No. 2, July 1972, pp. 103–23.

[30] Henry Hauser, *Germany's Commercial Grip on the World*, (London, 1917) p. 121.

[31] Ibid., p. 136.

[32] Ibid., p. 137.

[33] Ibid., pp. 128–9.

[34] *See* Table 3.5 in the Appendix to this chapter.

[35] *See* Table 3.5 in the Appendix to this chapter.

Table 3.2 Merchant shipping tonnage of the United Kingdom, 1840–1910

	UK fleet (million net tons)	UK share of world tonnage	UK share of world steam tonnage
1840	2.77	29.52	24.3
1850	3.57	39.47	23.0
1860	4.66	34.80	31.3
1870	5.69	33.94	42.3
1880	6.58	32.88	50.0
1890	7.98	35.83	49.2
1900	9.30	35.50	44.5
1910	11.56	33.37	40.0

Note: The American tonnage employed on the Great Lakes has been included for the purpose of these calculations.

Source: H. J. Dyos and D. H. Aldcroft, *British Transport: An Economic Survey from the 17th Century to the Twentieth* (Harmondsworth, 1974) p. 248.

must be reached that these states were beginning to be able to approach the levels of freight rates being offered by UK owners in the Baltic Exchange[36] and on liner routes.

These freight rates had fallen dramatically during the nineteenth century and were to continue to do so in real terms until 1904. The Isserlis Index,[37] which uses 1869 as its base, showed that rates had fallen to only 49 in that year. As the decline was substantially more than the reduction in the price level, the real cost of transport was constantly being lowered and, because this was especially evident on the longer voyages, the scope and range of world trade was significantly widened. It was the carriage of cargoes with a high bulk, low value that were affected most – *see* Table 3.3.

Britain's share in this growth of world trade was substantial although it tended to diminish as a percentage after 1860 even though it continued to rise in real terms at a rapid rate. *See* Table 3.4.

This vast increase in overseas trade in which Britain took such a prominent part can be attributed to many factors. Innovations in production techniques obviously played a significant role but, without the ability to sell in a wider market and obtain raw materials from distant sources, their impact would have been considerably reduced or even stifled. Serious weight must therefore be given to the thoughts of Douglass North who placed such great emphasis on the consequences of the reduction in the costs of ocean carriage:

[36] Thornton, *British Shipping*, pp. 133–4.

[37] L. Isserlis, 'Tramp Shipping, Cargoes and Freights', *Journal of the Royal Statistical Society*, Vol. CI, 1938, Part I, Table VIII, p. 122.

Table 3.3 Merchandise carried by sea, annual totals, 1840 and 1887 (in thousand tons)

Commodity	1840	1887
Coal	1400	49300
Iron	1100	11800
Timber	4100	12100
Grain	1900	19200
Sugar	700	4400
Petroleum	–	2700
Cotton	400	1800
Wool	20	350
Jute	–	600
Meat	–	700
Coffee	200	600
Wine	200	1400
Salt	800	1300
Sundries	9180	33750
Total:	**20,000**	**140,000**

Source: M. G. Mulhall, *Dictionary of Statistics*, 4th ed., (London, 1898), p. 130.

Revolutionary developments in transport have been an essential feature of the rapid growth of the western world of the past two centuries. Reduction in the cost of carriage has enabled specialization and division of labor on a national and international basis to replace the relatively self-sufficient economies that predominated in the western world two centuries ago. The striking role of the railroad in the nineteenth century is well known. However, it was water transport in which the bulk shipping of commodities began, and it was the development of ocean shipping that was an integral aspect of the growing economic interdependence of the western world, the opening up of the undeveloped continents, and the promotion of the settlement of the 'empty lands'. The declining cost of ocean transportation was a process of widening the resource base of the western world. The agriculture of new countries was stimulated (and that of old countries at least temporarily depressed), the specter of famine as a result of crop failure reduced, and the raw materials were provided for industrialization. In short, the radical decline in ocean freight rates was an important part of the redirection of the resources of the western world in the course of the vast development of the past two centuries.[38]

It would be hard, therefore, to dispute the view that improvements in ocean transport played a crucial, even decisive part, in promoting economic growth in the nineteenth century. Equally, however, it is clear that the reduction in

[38] M. G. Mulhall, *Dictionary of Statistics*, 4th Edition, London, 1898 p. 130.

Table 3.4 British and World Trade, 1840–1913

	British including re-exports	*British percentage of world*	*World*
1840	152.6*	27.25	560
1850	186.4*	23.20	800
1860	375.0	25.86	1450
1870	547.4	18.94	2890 (1872–3)
1880	697.7	–	–
1890	749.0	–	–
1900	877.5	–	–
1910	1212.5	–	–
1910	1403.5	16.79	8360
(*Declared value)			

Source: H. J. Dyos and D. H. Aldcroft, *British Transport: An Economic Survey from the 17th Century to the Twentieth*, p. 248.

costs only provided opportunities and these had to be grasped before progress could be achieved. Trade, in fact, could develop on a large scale only if many other conditions were conducive to growth, and it was here that Britain had a major role to fill.

The ability to manufacture and deliver goods at lower prices certainly stimulated demand but this could become effective only if the potential customer had the means of payment. To some extent, the problem was solved by the countervailing demand for raw materials and foodstuffs, but substantial additional improvements of purchasing power were created by the willingness of the industrial nations to offer credit. Britain's position as the prime manufacturer and carrier was then reinforced by the financial consequences of this policy, for the City of London became the major source of foreign capital during the nineteenth century.

The rise of world population from an estimated 906 million in 1800 to an approximate 1608 million in 1900[39] together with the increase in real incomes in the industrial and in the agricultural countries also helped to stimulate demand and thus promote trade:

> Changes in income levels have much to do with changes in demand and consequently with changes in the structure of output and the composition of foreign trade. As incomes rise, there is an increased demand for capital goods, manufactured consumer goods, and services, and a relatively slow expansion in demand for food, textiles and clothing. Moreover, rising living standards,

[39] Douglass North, 'Ocean Freight Rates and Economic Development, 1750–1913', *Journal of Economic History*, Vol. XVIII, No. 4, Dec. 1958, p. 537.

involving as they do changes in tastes, incomes and, consequently, in consumption patterns, not only influence the structure of domestic output but also affect the volume and composition of foreign trade. Thus the shift in the diet of the United States and other Western nations from cereals towards meat and dairy products as the standard of living rose was important both for the domestic producers of these commodities and for the trade flows that existed between these countries. Another example associated with the rise in real incomes is the increased demand for colonial products. Items of trade, such as sugar, tobacco, tea, coffee and cocoa, largely unknown to previous generations, came to be regarded as necessities during the nineteenth century, while the consumption of tropical fruits also became important for the first time towards the end of this period.[40]

Another important factor which aided both the development of commerce and the employment of shipping was the mass emigration movement from Europe. The reduction in the cost of travel was a vital element in permitting this to take place on a large scale although the outflow of pauper labour was in many cases assisted by private organizations or by state subsidy.[41] The subsequent needs of the migrants, their contribution to the productive capacities of their adopted lands and the remittances they sent to their relatives and friends at home all assisted in the creation of a new dynamic in world trade.

The consequences of these many interactive forces was that, after the 1840s, the growth of trade was faster than ever before: between 1840 and the early 1870s, it amounted to 400 per cent and to 1913 to 1400 per cent as compared with only 75 per cent in the period from 1800 to 1840.[42] To some extent, the growth of the world's shipping capacity may be regarded as an 'automatic response' to these developments but this did not guarantee that the additional tonnage would be either built in Britain or operated by British firms. In both cases, however, builders and owners were extremely successful in obtaining and retaining a massive share of their respective markets.

The British shipping operators, whether liner or tramp, proved to be quite adept in absorbing the technological improvements, and avoided the problems caused by premature obsolescence by exporting many of their redundant vessels. Foreign competition was largely defeated by the possession of the most sophisticated and advanced ships and by the adoption of such devices as the Conference System. Changes in the legal and financial

[40] A. M. Carr-Saunders, *World Population*, (Oxford, 1936) pp. 30–45.

[41] A. G. Kenwood and A. L. Lougheed, *The Growth of the International Economy, 1820–1960*, (London) p. 34.

[42] Ibid., p. 63.

framework enabled the owners to adapt to the capital requirements engendered by the increase in the scale of their operations, and their overall efficiency enabled them to cope reasonably well without the state subventions utilized by many other nations. Practically all of their tonnage was constructed in British yards, so shipbuilding shared in the progress of the shipping industry.[43] In addition, British builders consistently sold a substantial amount of their output to foreign buyers and, as late as 1913, this still amounted to 20 per cent of the total.[44]

The extent to which British shipping merely responded to changes in demand and the extent to which it led or initiated fresh developments must now be considered. On many routes the reduction in costs and improvement in service had the effect of increasing the demand precisely as theory dictates. An example of this was the replacement of the sailing packets on the North Atlantic run by the steamers of the Cunard Line. Without this intervention the trade would certainly have continued and even increased, but the scale would have been very much less. In the case of the Canadian timber trade the initial impetus was provided by the imposition of prohibitive duties on Baltic timber, but it was the rapid fall in rates that enabled these cargoes to stay competitive in the longer run. Fortunately for the Canadian timber producers, the further increase of this trade caused freight rates to fall even more, partly due to the economies of scale, and partly due to the better availability of back cargoes.[45]

Improvements in shipping certainly played an important part in promoting specific trades. The growth in the carriage of oil is a case in point. However high the potential demand, the transport of 40-gallon barrels has obvious limitations, and it required the introduction of bulk carriers if the business was not to be unduly restricted. Once the first tank steamer, built in 1886, proved a success, the potential demand then ensured that many similar vessels were constructed and, by 1912, 258 were in existence, with a further 480,000 tons under construction.[46] A similar account could be written of the growth of the refrigerated trades which, from tiny beginnings in 1880, have completely transformed the meat, dairy produce and fruit industries throughout the world.[47]

The impact of particular shipping lines on the economic development of West Africa, Latin America and the Far East has been well documented

[43] H. J. Dyos and D. H. Aldcroft, *British Transport: An Economic Survey from the 17th Century to the Twentieth*, (Harmondsworth, 1974) p. 249.
[44] *See* Table 3.6 in the Appendix to this chapter.
[45] S. Pollard and P. Robinson, *The British Shipbuilding Industry, 1870–1914*, (London, 1979) Appendix B, pp. 250–1.
[46] North, *Ocean Freight Rates*, p. 543.
[47] Kirkaldy, *British Shipping*, p. 120–9.

elsewhere.[48] In these cases, the shipowner and the producer had a community of interest to see that the landed-costs of their cargoes in Europe were at a price that encouraged their sale. The transport cost was a significant element in this price so it was in the shipowner's long-term interest to provide cost-effective shipping and, most importantly, to be satisfied with only a moderate return on capital.

It is clear from the foregoing that numerous examples of the shipowners' initiative in establishing new trades and commodities can easily be discovered. It is also certain that many instances of shipping lines providing facilities in excess of current requirements on existing routes can be discerned without difficulty. In spite of these particular cases, however, it still seems likely that most of the expansion of the British merchant navy came about as a direct result of the extension of British trade.

The matrix of economic, political and social forces which brought this about is extremely complex and does not lend itself to simple analysis. In general terms, a buoyant economy with overseas trade based on competitive price levels does seem to promote a vigorous mercantile marine. The corollary to this would also appear to be true. Thus, when the British economy lost its competitive edge after World War I and entered into a period of stagnation, this was characterized by a decline in its overseas trade. This then had very serious long-term consequences for the British merchant fleet for, while world tonnage rose from 43 to 68 million tons in the period 1913 to 1939, the United Kingdom's tonnage remained virtually static. The 'knock-on' effect on the British shipbuilding industry was even more adverse and immediate, and was to mark the beginning of a decline which reduced the British percentage of world construction from an average of 60 per cent in 1899–1913 to only 3.9 per cent in 1971–75 at a time when total launchings were rising substantially. These events suggest that there are obvious linkages between the state of the economy and the level of overseas trade, and that these variables do have a direct bearing on the health of the shipping industry. This is confirmed in a positive way by the Japanese experience for, during the post-war era when its exports have dominated world trade, its merchant fleet has risen from less than 2 million tons in 1950 to over 39 million gross registered tons in 1985.[49]

[48] Ibid., pp. 114–19 and p. 581.
[49] Davies, *The Trade Makers*; Edwin Green and Michael Moss, *A Business of National Importance – The Royal Mail Shipping Group, 1902–1937*, (London, 1982); F. E. Hyde, *Blue Funnel*, (Liverpool, 1957); A. McCrae and A. Prentice, *Irrawaddy Flotilla*, (Paisley, 1978); Marriner and Hyde, *The Senior John Samuel Swire*, and M. Murray, *Union Castle Chronicle, 1853–1953*, (London, 1953).
[50] Chida and Davies *Japanese Shipping*, p. 193.

In the final analysis, it would appear that trade and shipping react to each other in the form of a 'virtuous' circle in which it is impossible to be sure which is cause and which is effect.

Appendix

Table 3.5 Net Tonnage of the leading mercantile fleets of the world from 1850 to 1910, showing: (a) Sailing ship and steamship tonnage; (b) World's totals: (c) The British, United Kingdom, United States of America, and German percentage of the world's total; (d) These percentages also shown in terms of steamship tonnage, reckoning 1 ton of steam = 4 tons sailing. (The tonnage figures in this table are taken from *Progress of Merchant Shipping in the United Kingdom and Principal Maritime Countries*, (CJ. 6180, 1912.)

Countries		1850	1860	1870	1880	1890	1900	1905	1907	1910
United Kingdom	Sailing	3,396,659	4,204,360	4,577,855	3,851,045	2,936,021	2,096,498	1,670,766	1,461,376	1,113,944
	Steam	168,474	454,327	1,112,934	2,723,468	5,042,517	7,207,610	9,064,816	10,023,723	10,442,719
British possessions	Sailing	648,672	1,096,464	1,369,145	1,646,844	1,338,361	915,096	906,372	883,448	879,926
	Steam	19,157	45,817	89,200	225,814	371,189	532,188	696,430	814,808	926,399
British Empire	Sailing	4,045,331	5,300,824	5,947,000	5,497,889	4,274,382	3,011,594	2,577,138	2,344,824	1,993,870
	Steam	187,631	500,144	1,202,134	2,949,282	5,413,706	7,739,798	9,761,266	10,838,531	11,369,118
Russia (including Finland)	Sailing	—	—	—	655,771	560,267	556,614	511,518	564,721	581,316
	Steam	—	—	—	100,421	234,418	417,022	440,043	501,638	535,040
Norway	Sailing	298,315	558,927	1,009,200	1,460,596	1,502,584	1,002,675	813,864	750,862	628,287
	Steam	—	—	13,715	58,062	203,115	505,443	668,230	819,282	897,440
Sweden	Sailing	—	—	—	421,693	369,680	288,687	263,425	238,742	175,916
	Steam	—	—	—	81,049	141,267	325,105	459,664	532,515	596,763
Denmark	Sailing	—	—	168,193	197,509	189,406	158,303	149,310	141,035	131,342
	Steam	—	—	10,453	51,957	112,788	250,137	334,124	404,946	415,496
German Empire	Sailing	—	—	900,361	965,767	709,761	393,770	553,817	533,652	506,837
	Steam	—	—	81,994	215,758	723,652	1,347,875	1,915,475	2,256,783	2,396,733
Netherlands	Sailing	289,870	423,790	370,159	263,887	127,200	78,493	54,417	49,640	45,936
	Steam	2,706	10,132	19,455	64,394	128,511	268,430	356,890	398,026	488,339
Belgium	Sailing	33,315	28,857	20,648	10,442	4,393	741	2,844	964	3,402
	Steam	1,604	4,254	9,501	65,224	71,553	112,518	96,889	119,223	187,730
France	Sailing	674,228	928,099	917,633	641,539	444,092	501,175	676,193	662,828	636,081
	Steam	13,925	68,025	154,415	277,759	499,921	527,551	711,027	739,819	815,567
Portugal	Sailing	—	—	—	—	—	57,925	43,126	38,363	43,844
	Steam	—	—	—	—	—	51,506	58,077	62,675	70,193
Spain	Sailing	—	—	—	326,438	210,247	95,187	58,201	45,185	44,940
	Steam	—	—	—	233,695	407,935	679,392	685,680	676,926	744,517

Countries		1850	1860	1870	1880	1890	1900	1905	1907	1910
Italy	Sailing	—	—	980,064	922,126	634,149	371,164	541,171	468,674	432,695
	Steam	—	—	32,100	77,050	106,567	376,844	484,432	526,586	674,497
Austria Hungary	Sailing	—	—	279,400	258,642	138,796	52,736	39,565	37,658	32,235
	Steam	—	—	49,977	63,970	97,852	246,989	366,070	418,838	477,616
Greece	Sailing	—	263,075	398,703	—	226,702	175,867	145,312	145,283	145,284
	Steam	—	—	5,300	—	44,684	143,436	225,512	257,000	301,785
United States of America –										
(a) registered for foreign trade	Sailing	1,540,769	2,448,941	1,324,256	1,206,206	749,065	485,352	353,333	269,021	234,848
	Steam	44,942	97,296	192,544	146,604	197,630	341,342	601,180	602,125	556,977
(b) enrolled for river and lakes	Sailing	1,418,550	1,982,297	1,795,380	1,650,270	1,816,344	2,021,690	2,361,716	2,450,405	2,372,873
	Steam	481,005	770,641	882,551	1,064,954	1,661,458	2,316,455	3,140,314	3,677,243	4,343,384
China	Sailing	—	—	—	21,694	11,801	20,541	19,560	18,243	14,314
	Steam	—	—	—	—	29,766	18,215	45,617	57,604	88,888
Japan	Sailing	—	—	—	41,215	48,094	320,571	334,684	368,013	412,859
	Steam	—	—	—	—	93,812	543,365	938,783	1,116,193	1,233,785
Total		9,032,191	13,295,302	16,765,205	19,991,863	22,265,598	26,205,398	30,849,067	33,132,066	34,629,742
World's total	Sailing	8,300,378	11,844,810	14,111,006	14,541,684	12,016,963	9,993,075	9,559,194	9,126,113	8,435,874
	Steam	731,813	1,450,492	2,654,199	5,450,179	10,248,635	16,212,323	21,289,873	24,005,953	26,193,868
British percentage of world's total		46.86	43.33	42.64	42.25	43.51	41.02	39.99	39.79	38.58
United Kingdom do		39.47	34.80	33.94	32.88	35.83	35.50	34.80	34.66	33.37
United States of America do		38.58	39.51	25.02	20.38	19.87	19.70	20.92	21.12	21.68
German do		—	—	5.85	5.91	6.43	7.40	8.00	8.42	8.38
British percentage of world's total in terms of steamship tonnage, reckoning 1 ton steam =4 tons sailing		42.7	40.86	43.49	47.56	48.91	45.39	43.98	43.46	41.93
United Kingdom do		36.25	33.95	36.51	40.57	43.58	41.32	40.00	39.48	37.88
United States of America including (a) and (b) do		45.09	44.55	20.00	21.19	19.46	17.55	24.24	18.86	1961
German do		—	—	5.85	5.02	6.79	7.99	8.67	9.09	8.91

Source: A. W. Kirkaldy, *British Shipping*, reprinted by Augustus M. Kelley, (New York, 1970) Appendix XVII.

Table 3.6 Mercantile shipbuilding output of the chief shipbuilding countries 1892–1914 (in thousands of gross tons).

Year	UK	France	Germany	Holland	Italy	Japan	Norway	USA	World
1892	1110	17	65	14	14	–	25	63	1358
1893	836	20	60	1	11	1	17	27	1027
1894	1047	20	120	15	5	3	17	67	1324
1895	951	28	88	8	6	2	13	85	1218
1896	1160	45	103	12	7	8	12	184	1568
1897	925	49	140	20	13	7	17	87	1332
1898	1368	67	153	19	27	11	23	173	1893
1899	1417	90	212	34	49	7	28	224	2122
1900	1442	117	205	45	68	5	33	334	2304
1901	1525	178	218	30	61	37	37	433	2618
1902	1428	192	214	69	46	27	38	379	2503
1903	1191	93	184	59	50	35	42	382	2146
1904	1205	81	202	56	30	33	50	239	1988
1905	1623	73	255	44	62	32	53	303	2515
1906	1828	35	318	67	31	42	61	441	2920
1907	1608	62	275	69	45	66	58	475	2778
1908	930	83	208	59	27	60	53	305	1833
1909	991	42	129	59	31	52	29	210	1602
1910	1143	81	159	71	23	30	37	331	1958
1911	1804	125	256	93	17	44	35	172	2650
1912	1739	111	375	99	25	58	50	284	2902
1913	1932	176	465	104	50	65	51	276	3333
1914	1684	114	387	118	43	86	54	201	2853[a]

Source: S. Pollard and P. Robertson, *The British Shipbuilding Industry 1870–1914*. (Cambridge, Mass. and London, 1979) Table B.7, p. 249.
(Based on Lloyd's Register, *Annual Returns*.) Data for several countries unobtainable.

4

Exports and British Economic Growth (1850–1914)

Charles Feinstein

Introduction

In many accounts of British economic growth, the early and middle decades of the nineteenth century are seen as a period of successful expansion and prosperity, while those from 1870 to World War I are characterized as a period of retardation and relative decline. There is not much doubt that, in certain respects, Britain was indeed falling behind its industrial rivals by the closing decades of the century. As can be seen from column 3 of Table 4.1 , the United States, Germany, France, Sweden and Japan were all able to achieve appreciably more rapid rates of growth of output per head of population, and in all of these except France, industrial production also increased much more rapidly than in Britain (column 1 of Table 4.1).

The record with respect to retardation, in the sense of a slowing down relative to Britain's own previous growth record, is slightly more contentious. There is, however, some evidence to support this interpretation of deteriorating performance, particularly in the movement of industrial production given in row 3 of Table 4.2. This shows a rate of growth of 3.5 per cent per annum in early Victorian Britain, declining to less than 3 per cent per annum from 1856 to 1873, with a further fall to only 2 per cent per annum in the late-Victorian and Edwardian periods (1873–1913). For industrial output per worker (labour productivity), there was a corresponding deterioration in growth rates: from 1.9 to 1.6 to 1.0 per cent per annum (row 4 of Table 4.2). The late nineteenth century also witnessed a second major trend. As Table 4.3 (row 1) shows, there was a steady falling off in the rate of growth of

Table 4.1 UK growth relative to other countries, 1870–1913 (annual average percentage growth rates)

	Industrial production [1]	GDP [2]	GDP per head [3]
USA	4.7	4.2	2.0
Germany	3.9	2.8	1.6
Japan	4.4	2.5	1.5
Sweden	3.3	2.2	1.5
France	2.1	1.6	1.4
Belgium	–	2.0	1.0
United Kingdom	2.1	1.9	1.0
Netherlands	–	2.3	1.0
Italy	2.1	1.5	0.8

Sources: [1] B. R. Mitchell, *European Historical Statistics, 1750–1970* (Macmillan, 1978), p. 179; W. A. Lewis, *Growth and Fluctuations, 1870–1913* (Allen and Unwin, 1978), p. 273 (for the USA); and K. Ohkawa and M. Shinohara, *Patterns of Japanese Economic Development* (Yale University Press, 1979), pp. 278 and 302 (for Japan).

[2] and [3]: A. Maddison, *The World Economy in the 20th Century*, (OECD, 1989), pp. 119 and 128.

Table 4.2 UK growth relative to past performance, 1831–1913 (annual average percentage growth rates)

		1831–56	1856–73	1873–1913
Gross Domestic Product				
1	Output	2.0	2.2	1.8
2	Output per head	1.4	1.4	0.9
Industrial production				
3	Output	3.5	2.9	2.0
4	Output per worker	1.9	1.6	1.0

Sources: Rows 1–2: B. R. Mitchell, *British Historical Statistics, 1750–1970* (Macmillan, 1978) pp. 11–12 and 836–7.

Rows 3–4: Feinstein, *National Income, Expenditure and Output of the United Kingdom 1855–1965* (Cambridge, 1972), pp. T111–2 and T131, and author's estimates.

British exports: from 5.9 per cent per annum in 1831–57 to 3.5 per cent per annum in 1857–73 and 2.6 per cent per annum from 1873 to 1913. The rate of growth slowed most markedly in exports of textiles [rows 2(a) and (b)].

From 1873 to 1913 the growth of cotton exports was barely half what it had been from 1857 to 1873, and exports of other textiles, particularly woollens and worsteds, were almost stagnant. The export performance of iron and steel, machinery and other metal goods [row 2(c)] was somewhat better. They recovered from the very low rate to which they had fallen in 1857–73, but were still less than half the pre-1857 rate.

Table 4.3 Growth of volume of United Kingdom exports, 1831–1913 (annual percentage growth rates)

	1831–1857	*1857–1873*	*1873–1913*
1 Total exports	5.9	3.5	2.6
2 Exports of manufactures of which	5.7	3.1	1.6
(a) Cotton textiles	5.4	3.0	1.7
(b) Other textiles	5.5	3.1	0.3
(c) Iron and steel, machinery, and other metal goods	6.7	2.3	3.1
(d) Other manufactures	5.8	4.8	3.8
3 (a) Imports of manufactures	3.2	8.1	3.7
(b) Exports less imports of manufactures	6.1	2.3	1.3
4 Exports of coal	10.5	3.8	4.6

Sources: Row 1: A. H. Imlah, *Economic Elements in the Pax Britannica* (Harvard, 1958), pp. 95–8.
   Rows 2–4: W. Schlote, *British Overseas Trade from 1700 to the 1930s* (Oxford, 1952), pp. 131–5 and 147–53.

This coincidence in timing has led many writers to conclude that these two trends in industrial output and productivity, and in exports, were causally related. Proponents of this view argued that, in the earlier part of the nineteenth century, foreign trade played a strong and positive role in promoting British industrialization, and Britain thus experienced 'export-led' growth. This was possible during these decades because Britain enjoyed a monopoly in the supply of almost all manufactured goods, from cotton cloth and ceramics to iron rails and machinery. In the late nineteenth century, by contrast, it is suggested that this 'engine of growth' moved into reverse. When foreign nations developed their own manufacturing capacity, the consequent decline in the rate of growth of British exports exercised a harmful effect on Britain's growth, creating what might be called 'export-re-tarded growth'.

The proposition that foreign industrialization had adversely affected British economic growth in the late nineteenth century has been widely advanced. In 1949, for example, Lewis stated that, 'The principal reason for the relative stagnation of British industry was that Britain had ceased to be the workshop of the world'.[1] His analysis was endorsed by Coppock: 'the deceleration of growth of production and productivity was caused by a decline in the trend rate of growth of UK exports, which in turn was associated with the emergence of the USA and Germany as serious industrial competitors'.[2] Matthews expressed a broadly similar view, observing that the emergence of foreign competitors, 'offers a straightforward explanation of decelerating British growth in terms of the pace and nature of overseas growth', although he also noted that there were some important qualifications to the argument.[3]

These general propositions were reinforced by an innovative, quantitative assessment of the effect on Britain's industrial growth of the slow-down in exports, undertaken by Meyer. He concluded from this that, 'if British exports had continued to grow in the last quarter of the century as they had in the third, English industrial output would have more than maintained the rapid pace of earlier years'.[4]

From 1970, however, this interpretation of Britain's nineteenth-century growth was strongly challenged by McCloskey. In a series of coruscating articles and rejoinders to critics he argued that exports did not matter very much, either as a source of rapid growth in the earlier part of the century or as a reason for declining growth rates after 1870.[5] In his view, it was

[1] W. A. Lewis, *Economic Survey 1919–1939*, (London, 1949) p. 75.

[2] D. J. Coppock, 'The causes of the Great Depression, 1873–96', *Manchester School*, 29, 1961, p. 221, *see* also ibid., 'The climacteric of the 1890s: a critical note', *Manchester School*, 24, 1956.

[3] R. C. O. Matthews, 'Foreign trade and British economic growth', *Scottish Journal of Political Economy*, XX, 1973, p. 198.

[4] J. R. Meyer, 'An input-output approach to evaluating the influence of exports on Britain's industrial production in the late nineteenth century', *Explorations in Entrepreneurial History*, VIII, 1955.

[5] The first and most substantial statement of his views was given in D. N. McCloskey, 'Victorian Britain did not fail', *Economic History Review*, XXIII, 1970, pp. 446–59. *See* also 'Britain's loss from industrialization: a provisional estimate', *Explorations in Economic History*, 8, 1970–71, pp. 141–52; and 'Magnanimous Albion: Free trade and British national income, 1841–1881', *Explorations in Economic History*, 17, 1980, pp. 303–20. These articles were reprinted, together with certain additional material and several controversies with critics of the 1970 paper, notably W. A. Kennedy and N. F. R. Crafts, in *Enterprise and Trade in Victorian Britain*, (London, 1981) chapters 5–9. The argument is also summarized in C. K. Harley and D. N. McCloskey, 'Foreign trade: competition and the expanding international economy', in R. C. Floud and D. N. McCloskey (eds), *The Economic History of Britain since 1700, 2. 1860 to the 1970s*, (Cambridge, 1981), pp. 50–69.

domestic accumulation and productivity, not free trade and the expansion of exports, which were the determinants of mid-Victorian prosperity; and it was limits to the supply of labour and capital that explained the subsequent deceleration.

The issue was taken up again by Matthews and others in the context of a major study of British economic growth from 1856 to 1973. They found that the pre-1914 deceleration in exports generated a decline in the rate of growth of demand and also had significant supply-side effects on capital accumulation and total factor productivity (TFP). They also emphasized, however, the adverse impact of internal factors unrelated to movements in exports, and concluded, 'The effects of autonomous decline in the rate of growth of TFP and the effects of foreign trade thus both remain of importance in explaining the course of events'.[6]

The relationship between exports and domestic growth during the course of the nineteenth century has thus been a controversial topic and raises many issues. It is only one aspect of this: the alleged retardation of growth in late-Victorian and Edwardian Britain, which is taken as the theme for this chapter. As a preliminary to the exploration of this question, the next section is devoted to clarification of some of the major implications of what I shall call the 'traditional hypothesis', linking the deceleration in British growth to foreign industrialization. This hypothesis is shown to rest on four propositions, to each of which there is a plausible alternative which needs to be considered. The strength of the case for each of these propositions and for the rival version is then explored and tested against the available evidence in the subsequent two sections. Finally, the main conclusions of the analysis are summarized in the Conclusion.

Possible Relationships between Trade and Growth

Before we turn to study the actual historical record, it will be helpful to clarify the underlying analysis, and to distinguish a number of different ways in which exports and growth might be related. The traditional explanation for the retardation of growth in late-Victorian Britain rests on four crucial propositions:

1   that the changes which initiated this deceleration in export growth rates had their origin in the process of foreign industrialization, and were

[6] R. C. O. Matthews, C. H. Feinstein and J. C. Odling-Smee, *British Economic Growth, 1856–1973*, (Oxford, 1982), pp. 447–65. For a brief explanation of the concept of total factor productivity see below.

essentially independent of developments within Britain (or, to use an economists' term, the causes of the deceleration were exogenous);

2 that the dominant effect of this extension of industrialization to other countries was increased competition for Britain, and a resultant loss of markets;

3 that, if this had not occurred, it would have been possible to expand output to meet a hypothetically higher level of overseas demand without a corresponding reduction in production for the home market;

4 that a consequence of the slower growth of exports was a deterioration in Britain's performance in relation not only to output but also to productivity.

All of these components of the traditional hypothesis are theoretically plausible, but it does not necessarily follow that they provide an accurate and comprehensive representation of what actually happened in the specific circumstances of the late nineteenth century. Each could be countered by alternative propositions leading to different explanations for retardation. The remainder of this section is designed to clarify some of the possible alternatives to the four propositions, and to identify the specific questions that need to be addressed to determine the relative merits of the conflicting analyses. In the case of propositions (1), (2) and (4), the alternatives are not necessarily completely inconsistent with the traditional view: what is at issue is essentially either the relative importance of the respective propositions, or their application to particular commodities or sectors within aggregate production and trade. The alternative to proposition (3), however, essentially represents a directly contradictory interpretation of the causal relationships, so that there is little room for compromise; one or other version must be discarded.

The alternative to the first proposition is that the source of the deceleration in export growth rates was not exogenous, but endogenous. In other words, the direction of causality was not from loss of markets to slower growth, but from adverse factors within Britain to loss of markets. Suppose, for example, that over the course of the century there had been a deterioration in the quality of British management, such as might have occurred if the deficiencies of third-generation entrepreneurs were as great as is often alleged; in Landes's graphic description: 'tired of the tedium of trade, and flushed with the bucolic aspirations of the country gentleman . . . they went through the motions of entrepreneurship between the long weekends; they worked at play and played at work'.[7] Such a deterioration could have initiated

---

[7] D. Landes 'The Unbound Prometheus', in J. Habakkuk and M. M. Postan (eds), *Cambridge Economic History of Europe*, VI, pt I, *The Industrial Revolution and After*, (Cambridge, 1965), p. 563.

a decline in the rate of growth of productivity, leading to reduced competitiveness, higher prices for British traded goods than those charged by her rivals for similar products, and thus a slower rate of growth of exports. To the extent that there was a causal link running in this direction, trends in foreign trade could be explained by what happened in Britain, but the slower growth of output could not be attributed to the effects of foreign industrialization.

Once the process of decline in export growth was under way, there could, of course, have been a feedback, leading to cumulative interactions between domestic factors and exports. On this alternative version of the story, however, the initial source of the decline would have been domestic, not external, forces. The key question which has to be investigated, therefore, is whether or not there are good grounds for thinking that the source of the initial decline in the growth of exports was primarily exogenous or endogenous.

As a counter to the second proposition, it might be suggested that, as other countries industrialized, so their incomes increased, and the rest of the world was able to purchase more goods and services from Britain. To the extent that this occurred, we could regard the effects of foreign industrialization as complementary, not competitive. At a disaggregated level it might be expected that there were competitive effects for some commodities, and complementary effects for others; but for exports as a whole, one or other of these effects must prevail. The question, therefore, is which of these effects was dominant in the overall fortunes of British exports.

Underlying the third proposition is the assumption that in the relevant period there was always a significant element of spare capacity, of slack, in the British economy. The contrary argument would be that the available supplies of labour and of capital were in fact always extremely close to full employment so that growth could not have been more rapid even if demand had been greater. This claim: that the growth of output was effectively constrained by lack of resources, not by lack of demand, was the crux of McCloskey's challenge. If he is correct, any deceleration of demand would have been of no significance, and the traditional hypothesis would have to be abandoned. Thus, the critical question is whether or not there were significant unemployed (or underemployed) resources available in late-Victorian and Edwardian Britain.

The final element in the traditional hypothesis requires that a significant causal link can be established between the deceleration of exports and domestic retardation. In the absence of supply constraints, any fall in the rate of growth of demand will almost inevitably reduce the rate of growth of output, but the impact on productivity (i.e. on the efficiency with which that output is produced) is more problematical. It is not difficult to suggest possible ways in which a slower rate of growth of output, consequent on the deceleration of exports, would harm productivity growth. This could occur, for example, through its adverse effects on investment in new equipment or on the opportunities for innovation and structural change. As we have already noted in relation to proposition (1), however, it is also possible that there were sources of a deterioration in performance stemming directly from domestic weaknesses. These alternative explanations for retardation are not mutually exclusive, so that what is at issue is whether it can be shown that there was a link between demand and productivity; and if so, whether it was a significant cause of the slow-down in productivity, relative to other possible endogenous factors which might also have operated in this period.

Even this limited selection of issues involves a complex analytical and empirical investigation, but it is by no means complete. Other factors – for example, the extent of foreign investment, or the institutional arrangements for settling international transactions – were also relevant, and will be referred to where appropriate. The purpose of this chapter, however, is restricted to an exploration of some aspects of the links between growth and trade specified above; it is not possible here to undertake a comprehensive assessment of all the determinants of these two variables. In view of the critical importance for the traditional hypothesis of proposition (3), and the significance of McCloskey's alternative argument from the supply side, it is desirable to deal first with this issue. There would be no point in considering the further implications of a possible lack of demand induced by poor export performance if in fact the growth of the economy was effectively constrained by lack of resources.

Was there a Supply-side Constraint?

As we have noted, the challenge to the traditional view that loss of export markets had significantly depressed Britain's rate of growth was mounted by McCloskey in the 1970s. There were two main parts to his argument, one an empirical observation, the other a hypothetical deduction. His empirical claim was that British growth was constrained from the supply side by a lack of resources, not from the demand side by a lack of markets. His case for this was made as follows:

> If faltering export demand after 1872 held back the growth of the British economy there would have been increasing unemployment as actual output, cut by the insufficiency of aggregate demand, fell more and more behind potential output. But unemployment after 1872 was low and did not increase

with time: the trade-union figures suggest that unemployment late in the period 1872–1907 was lower than it was early in the period.[8]

Measurement of the state of the labour market is a more complex matter than this allows, however, and there are several reasons for doubting whether the absence of rising unemployment in the trade union figures is sufficient to demonstrate that any higher rate of growth would have been inhibited by lack of labour.

First, the trade union figures cover only those workers – predominantly the skilled – whose earnings were high enough for them to pay union dues in return for unemployment benefits. It omits millions of unskilled and casual workers for whom, in the view of Beveridge, 'there appears to be always and everywhere an inexhaustible excess in the supply of labour over the demand'.[9] Secondly, recorded unemployment is only one indicator of the balance between demand and supply in the labour market. During the four decades after 1871 over 5,000,000 people emigrated from the United Kingdom, many of whom might have remained at home if the demand for labour had been higher. Similarly, greater demand in the labour market might have increased the proportion of women and girls willing to enter paid work. Thirdly, the argument about export retardation is essentially concerned with the industrial sector, and the critical issue is thus the potential rate of growth of the labour supply for industry, not for the economy as a whole. Given the presence in late-Victorian Britain of many low-paid, low-productivity workers – including, for example, some 2,000,000 domestic servants – it does not seem unreasonable to postulate that greater pressure of demand for industrial goods would have encouraged a transfer of labour into higher-productivity jobs in industry.

The second part of McCloskey's case turned on his estimate of the GDP growth rate which would have been achieved if exports had maintained their pre-1872 growth rate right through to 1913. The outcome of this hypothetical exercise was 3.71 per cent per annum. He then sought to demonstrate that Britain could not possibly have achieved such fast growth. This was based on his claim that the supply of labour and capital, and the pace of productivity change, were not sufficiently responsive to permit a hypothetical rate as high as that. For the purpose of this demonstration, he adopted the widely used 'growth-accounting' framework. Because this growth-accounting exercise plays a fundamental role, in McCloskey's rebuttal of the traditional hypothesis and in our comments on his arguments, we must make a short

[8] McCloskey, 'Victorian Britain', p. 448.
[9] W. H. Beveridge, *Unemployment, a Problem of Industry*, 2nd ed., (London, 1930), pp.69–70.

digression from the main theme to explain what it involves. Growth accounting relies on certain standard – if controversial – assumptions about the way in which the growth of output depends on the growth of labour and capital inputs and of productivity, and thus provides a useful means of identifying the proximate sources of growth.

The economic relationship – or production function – underlying the growth-accounting approach can be expressed in the form:

$$\hat{Q} = \alpha\hat{L} = \beta\hat{K} + \hat{A} \qquad (4.1)$$

$\hat{Q}$, $\hat{L}$ and $\hat{K}$ are the rates of growth of output, labour and capital. A is the rate of growth of total factor productivity (TFP), and is sometimes referred to as the residual, because it reflects all those contributions to the growth of output which are not captured by the measures of L and K; for example, improvements in the quality of the labour, or certain forms of technical progress. α and β are the respective output elasticities; i.e. they measure the relationship between an increase in the respective inputs and the growth of output. Thus, if $\alpha = 0.6$, this tells us that, if labour (L) increases by (say) 10 per cent, then output (Q) increases by 6 per cent. The particular form of the relationship used by McCloskey (known as the Cobb-Douglas function) has the property that the elasticities α and β add up to 1. As can easily be seen, this means that if L and K each increases by (say) 10 per cent then Q also increases by 10 per cent; in other words, the economy operates under constant returns to scale.

For the economy as a whole the *actual* rate of growth of output (GDP) over this period was 1.8 per cent per annum; and the growth rates for labour (measured in person-hours) and capital were respectively 0.9 and 2.0 per cent per annum. With values of 0.57 and 0.43 taken for α and β, the rate of growth of total factor productivity would have been 0.45 per cent per annum. This is derived by rearranging equation (4.1) as follows:

$$0.45 = 1.8 - (0.57)0.9 - (0.43)(2.0) \qquad (4.2)$$

Using this growth-accounting framework, McCloskey attempted to demonstrate that the economy could not possibly have grown at the hypothetical rate of 3.71 per cent per annum. To show this he considered each of the three sources of growth – labour, capital and total factor productivity – in isolation. By taking each separately he has no difficulty in showing that no one supply-side factor could have been increased sufficiently *by itself* to bring about the hypothetical growth of output. For example, he calculated that if capital and productivity had made no contribution, the labour-force required would have had to be twice as large as it actually was and two-fifths larger than the entire population aged 15 and over! Similarly, if labour and productivity had made no contribution, the proportion of income made available by savers for domestic investment would have had to increase from its actual level of about 6 per cent to an impossible 42 per cent to provide the necessary increase in capital.

This *reductio ad absurdum* procedure is not as conclusive as it may seem at first sight, however. In the first place, the hypothetical target of 3.7 per cent per annum is more than double the actual rate for 1873–1913 and seems unreasonably high. A more feasible target of, say, 2.5–3.0 per cent per annum would still have eliminated any deterioration in British economic performance as measured by the growth of output. Secondly, and more crucially, there is no good reason to take each contribution on its own in this way.[10] A more appropriate approach would be to ask what might have been achieved with plausible increments in all three sources of growth combined, each arising partly from independent responses to the postulated higher rate of growth of demand, and partly from endogenous links between them. For example, if there had been a slightly faster increase in the labour supply, then this might have encouraged greater increments in the supply of capital, and this in turn might have generated more rapid total factor productivity increase.

To explore the implications of these two counter-arguments we can take the growth-accounting relationship set out above, and compare the actual growth over the period 1873–1913 with a different hypothetical alternative to the one posed by McCloskey. There are obviously numerous possible counterfactuals (i.e. hypothetical alternatives); to illustrate one plausible case let us assume:

1 that the rate of growth of the labour supply could have been increased from 0.9 to 1.3 per cent per annum. This does not seem unrealistic, given the scope for reductions in both unemployment and emigration.

2 that the rate of growth of the stock of fixed capital could have been increased from 2.0 to 2.75 per cent per annum. With a constant capital/output ratio of 3.2 this would have required an increase in the domestic saving ratio from about 6 per cent to a little under 9 per cent; this again seems quite plausible allowing either for lower consumption or for the possibility that some savings might have been diverted from foreign to home investment. It is also possible that some investment might have been switched from dwellings to more productive assets, with a consequent lowering of the capital/output ratio.

3 that the rate of growth of total factor productivity increased from 0.45 to 0.8 per cent per annum, a decent – but by no means an extravagant – improvement.

[10] McCloskey acknowledges this feature of his method in his debate with Kennedy, *Enterprise and Trade*, p. 125.

If the output elasticities, α and β, were unchanged, this hypothetical version of the growth equation would then be:

$$(0.57)1.3 + (0.43)(2.75) + 0.8 = 2.7 \tag{4.3}$$

On this basis it would thus have been possible for GDP to grow at a rate of 2.7 per cent per annum.[11] This would have been well below the growth rate in the United States and about equal to that in Germany (*see* column 2 of Table 4.1). In contrast to the rate of 2.2 per cent per annum in the preceding period 1856–73, it would have meant a slight improvement rather than a slow-down in growth. This is not in any sense a definitive estimate, but is intended only as one illustration of a plausible counterfactual. It is in my view, however, sufficient to overturn McCloskey's argument that the Edwardian economy was *necessarily* constrained by lack of resources. It thus remains relevant to explore further the possible consequences of the slow-down in exports.

Testing the Strength of the Traditional Hypothesis

With the way open for the possibility that output *could* have grown more rapidly if required by more buoyant demand, we can now take up the issues raised by possible objections to the three remaining propositions underpinning the traditional hypothesis that the competitive effect of slower growth of exports was a principal cause of retardation.

The role of exogenous factors

The possible counter-argument suggested to proposition (1) was that the causes of the deterioration in Britain's export performance were located in forces *within* the domestic economy. Some such forces may well have existed, but that does not in itself preclude the operation of external factors, and there were unquestionably powerful *exogenous* causes that contributed significantly to the decline in exports. The crucial development was the sustained and substantial expansion of manufacturing in other countries, notably the United States, Germany, France, Belgium, and the Netherlands. This inexorable and inevitable historical process was accelerated by the zeal with which these countries abandoned the free-trade precepts which Britain continued to proclaim and to practise so enthusiastically. Instead, her rivals resorted to

---

[11] The corresponding growth rate for labour productivity (GDP per hour) would be 1.4 per cent per annum, appreciably better than the actual rate of 0.9 per cent per annum.

tariff barriers to shelter their infant industries, particularly in textiles, iron and steel, and other staple manufactures. The adoption of protection reinforced the development of the newly industrializing countries, hastened the exclusion of British products from their home markets, and brought forward the time when Britain had to face effective competition not only in third countries, for example, from American products in Canada and Latin America or German goods in eastern Europe, but even in Britain's own home market [*see* row 3(a) of Table 4.3].

The process of advancing foreign manufacturing capacity, protected by tariffs, was not to any significant extent dependent on Britain, and Britain could not have done anything to prevent it. It is sometimes suggested that Britain contributed to its own decline, by supplying the initial industrial and transport equipment needed to start the process of manufacturing abroad, and by lending capital for investment, notably for railways in the United States. But neither of these was a vital factor in the successful industrialization of the major foreign powers. Without British involvement, the process might have been slightly delayed but countries as richly endowed with human and natural resources as the United States or Germany would certainly have achieved industrialization without substantial assistance from abroad, just as Britain had done.

We conclude, therefore, that the impact of this progress abroad was a powerful and significant exogenous influence on Britain's exports from the last quarter of the nineteenth century onwards. This applies particularly to steel and to engineering products, which might otherwise have played a role in the continued growth of the British economy similar to that played by cotton textiles in the first half of the century. The effects of foreign industrialization can also be seen in Britain's trade in cotton piece goods, woollen and worsted cloths, alkalis and other chemicals, pottery and glassware, furniture, and numerous other products.[12]

The complementary and competitive effects of foreign industrialization

The question raised in relation to proposition (2) was whether the effects of foreign industrialization were predominantly competitive or complementary. There is no reason to doubt that, as foreign industry expanded, it raised incomes abroad, and so created higher demand for British products. This can be seen in mid-century trade in railway equipment, machinery, and other capital goods, and in certain consumer goods. To the extent that this occurred, it meant bigger markets and more profitable production. There

---

[12] For detailed analysis of these issues *see* S. B. Saul, *Studies in British Overseas Trade 1870–1914*, (Liverpool 1960).

were also indirect benefits, as industrialization abroad increased demand for raw materials, and the suppliers of these primary commodities were in turn enabled to increase their purchases of manufactures from Britain. It is equally certain, however, that over time these gains were increasingly offset by loss of markets once the industrializing countries achieved selfsufficiency and moved on to compete with Britain in sales to third countries.

One indication of this process is found in the changes in the destination of British exports. In Table 4.4 the countries purchasing goods from Britain have been grouped under three broad headings: industrial, developing and agricultural. A more detailed breakdown within these headings is shown in Table 4.1 The principal countries classified as industrial are Germany, France, the Netherlands, Belgium, Switzerland, and the United States. The countries classified as developing are those which were still primarily agricultural, but whose incomes were rising on the back of rapidly expanding exports of primary products. This includes the four Dominions of Canada, Australia, New Zealand, and South Africa, together with the Scandinavian countries, Russia, and the Argentine. The third heading covers the remaining countries of southern Europe, Asia, Africa, and South America.

Table 4.4 Destination of United Kingdom exports (Percentage of values at current prices)

	Industrial countries [1]	*Developing countries* [2]	*Agricultural countries* [3]
1855–64	44	17	39
1866–74	47	16	37
1875–84	43	21	36
1885–94	42	22	36
1895–1904	38	26	35
1905–13	36	27	37

Note: Exports include re-exports.
Source: As for Table 4.1.

The analysis of this trade data is not entirely straightforward. The long-run movements in which we are interested are frequently distorted by short-term events – most notably wars, but also such factors as harvest fluctuations, financial crises, gold discoveries, and fluctuations in Britain's own foreign lending – and this makes it difficult to discern the underlying trends. To eliminate these distorting factors as much as possible, the figures are summarized in Table 4.4 in the form of decennial averages. These figures reveal two very striking trends over the period from the middle of the nineteenth century to 1913.[13]

There was a dramatic fall in the proportion of exports to the industrializing countries. At their peak in 1865–74 these countries purchased 47 per cent of British exports; by 1905–13 the weakening of Britain's competitive position in these markets had reduced this to 36 per cent. By far the greater part of this decline occurred in exports to industrial Europe, where the corresponding fall was from 35 to 24 per cent. The pattern of trade with the United States was somewhat different. The share of exports continued to rise until the early 1890s but, after the introduction of the McKinley (1890) and Dingley (1897) tariffs, both of which raised the level of duty and extended the range of goods protected, British exports rapidly lost ground. The compensating gain was made in the redistribution of Britain's trade to the developing countries. The share of her exports sold to these regions climbed from 16 per cent in 1865–74 to 27 per cent by the end of the period. The biggest rise was in the proportion purchased by the four Dominions, but the percentage taken by the Scandinavian countries, Russia and the Argentine also increased.

By contrast with these striking changes in the direction of Britain's trade, the overall share of exports to the remaining agricultural countries was roughly stable. There was some increase in the share going to parts of Africa and Asia (though not to India), offset by a reduction in the proportions going to southern Europe, Turkey and the Middle East, and to Central and South America.

A second pointer to the damaging effect of the growing competitive pressures on exports in the late nineteenth century is seen in the behaviour of prices. One measure of this pressure is evident in the decline in British export prices relative to those for all British goods. With 1873 as 100, the ratio of export prices to prices for all goods and services had fallen by the mid-1890s by almost 30 per cent, but then recovered slightly in the remaining years to 1913.[14] Some part of this decline can be explained by the steep fall in the price of the import content of exports (for example, in the price of raw cotton), but the intensified competition in export markets also helps to

---

[13] It would be better if we could examine trends in the *volume* of exports, but this information is not available by country and we must use the series at current prices. It should also be noted that the figures include both exports of British products and re-exports of imported goods. Exclusion of the latter would lower the absolute level of sales to the industrializing countries, but would not alter the strength of the fall over time in their share of exports; *see* W. Schlote, *British Overseas Trade from 1700 to the 1930s*, (Oxford, 1952), p. 82.

[14] C. H. Feinstein, *National Income, Expenditure and Output of the United Kingdom 1855–1965*, (Cambridge, 1972) p. T132 for the GDP deflator; A. H. Imlah, *Economic Elements in the Pax Britannica*, (Harvard, 1958) pp. 97–8 for the export price index.

account for this trend. A similar measure of growing competitive pressure is given by the relative trends in the export price indices of the United States and Britain. Between 1879–81 and 1911–13 the average level of United States export prices for manufactured products fell by 20 per cent relative to British export prices.[15] Despite any reservations there might be about the accuracy of these series, the downward trend in relative United States prices affords a vivid indication of the problems British manufacturers faced in trying to compete with the United States, in their respective home markets and in third countries.

There is one further point to be made in discussion of the complementary effects of foreign industrialization. A striking feature of the post-1873 period was the degree to which industrialization abroad generated an increasing demand for Britain's one important raw material, coal (*see* row 4 of Table 4.3). This increase in foreign demand was beneficial for output and employment in South Wales and other coal-exporting regions, but there was another, more complicated, effect which may have been less helpful. The buoyant foreign demand for coal strengthened Britain's balance of payments on current account, adding to the surplus generated by the substantial flows of interest and dividends received from Britain's rapidly rising stock of foreign investments. This surplus on current account created a transfer problem equivalent to the modern 'Dutch disease' experienced by the Netherlands, Britain, and other countries with a large current-account surplus produced by substantial oil exports. Under the nineteenth-century system of fixed exchange rates, such a surplus could not cause a direct appreciation of the value of sterling, but it would have had the effect of increasing prices of British tradeables relative to those of the borrowing countries. This would have reduced the competitiveness of British manufactures and made exporting of manufactures more difficult.[16]

The link from exports to productivity

The final issues to be considered are those arising from the fourth proposition, linking the decline in export growth to retardation in output and in productivity. The preceding argument has shown that there were powerful

[15] Imlah, *Economic Elements*, pp. 97–8; R. E. Lipsey, *Price and Quantity Trends in the Foreign Trade of the United States*, (NBER, Princeton, 1963) pp. 142–3. With the average for 1879–81 set as 100 in both cases, the US index for 1911–13 had fallen to 71 by 1893–97 and then rose slightly to 78 in 1911–13, whereas the British index fell less (to 80 in the mid-1890s) and rose more (to 97 in 1911–13).

[16] *See* further R. E. Rowthorn and S. Solomou, 'The macroeconomic effects of overseas investment on the UK balance of trade, 1870–1913', *Economic History Review*, 44, 1991.

exogenous factors at work serving to slow down the rate of growth of British exports of manufactures. It is easy to see that this would have caused a corresponding decline in the rate of growth of *output* unless there was a compensating rise in the rate of growth of home sales, and there is no obvious reason why that should have occurred. But why should it have had an adverse effect on the rate of growth of *productivity*?

There is a number of reasons that can be suggested. First, the slower growth of output caused by reduced exports and home sales would have had an adverse effect on investment in fixed assets.[17] One reason for this to occur would be because slower growth of demand would reduce the rate at which firms needed to expand their capacity, so that less new plant and equipment was installed. Because many forms of technological change are embodied in new equipment, this in turn would mean that the rate of technical progress – and thus of productivity – was diminished. Another factor leading to the same outcome would be the consequences for industrial profits of the fall in the relative prices of manufactured exports noted above. This would cut deeply into profits, and reduce the funds available for reinvestment. Support for these propositions can be found in estimates of the stock of domestic fixed capital in United-Kingdom manufacturing. These show a downward trend in the rate of increase, from 4.2 per cent per annum between 1830 and 1856, to 2.8 from 1856 to 1873 and 2.2 from 1873 to 1913.[18]

Secondly, slower growth could adversely affect the climate of opinion, making it more difficult to introduce changes; for example, in work practices. In a slow-growth economy everyone becomes more defensive, more anxious to preserve the *status quo*. It becomes harder for workers to accept the need to exploit to the full the potential benefits of mechanization when this threatens jobs in an already difficult situation; harder for new firms to enter an industry; harder for more dynamic entrepreneurs to start up in new businesses or to get to the top in existing ones. There is generally a much less favourable environment for innovation, restructuring and technical change than in countries where demand is growing rapidly. These consequences

---

[17] *See* especially P. Temin, 'The relative decline of the British steel industry, 1880–1913' in H. Rosovsky (ed.), *Industrialization in Two Systems: Essays in Honour of Alexander Gerschenkron*, (Chichester, 1966). Temin argues that the higher costs of British steel were the result of the slow rate of growth in Britain, not its cause, and that this worked through the mechanism of a slower rate of growth of the capital stock.

[18] C. H. Feinstein, 'National statistics, 1760–1920' in C. H. Feinstein and S. Pollard (eds), *Studies in Capital Formation in the United Kingdom, 1750–1920*, (Oxford, 1988), p. 448.

of slower growth thus block off precisely the changes that are necessary to meet the challenge from abroad.[19]

There is thus sufficient reason to believe that at least some part of the slow-down in industrial productivity growth can be explained by the adverse impact of foreign competition on the markets for British exports. It is also clear, however, that external factors were *not* the only cause of slower productivity growth in this period. In the important textile industry, for example, quite different forces were at work. By the 1860s, the process of mechanization – in which steam power replaced spinning and weaving by hand – had effectively been completed. The initial benefits of this transformation, in terms of increased productivity and sharply reduced prices, were very large indeed but, once the process of mechanization had been completed, some slowing down was inevitable. No subsequent innovations could have such a powerful effect. The decline in the rate of growth of productivity was in this respect essentially independent of foreign industrialization.

Another significant sector where the rise of foreign competition was largely irrelevant for productivity performance was the mixed group of 'new industries'. Britain had never enjoyed a monopoly of the production of products such as bicycles and motor cars, or synthetic dyes and other chemicals, and cannot attribute failure to expand more rapidly to loss of overseas markets. There were also some industries where foreign competition proved beneficial, as progress abroad, notably in the United States, generated technological innovations. Examples of this include printing, footwear manufacture, and furniture-making. In these industries, foreign innovations, in machinery and in production techniques, were eventually adopted in Britain – though often only after a prolonged struggle with a reluctant labour-force – with significant consequential advances in productivity.

A further objection to the argument attributing primary responsibility for retardation in domestic performance to the decline in the rate of growth of exports is the awkward fact that exports of almost all manufactured products (except cotton textiles) enjoyed quite a sharp revival after 1899 (*see* Table 4.5). For exports as a whole, the rate of growth accelerated from 2.1 per cent per annum between 1873 and 1899 to 3.6 per cent per annum from 1899 to 1913.

This Edwardian revival in export growth rates thus saw a return to the standards of 1857–73. Yet, in this same period, the pace of productivity improvement showed none of the gains that might have been anticipated

---

[19] *See* Matthews, Feinstein and Odling-Smee, *British Economic Growth*, pp. 458–65 for further discussion of the effects of slower export growth on domestic investment and productivity.

Table 4.5 Growth of volume of United Kingdom exports, 1873–1913 (annual percentage growth rates)

	1873–1899	1899–1913
1 Total exports	2.1	3.6
2 Exports of manufactures *of which*	1.6	2.7
(a) Cotton textiles	1.7	1.6
(b) Other textiles	−0.4	1.5
(c) Iron and steel, machinery, and other metal goods	2.9	3.4
(d) Other manufactures	3.4	4.7
3 (a) Imports of manufactures	4.5	2.1
(b) Exports less imports of manufactures	0.4	3.1

Sources: As for Table III.

from the strong versions of the demand-side arguments. On the contrary it slowed even further.[20] It would no doubt be possible to suggest factors that might have caused lengthy time-lags in the response of productivity to a more rapid rate of growth of demand. This would help to account for the absence of the relationship postulated by the traditional hypothesis, but would still cast considerable doubt on the validity of that hypothesis.

Conclusion

This chapter has tried to underline the need for a balanced view of the role of exports. The relationship between trade and growth in the late nineteenth century was complex and many sided, with causal links flowing in both directions. The strong claim that the impact of exports on demand was irrelevant because output was constrained by supply cannot be sustained, but the extreme demand-side arguments associated with what we have called the traditional hypothesis also fail to withstand close scrutiny.

The support frequently given to this hypothesis can be explained by the strength of the evidence in favour of the first two of its underlying propositions. Foreign industrialization, assisted where necessary by tariff protection – both processes Britain was powerless to prevent – was the principal reason for the slow-down in British exports from the remarkably rapid rates enjoyed before mid-century. And the resulting growth of industrial capacity did have far-reaching competitive effects which outweighed any

[20] *See* further the discussion in C. H. Feinstein, 'What really happened to real wages? Trends in wages, prices, and productivity in the United Kingdom, 1880–1913' *Economic History Review*, 43, 1990.

gains to Britain's trade from rising incomes abroad. Our analysis has also upheld the validity of the third proposition, and has suggested that, if demand had not declined, Britain would have been able to find the resources needed to supply a larger volume of goods and services.

It is, however, the final step in the argument that proves to be the weak link in the case for the traditional hypothesis. The crucial fourth proposition, attaching special weight to export retardation as the dominant cause of the productivity slow-down, cannot be sustained without substantial qualification. The historical evidence indicates that the causes of this much-debated phenomenon in fact varied greatly from sector to sector. There were certainly some cases where the loss of export markets did have a significant adverse effect although, even in these industries, it seems likely that autonomous internal trends were also relevant. The performance in the major industries of steel-making and engineering illustrates this situation. There were also important sectors, such as cotton textiles or the new industries, however, where it was internal factors, not trends in exports, that were primarily responsible for the slower growth of output and productivity. In yet other industries, such as shoemaking, the challenge from abroad evoked a positive response leading to improved productivity performance.

Further research into individual industries and sectors is needed before a final balance can be struck. For the present, we conclude that the adverse, competitive, effect of foreign industrialization did create severe problems for British growth, but that it must be regarded as only one of the factors responsible for the retardation of late-Victorian and Edwardian Britain.

5

Trade Policy and Growth: some European Experiences (1850–1940)

Forrest Capie

Claims are sometimes made that trade policy has had a significant role to play in nations' fortunes. In this chapter we consider some of the experiences in Europe in the period 1850–1940. How did trade policy develop and what was its impact? On the first part of the question, the main conclusion is that there are many factors at work in shaping commercial policy but they can, in the main, be covered by interest-group activity and the power of ideas. The outcome, of course, depends upon the relative strengths of the participants and on the persuasiveness of the ideas. The impact of policy has always been difficult to assess but the most general conclusion here is that there is little association between policy and performance in any one country, but that protection has been damaging in the aggregate.

Trade Policy in the Nineteenth Century

The modern world economy evolved in the course of the nineteenth century. Following the Napoleonic Wars at the beginning of the century, Britain emerged as the leading industrial country and adopted free trade in the 1840s. Other countries were encouraged to follow, and a period of trade liberalization followed. Then there was a collapse into protectionism in the closing years of the century.

The role of interest groups in these changes in commercial policies is clear. There are many specific studies of these for different countries at different times, and they are undoubtedly useful in helping to explain the pattern of commercial policy that emerged in the course of the nineteenth century. Interest groups were influential in Britain in the first half of the century in the implementation of free trade, and equally so in Germany in the implementation of protectionism. But there were other factors at work, such as war and recession. Free trade emerged slowly after the long period of mercantilist philosophy that had dominated economic thought in the seventeenth and eighteenth centuries. Though, of course, protectionism should not be regarded as perfectly synonymous with mercantilism.[1]

Kindleberger has argued that the rise of free trade in Europe owed much to the British influence, and regarded it as part of a general response to the breakdown of the manor and guild system together with a quite widespread concern with the promotion of exports.[2] Export taxes had once been common, sometimes on machinery, but more often on goods which were inputs in domestic production. Different countries had different experiences but in France and in Germany the exporting interests were powerful enough to make the case successfully for the removal of export taxes. But, in the end, it was 'Manchester' interests and the political economists that persuaded Britain, and Britain persuaded Europe by precept and example.

In the supposedly high tide of *laissez-faire*, there were many powerful competing forces; interest played its part and state intervention in some form or other was never far away. Free trade was in part the product of interest, but even more so was the drift back to protection in the late nineteenth century. In the 1870s, some of the exporting interests in Europe suffered changing fortunes. These exporting interests had been instrumental in the introduction of free trade in the 1850s, and the changes they suffered undoubtedly lay behind the widespread reversal of free-trade policies that came in the 1870s. The root cause was the arrival, from the 1870s onwards, of New World grain in European markets, and the damage that did to the agrarian interests – which were still politically powerful – there.

The comparative decline of free trade in Europe in the late nineteenth century has occasioned a great deal of research. Of some importance in this was the work of Gerschenkron.[3] The proposition that Gerschenkron advances is a challenging one – no less than that, if Germany had fully embraced free trade in the mid-nineteenth century, it would probably not have turned out the militaristic power that it did in the twentieth century. His thesis is

---

[1] R. Davis, 'The Rise of Protectionism in England 1689–1786', *Economic History Review*, vol. 19 (1966), p. 306.

[2] Charles Kindleberger, 'The Rise of Free Trade in Western Europe 1820–1875', *Journal of Economic History*, vol. 35, (1985).

[3] A. Gerschenkron, *Bread and Democracy in Germany* (Cornell, 1943, 1989).

that the large east Elbian farmers (the *Junkers*) were powerful enough in the middle of the century to secure protection for agriculture and to strengthen their position further. Their feudal and reactionary role and persistent political influence were the major impediments to liberal democracy in Germany. Prussian power had been built up in the eighteenth century and, in the process, landlords were given increasing control over their tenants. *Junkers* had emerged with disproportionate political power, and that is what lies behind the introduction of the tariff to save their grain production when the New World was opening up. Although there were many groups aligned against them, the *Junkers* were powerful enough to carry the day though it did require making an alliance with industry. These sorts of pressures were widespread and were instrumental in bringing about shifts in mood. But ideas, good and bad, have also been important in preparing the way for the introduction of protection, although they may have taken a long time from conception to delivery of legislation.[4]

An additional part of the explanation, that has often been said to trigger the implementation of protection, is recession. Falling profits, prices and output, and rising unemployment provide the ideal conditions in which to find culprits abroad, and governments can win domestic favour more easily by giving protection in these conditions. A specific attempt at testing the connection between economic recession and tariffs in the nineteenth century was made by Gallarotti.[5] He examines three countries – Germany 1853–1914, the United States 1800–1914, and the United Kingdom 1800–1914 – to discover the influence of the business cycle on tariff legislation. His tests are the degree of association between years of expansion and changes in such legislation. The actual technique is to divide the periods into quinquenniums and then take the average number of years of expansion and contraction within each quinquennium and associate that with the major tariff changes that take place. He claims to find a degree of association between contrac-tionary phases in the business cycle and legislation increasing protection. As might be imagined, the test is a little tangled and the results are at best weak.

The most reliable guide to business-cycle chronology for France and Germany is found in Burns and Mitchell.[6] Superimposing the major pieces of protectionist legislation on their chronology provides no unambiguous picture. The first important French tariff came in 1885, three years after a peak in the business cycle and two years before the next trough; and the

---

[4] David Henderson, 'The Evolution of the World Trading System' in John Llewllyn and Stephen J. Cotter (eds), *Economic Policies for the 1990s* (Oxford, 1991).

[5] Guillio Gallarotti, 'Towards a Business Cycle Model of Tariffs', *International Organisation*, vol. 39.

[6] A. F. Burns and W. C. Mitchell, *Measuring Business Cycles* (New York, 1946).

comprehensive Meline tariff was introduced in 1892, two years after a peak. The German figures for tariffs and growth follow the hypothesis a little more closely but still not very convincingly.

That said, it is nevertheless difficult to believe that the broad movements in tariff policy throughout the world in the late nineteenth century, and possibly later, have not been connected with longer-term trends in performance. The general impression would be that periods of prosperity have promoted free trade, while long periods of depression have encouraged protection. There certainly seems to be a close association over the longer run between prosperity and free trade.

For the United Kingdom there was a long decline in protectionist measures from mercantilism through to *laissez-faire*. From 1840 to 1920, there is no significant rise in protection (despite considerable and frequent recessions – a business cycle of clear and regular periodicity, and many would argue, periods of secular decline). Indeed, the trend from 1860 to 1970 is clearly downwards at a low level and without variation except of course for the inter-war behaviour that Lindert has labelled 'Depression Duties'.[7] I return to that later but, leaving that episode aside for the moment, there is no obvious support for the relationship between protection and recession in Britain.

What of depression and protectionist trade policies in continental Europe in the second half of the nineteenth century? Two features are well known. The first is that the late nineteenth century saw a growth of protectionist sentiment and of protectionist measures; and the second is that the period 1873–96 is frequently characterized as the Great Depression. Is there a relationship between the two?

The Depression

There is no doubt that the 1870s decade was one of low growth. The worst years were usually 1873–79 but some countries suffered into the 1880s. Table 5.1 shows the rates of growth of total income and income per head across the period 1860–1914, and there is no doubt about the severity of the depression experienced in the 1870s. The story that is commonly told is of an intensive boom in the very early 1870s relating particularly to capital goods industries and that there followed around the world a long period (sometimes said to be 20 years or so) of depression. The period has attracted a lot of attention with a variety of explanations (both monetary and real) put forward for the long deflation – for it was primarily a long downswing in prices. Kondratieff's long swing was essentially a price cycle.

[7] Peter H. Lindert, *International Economics* (Irwin, 1991).

Forrest Capie

Table 5.1 Income growth in European countries, 1860–1910
(% per decade)

Country	1860s (a)	(b)	1870s (a)	(b)	1880s (a)	(b)	1890 (a)	(b)	(1900–10) (a)	(b)
Great Britain		12.4		8.3		15.4		12.3		2.6
Germany	28.5	20.3	18.3	4.0	34.6	21.0	36.0	19.0	31.1	10.3
France	22.9	19.6	18.0	6.2	10.5	11.0	17.6	17.3	20.0	12.6
Italy	6.6	3.5	10.8	0.0	13.1	0.0	11.4	7.7	16.0	9.2
Russia		6.8		0.0	16.0	9.1	68.5	23.9	31.3	16.4
Austria			24.7		19.4		11.4			8.4
Netherlands			19.6		8.6		9.4			13.3

Source: (a) from Mitchell (1987); total growth of GDP (b) calculated from Crafts (1983). *Per capita* growth (c) from Falkus (1972).

One of the *real* (i.e. as opposed to monetary) explanations for depression in Europe is that vast amounts of grain from the United States and other New World areas were landed in European countries in the 1870s following the extension of the prairie in the United States as well as the transport revolution. With the United States maintaining high tariffs on manufactured goods, Europe was plunged into a deflationary spiral. Given the nature of this two-pronged 'attack', European industry and agriculture joined together – the alliance of 'rye and iron' – to seek tariff and non-tariff protection.

A growth in protectionist sentiment

There certainly was some turn-round in policy following the gains of free trade so recently achieved in the 1850s, 1860s and early 1870s. In 1879, the Germans put duties on iron and steel. In 1885 and 1887 industrial and agricultural duties were raised. The French raised agricultural duties in 1885 and 1887, too, and in 1892 introduced the comprehensive Meline tariff. The Austro-Hungarians' tariffs were still moderate in 1878 but they were raised in 1882 and 1887. The Italians, who had low rates in 1878, introduced a high general tariff in 1887 and raised it still higher in 1894. In addition, there was a breakdown of most-favoured nation treatment and outbreaks of tariff wars in Europe, notably between the French and the Italians, and the Russians and Germans.

All of this meant that, between 1875 and 1895, duties on manufactured articles in Europe as a whole were raised. There were some attempts to reverse this process but the general trend was one of intensification so that, by 1913, the average levels of tariffs in continental Europe ranged from 10 per cent to 40 per cent, with the Germans being at the lower end of the range, the French around 20 per cent, and Russians and Spanish at the top. There is evidence for the case that some prolonged periods of hardship were followed by protectionist policies in many countries.

Economic historians are justifiably cautious about reading the pattern of events from the statute book, however, and tariff legislation is no exception. It did not necessarily translate into corresponding duties. The legislation should be contrasted with actual protection provided as captured in the ratio of duties to imports. Measuring protection is difficult but this measure has its uses and it reveals relatively little change across the period. The direction is unmistakably upward but the extent is not always large. By this measure, French ratio moved from 5 per cent to 8 per cent; German from 6 per cent to 8 per cent; Italian from 8 per cent to 10 per cent. The British ratio rose very slightly, too, but at a lower level.

In summary, in Europe in the second half of the nineteenth century, protectionist measures increased. They came mostly in the 1880s and 1890s. And, while there may not have been the great depression that was formerly the characterization of the period, the 1870s and 1880s do seem to have experienced a particularly deep and prolonged downswing. A greatly reduced agricultural sector, together with migration, may have helped Britain escape the consequences of protectionist pressure but other Europeans were not so well placed. There, the increasing size of industry and increasing concentration of industry were probably important, as was the disproportionate political power of agricultural interests.

Policy and Growth

What impact did protection have in the late nineteenth century? Did it improve the economic performance of the countries where it was introduced? Did countries with protectionist trade policies have faster rates of economic growth than they would otherwise have had, and faster than non-protectionist countries? These questions are not easily answered but the accumulating evidence suggests that the impact was small, weak and possibly even perverse. The immense difficulties in trying to estimate the effects of the tariff should always be recognized.

One attempt at establishing the relationship between protection and growth was that of Bairoch.[8] Bairoch did not use data on protection but simply classified some European countries (France, Germany, and Italy) as

[8] P. Bairoch, 'Free Trade and European Economic Development in the 19th Century', *European Economic Review*, (1972).

being either 'free trade' or 'protectionist' in different periods. The free-trade periods were, for each of these countries respectively: 1860–90; 1862–79; and 1863–87. He then compared their growth rates in those periods with growth before and after, in what by definition, were protectionist periods. The trouble with this is that commercial policy is seen as being either switched on or off, when in fact it is a continuum. Bairoch's study cannot take account of varying degrees of protection. Nevertheless, he felt able to conclude very strongly that liberalizing trade was damaging.

It is possible to be more precise than Bairoch was. As a first step, the growth of GDP and industrial production by decade, together with average tariff levels, can be compared more carefully. Table 5.2 provides the data for seven countries for as much of the century as there is data. It would be impossible from a comparison of these data to reach a conclusion in the way that Bairoch did. High-growth decades often went with big reductions in tariffs. This may be so because high growth is the cause, even if with some lag, of the reduced protection.

It is also interesting to note from the table that, aside from Russia, there is a lack of any great difference in the degree of protection captured in these measures for the European countries. Britain, supposedly free trade, had a gently declining ratio of around 4 per cent. The French ratio did rise to 12 in 1890 but was closer, on average, to 8. That is certainly twice the British level but it should also be remembered that Britain was a more open economy, and a comparison with GDP would narrow this difference. The German ratio was always slightly lower than that of the French. Even Italy, often singled out for its destructive protectionism, finishes the period not far out of line with the French.

There are annual data on these variables on protection, and on growth for several countries for the important 40 years or so before World War I. The data, it must be stressed again, are somewhat fragile. But, bearing that in mind, and exercising due caution over the results, it is possible to carry out a more rigorous examination by regression analysis. The hypothesis that economic growth was a function of protection can be tested. The test can be made to accommodate the plausible assumption that it was the previous period's (or the period's before that, or an accumulation of weighted amounts of previous periods') protection that contributed to the current period's economic growth. When such tests are run for Germany, Italy, the United Kingdom and Russia, (the countries where there were long enough runs of reasonably good data) we find that there is no explanation of growth to be found in protection.[9] The statistical results of the exercise turn out to

---

[9] Forrest Capie, 'Tariff Protection and Economic Performance' in J. Black and A. Winters (eds), *Policy and Performance in International Trade* (Macmillan, 1983); *idem, Depression and Protectionism: Britain Between the Wars* (Allen & Unwin, 1983).

Table 5.2 Nominal tariff rates: (a) total duties as a percentage of exports, and (b) economic growth per decade.

Decade	US (a) Nom.	(b) GDP	IP	France (a) Nom.	(b) GDP	IP	Germany (a) Nom.	(b) GDP	IP	Italy (a) Nom.	(b) GDP	IP	UK (a) Nom.	(b) GDP	IP	Japan (a) Nom.	(b) GDP	IP	Russia (a) Nom.	(b) GDP	IP
1820	46				22	4.1									36.4						
1830	25				22.4	19.1								20.5	33.3						
1840	24	61			17.8	30.9							34	21.6	33.3						
1850	21	57		12	13.1	25.7		28.7	36.6				15	27.6	9.3	26					
1860	36	28		5	22.9	3.4	8	28.5	46.2	8	6.6	25	8	22.9	26.8	17					25
1870	31	60		4	18.0	19.6	6	18.3	23.8	9	10.8	7.7	5	15.9	15.6	14					50
1880	30	47		7	10.5	5.9	8	34.6	48.1	16	13.1	8.5	5	17.3	18.3		55.2	15.7	25	16.0	45.5
1890	24	36		8	17.6	12.6	9	36.0	48.8	15	11.4	29.8	5	21.7	25.0		65.3	285.5	34	68.5	85.3
1900	25	52		8	20	19.8	8	31.1	45.8	10	16.0	55.7	5	10.2	6.5		11.1	53.0	30	31.3	32.3

Source: Capie (1983a). By courtesy of Macmillan Ltd, London.

be very weak, and that should not be surprising. Economic growth is not well understood but, by any reckoning, there would be a very long list of factors that would come above commercial policy in the explanation. Commercial policy is notoriously hard to police and enforce, and examples abound on the ways in which firms get around trade barriers facing their exports.[10]

The Extent of Openness

The weakness of the regression results, together with the earlier superficial examination of the data for more countries over a longer period, suggest that the conclusion that protection did not improve economic performance is warranted. What other kind of evidence can be marshalled? One possibility lies in import ratios – the ratio of imports to total output. If, as is usually asserted and the evidence does support, protection was rising in the late nineteenth century and growth was improving, then import ratios should have been falling. An advantage of these ratios is that they embody all the protectionist measures contributing to changes in imports, and so overcome some of the deficiencies of the previous measure, though at the same time they are clearly the outcome of a number of other factors.

These ratios are presented in Table 5.3. They are for the seven countries that made up the great bulk of the world economy in the period. The ratios for all the countries, except the United States and the United Kingdom, are stable or rising between 1850 and 1900. (Export ratios and, therefore, total trade ratios were similar). The exceptions are interesting. The United States has a falling ratio (implying less and less openness) and yet duties/imports were falling throughout. More interesting is the fact that the United Kingdom also has a falling trade ratio when it was the country holding to free trade. It could be argued that other factors dominated, but the result as it stands lends more weight to the suggestion that protection was not as effective as is sometimes claimed.

A qualification needs to be made, however. The ratios were calculated using current price data (in the absence of consistent constant price data). Volume data for the United Kingdom show an import ratio rising quite steeply from 19 per cent in 1870 to 28 per cent in 1913. The same is true for the United States. Lipsey showed that, using constant price data, the United States actually became more open,[11] and that agrees with the

[10] Walter Kirchner, 'Russian Tariffs and Foreign Industries before 1919', *Journal of Economic History*, (1981).

[11] Robert E. Lipsey, 'Price and quantity trends in the foreign trade of the United States', (Princeton, 1963).

protectionist measure being in decline. Thus, although the United States introduced more tariff legislation (though some small reversals were made before World War I) and talked protectionist language, the indication contained in the duties collected as a percentage of imports, showing relatively declining protection, is supported by the import ratio in volume terms (the better measure) actually rising.

Table 5.3 Trade ratios

	France		Germany		Italy		UK		US		Japan		Russia	
Decade	M	X	M	X	M	X	M	X	M	X	M	X	M	X
1840–50	4.7	5.6					18.2	14.1	8.9	5.9				
1850–60	8.7	8.3					24.9	19.5	9.8	5.6				
1860–70	9.0	9.5			9.2		30.7	23.7	9.1					
1870–80	11.6	11.8			9.3		28.0	21.6	8.5	6.2				
1880–90	14.5	13.4	17.4	15.8	10.4		28.2	21.5	8.0	6.7	5.1		6.5	
1890–1900	14.5	13.6	18.1	14.1	9.8		26.4	18.1	7.3	6.9	8.3		5.9	
1900–10	15.2	15.1	18.3	16.8	13.1		26.9	19.3	5.9	6.8	13.5		6.0	

Note: M imports, X exports.
Source: Capie (1983a). By courtesy of Macmillan Ltd, London.

The kind of evidence presented above is inclining one way – it shows that, in some of the literature, protectionism has not been measured as well as it might have been, and that the best measures show that it has not had the large positive impact sometimes claimed. An alternative approach to measuring protection is found in the effective rate of protection which captures the relationship between the net tariff and the value added in production. When the evidence, such as it is, for effective rates of protection in the nineteenth century is considered, more support for the weakness of protection is found.[12]

Several factors were operating to produce these results. One was the habit of the time of placing tariffs on primary products and raw material inputs – operating to reduce the net tariff. Another was the use of specific tariffs in a period when prices were falling and so depressing further the net tariff calculation. And a third was the fact that value added was in general rising over the period and so depressed the overall impact of protection.

[12] Forrest Capie (ed.), *Protectionism in the World Economy* (Edward Elgar, 1992); G. Toniolo, 'Effective Protection and Industrial Growth: The Case of Italian Engineering 1898–1913', *Journal of European Economic History*, vol. 6, (1977); S. B. Webb, 'Tariffs, Cartels, Technology and Growth in the German Steel Industry 1879–1914', *Journal of Economic History*, vol. 40 (1981).

Another point that should be made concerns exchange rates. In 1870, of these major industrializing countries, only Britain was on the gold standard. Most of Europe was on a silver or some bimetallic standard. Among some others, Russia had the appearance of being on a metallic standard but, in fact, operated on a depreciated paper currency. In the course of the 1870s, a fall in silver prices took place largely as a result of the increasing American output of silver and that in turn led to the depreciation of silver currencies. Similarly, for those with a bimetallic standard, silver replaced gold and those currencies also depreciated.

Some trading advantage (of a protective kind) therefore followed for those depreciating, as against gold, but the instability of the exchange rates that accompanied this encouraged countries to adopt the gold standard. Germany led the way in 1871 and the others followed. France moved towards gold but still held to a form of bimetallism. Russia and Japan did not, in fact, adopt the gold standard until the late 1890s. The gold purchases made by the countries adopting the gold standard added to the pressure on the remaining silver currencies to such an extent that, by the end of the 1870s, the major industrial countries had effectively adopted the gold standard. In other words, in the closing quarter of the nineteenth century, almost coincident with the rise in protection, was the widespread adoption of the gold standard, and countries that adopted it relinquished whatever flexibility they had from the previous arrangement.

Tariff policy is non-monetary but its effect depends upon fixed or floating exchange rates. Brunner showed that the unambiguous effect of higher tariffs with fixed exchange rates was to increase the domestic money supply and lower foreign money supply.[13] Therefore, whatever benefits accrued from the raising of tariffs in the 1880s and 1890s by those who adopted the gold standard, there was the offsetting factor of rising money supply raising prices and hence reducing competitiveness. The final result would represent another negative effect for the tariff.

In summary, this examination of quite a wide array of evidence on the impact of protection (very largely the tariff) in the nineteenth century, points to the fact that the tariff did not have a significant economic impact on the economies in which it was introduced. Their growth performance was not enhanced; but neither does much individual damage appear to have been done to their performance. Individual industries would have been assisted in the short run and then probably handicapped in the long run. It is worth

[13] K. Brunner, 'A Fisherian Framework for the Analyses of International Monetary Problems' in Michael Parkin and George Zis (eds), *Inflation in the World Economy* (Manchester, 1976).

reiterating here, though, that there is no evidence for the assertion that countries prospered behind high protective walls.

There is one further area of explanation, and that is that there were exogenous factors at work operating to offset the impact of protection. If transport costs fall, for example, that has the same impact as a decrease in every affected country's tariffs. With the spread of railways and the revolution in shipping, transport costs were tumbling in the late nineteenth century. Furthermore, any change that reduces risk or the transaction costs of trade will have similar effects. It could easily be argued that the world grew more stable across this period, 1880–1913.

If this argument is correct, why is there often a fuss made about the role of protection? The answer surely is that the problems that arose were essentially political, though none-the-less serious for that. The international climate that was generated carried considerable dangers for international trade. Thus, where it was once believed that late-nineteenth-century protection was high, that should now be modified. The fact that there is no clear relationship found between protection and economic performance therefore becomes less surprising. Equally, there is no denying that protectionist talk and legislation went hand in hand with nationalism, and that wrecked the world economy in the war of 1914–18.

Inter-war

In the years between the two world wars there was considerable turmoil in the international economy. A variety of problems dogged the immediate post-war recovery of many countries and severely hampered the progress of international economic relations. A principal legacy of financing the 'Great War' was differential inflation rates and price levels in 1919–20 and hence exchange-rate problems. There had also been soaring domestic and international debt and diminished resources with which to service that debt. Domestic production and international trade patterns were badly disrupted. Added to all this was the burden of reparation payments for some and the difficulties of transfer for others. Protection followed. The creation of new states in Europe increased protection as these countries also sought to protect their own industries. In the decade after the war there were increases in tariff levels generally as the figures (duties as a percentage of dutiable imports) in Table 4. show.

The League of Nations was impotent in the face of such determined action by individual countries. World economic conferences were organized by the League in 1927, 1929, and 1930. These were all quite realistic in their ambitions, aiming to get rid of non- tariff barriers to trade and prevent any

Table 5.4 Tariff levels in 1913 and 1931

	1913	*1931*
Germany	16.7	40.7
France	23.6	38.0
Italy	24.8	48.3
Austria	22.8	36.0
Czechoslovakia	22.8	50.0
Hungary	22.8	45.0
Spain	37.0	68.5
United States	41.0	53.0

Sources: Liepeman, H., *Tariff Levels and the Economic Unity of Europe* (New York, 1938); Humphrey, S., *American Imports* (New York, 1955); Conybeare, J., *Trade wars: The Theory and Practice of International Commercial Rivalry* (New York, 1987).

further increases in tariff levels. They all failed. Leaders invariably came away from the conferences making high-sounding statements and all in apparent agreement with one another on the need to bring about increased free trade. But they returned to their countries unable to resist the political pressures that awaited them. In 1933, at yet another world economic conference, held in London, an attempt at a tariff truce was made but failed.

The great depression of 1929–32/33 was truly world-wide but there was a considerable range of experience. The British suffered only relatively mild setbacks while most of Europe fared badly. Both the US and the UK used the depression as an excuse to adopt protectionist measures. Their actions brought dismay around the world and provoked the tariff wars that accompanied the trade collapse in the following decade. Britain's adoption of protection was especially important for Britain had long been the foremost exponent of free trade and its leading exemplar.

The protectionist stance of the United States and the United Kingdom – one the largest and richest, and the other the oldest and most committed free trader – produced dire results in the following few years. Around the world (and even across much of the United States) there was near despair at the passing of the Hawley-Smoot Act. The *New York Times* (11 February 1932), reported the view that, in passing the Hawley-Smoot Act, 'war was declared by the Republican Party against the rest of mankind'. And equally there was dismay at the action of the British. Of course, many other countries were highly protectionist but, at that time, any lead on trade liberalization had to come from these two. When the leading economies in the world took such action, it was widely regarded as further evidence of the breakdown in international trading relations.

The passing of the Hawley-Smoot Tariff provoked immediate and widespread recriminations and some retaliatory protectionist measures. Thirty nations immediately protested against the new tariff and many imposed countervailing tariffs within a week. The following examples give a flavour of what happened.

Italy immediately boycotted a range of American goods and raised their duties on others including cars, car parts, radios and so on. Italy also by decree switched the source of its imports to other countries. It specified the countries that imports could be purchased from as only a dictatorship could. The French followed suit. Indeed, to some extent, they set the pace. The French Minister of Commerce, Louis Rollin, made a speech on 30 April 1931 which declared that retaliation was the current basis of French commercial policy.[14] The particular approach of the French was the use of quotas, that is the imposition of maximum quantities of goods which could be imported from specified countries. This got around some of the constraints of important trade treaties that the French had signed. The first decree was issued in 1931, and many others followed, establishing quotas on a wide range of raw materials and foodstuffs. Others were introduced in 1932 on manufactured goods and, in total, hundreds of items were covered.

The Germans were particularly aggrieved at the actions of the Americans and the British, believing that they, the Germans, had been singled out for treatment. In the course of 1932, they raised their tariffs by 100 per cent and drove their imports down to the levels of 1898. There were many claims at the time that the rising unemployment in Germany was a direct result of these American and British protectionist measures. While it is difficult to provide evidence to support these claims, the economic climate contributed to Germany becoming a totalitarian state that strictly regulated trade, usually bilaterally, and also implemented a regimented payments system.

The Swiss believed that their watch industry had been singled out for discriminatory treatment and, indeed, that it was placed in jeopardy as a result of the increase in American duties of 300 per cent. The Swiss therefore boycotted American products. The Spanish, too, took action by immediately withdrawing most-favoured-nation treatment.[15]

When tariffs were insufficient to stem the flow of imports, countries followed the French example and turned to quotas. Sixteen European countries were using quotas on a wide range of products by the middle of the 1930s. Some of the duties imposed led to bilateral, as opposed to multilateral, exchanges, and they encouraged the formation of trading blocs.

[14] S. H. Bailey, 'The Political Aspect of Discrimination in International Economic Relations', *Eca* (1932), 89–115, p. 96.
[15] M. Gordon, *Barriers to World Trade: A Study of Recent Commercial Policy* (Kellen, 1941).

Barter agreements increased as did clearing agreements – designed to balance the exchanges between the two participating countries. There had been no agreements of that kind in 1929. By 1937 almost an eighth of the world's trade came under such agreements.

International Trade

As we noted following, World War I, there were various forces disturbing international trade. Debt and reparation payments, central European hyper-inflation, wartime import substitution, and so on, all played a part. In many countries, demand was depressed and yet great advances in technology had resulted in hugely expanded agricultural and primary produce output. Combined with the post-war glut of shipping, this resulted in tumbling prices for these products. By the time of the re-establishment of the gold standard, however, many of the problems appeared to be diminishing somewhat, and trade began to grow steadily.

World trade was on a gently upward trend from the middle of the 1920s until the peak in activity in 1929. Taking 1929 as the base year of 100, world trade had grown from 94.3 in 1925, that is, by over 6 per cent in four years – steady, given the generally fragile state of the world economy. In the next few years, though, there was the most dramatic destruction of trade in the history of the world economy. By 1932 that index had fallen to 39.1 – a fall of over 60 per cent in the real value of world trade in just three years. It continued to fall for the next two years reaching its nadir of 34 in 1934. There was some improvement in the next few years so that the index stood at 40.5 in 1938. But that means that world trade in 1938 was still 60 per cent below the point it had reached in 1929.

Not all of the blame for this collapse should be put at the door of the Hawley-Smoot trade wars. The US depression of 1929 to 1933 was the deepest ever, and the fall in income was undoubtedly responsible for much of the fall in world trade. Thereafter, that is, after the initial fall in income in all countries, from 1929 onwards, the two elements were inextricably bound up in driving trade and income down further. The tariffs imposed, by raising prices, reduced the demand for goods and so reduced the income earned by the exporters of these goods. That, in turn, depressed their demand for other countries' products and so the downward spiral went on.

It is difficult to disentangle the relative contribution of each element, but some indication can be gained from the following. At the end of the 1930s, most countries had surpassed by some distance the level of GDP they had reached in 1929. World output was approximately 20 per cent higher in 1938 than the 1929 figure. And yet, as we have seen, trade was 60 per cent lower.

Thus trade, which is usually closely tied to income, was dramatically damaged. The loss of income that resulted from trade restrictions must be judged to have been substantial. There is also the further point that protection produces a misallocation of resources and so depresses economic welfare further.

We take a closer look here at the British case. What led Britain to adopt such a policy, one that had had no place in British economic life for so long? This is a question that has long been debated, with a variety of answers given. These answers chiefly take the following forms. It was a desperate measure in the face of one of the worst economic recessions in economic history. Some find that too strong, and suggest that the forces working for protection had been gaining strength in the 1920s – indeed from as early as World War I.[16] According to this latter account, the return to protection was likely even without the depression of 1929–32. The third explanation emphasizes the longer term. It draws on the fact that there are always groups who benefit from protection and, where they can acquire power, they are likely to encourage protectionism and adopt protectionist measures. We incline to the last mentioned.

Be that as it may, a National Government, but one dominated by the protectionist Conservatives, came to power in Britain in the autumn of 1931 and immediately found an excuse for introducing very high tariffs. They claimed that the scale of imports in October of that year were such as to constitute dumping, and something must be done about them. In fact, the evidence was slender to say the least. They compared manufactured imports coming into the ports of London and Harwich in October 1931 and the first few days of November with those of the corresponding period in 1930. There was not much difference for October but the early part of November did show an increase. On the strength of this, the Abnormal Importation (Customs Duties) Bill was introduced in Parliament on 16 November and came into force on 25 November. Duties of 100 per cent were permitted because the Act was designed not to tax, but to prevent goods coming in. There was no good evidence of dumping. The likelihood is that importers were acting to beat the widely rumoured imposition of a tariff.

The British return to protection after almost 80 years can be seen as a triumph for the business pressure that had its origins in the years before 1914 and whose real foundations are found in World War I. Thereafter, throughout the 1920s, the pressure built up steadily. The performance of the economy between 1929 and 1932 was not the real cause. Unemployment was

---

[16] Capie, 'Tariff Protection and Economic Performance', *Policy and Performance* (1983); *idem, Depression and Protectionism* (1983); E. B. McGuire, *The British Tariff System* (Methuen, 1951).

exploited, and spurious dumping concocted to pave the way for the protectionist measures the Conservatives had long favoured.

Inter-war Impact

In the 1930s the British economy grew faster than at any time in the previous half-century. Over the period 1929–37 the economy grew at more than 2 per cent per annum. That was faster than in the 1920s (1924–9) which, in turn, was better than anything since the 1870s. The depression of 1929–32 in Britain was not severe, not as deep as that of 1920–1, and mild compared with most other countries. That partly accounts for the good performance over the whole cycle. But more important was the very strong upswing of 1932–7, one of the strongest in British economic history. The economy grew by 24 per cent in that short period.

What brought about this remarkable growth? The tariff and some other protectionist measures were introduced in 1932 and many have been content to argue *post hoc ergo propter hoc* that it was protection that was responsible. The main objection to this is that a whole host of other factors might equally contend for that position. This was a time when a great deal was heard about managing the economy. A number of policies was introduced and, as usual, there were some exogenous factors that also operated. Where the whole explanation lies is not easy to determine, and this is not the place to pursue it. Our purpose here is to consider the part that the tariff might have played.

Some early assessments of the tariffs, which relied on rather casual investigations, found favourably. Some attributed the fall in imports directly to the tariff. Alfred E. Khan claimed that imports of manufacturers were reduced by 60 per cent inside 18 months.[17] Arthur Lewis felt that the tariff was too low to be of much use.[18] Benham, one of the most distinguished contemporary investigators, believed that the way in which the tariff assisted recovery was by stimulating investment in iron and steel.[19] This is of particular interest in view of some specific results that we shall turn to in this section. Finally, in a lengthier study, Richardson concluded that, 'the effects of the general tariff were not very significant'.[20]

The use of effective protective rates has again proved useful in assessing the impact of the tariff.[21] The results on effective rates have become quite

---

[17] Alfred E. Khan, *Great Britain in the World Economy* (New York, 1946).

[18] W. Arthur Lewis, *Economic Survey 1919–1939* (London, 1949).

[19] F. C. C. Benham, *Great Britain Under Protection* (New York, 1941).

[20] H. W. Richardson, *Economic Recovery in Britain, 1932–39* (London, 1967), p. 408.

[21] Capie, *Protectionism* (1992).

widely accepted and suggest that the impact of the tariff must have been slight. But, while they have added to our understanding of the role of the tariff in economic performance, they have not gone unchallenged. Some objections have been made to the restrictive assumptions employed in the effective protection model,[22] and some dispute has arisen over the precise amount of inputs in some industries.[23] These complaints have, however, led to some alternative explorations of the issue and yielded some interesting results.

For example, in one of these other approaches, Foreman-Peck used a simple Keynesian model to assess the effects of the tariff on the overall level of demand. He therefore estimates the reduction in imports brought about by the tariff between the years 1930 and 1935. He found a 32.7 per cent fall in manufactured imports in a period when income rose by 6 per cent. Having estimated a propensity to import manufactured and semi-manufactured goods of 1.44, Foreman-Peck employs that to show that income should have raised imports by 8.6 per cent. Therefore, protection was actually responsible for a fall in imports of almost 41 per cent, the income rise bringing it back to an actual level of 32.7.

There would therefore have been a switch to domestic goods as a result of the tariff. And, added to that, some multiplier should be used to estimate and indicate the overall contribution of the tariff. Foreman-Peck uses Kahn's multiplier estimate of 1.75. This leads to the conclusion that 2.3 percentage points of the total rise of 24 per cent can be attributed to the tariff.

One problem with this approach is the attribution of the fall in imports to the tariff. Although the British economy was not in serious recession, a large part of the rest of the world industrial economy was, and world trade had collapsed dramatically between 1929 and 1932, and had slipped further by 1935. British imports fell from a value of £1044 million in 1930 to £861 million (17.5 per cent) *before* the tariff was imposed. Income fell by 5.6 per cent that year which, on these figures, should have brought about an 8 per cent (approximately) fall in imports. Something else must account for the bulk of the fall. Imports fell by a further 18.5 per cent to £702 million in 1932 when, for most of that year, tariffs were at their initial level of 10 per cent. The following year there was another fall but some of that must be attributed to the exchange rate. Thus, even without the tariff, imports were falling, and we must look elsewhere for the explanation. We should not attribute the fall in imports exclusively to the tariff and so must modify any

---

[22] Foreman-Peck, 'The British Tariff' (1981).

[23] M. Kitson and S. Solomou, *Protectionism and Economic Revival: The British Interwar Economy* (Cambridge, 1990).

expenditure-switching calculation and income-generating effects that are said to be attributable to the tariff.

Britain had returned to a gold standard in 1925 and remained on that standard until September 1931. The debate on protection had taken place in the context of a fixed exchange-rate regime. International trade theory deals with the differential impacts that can be expected from tariffs under fixed and floating exchange-rate regimes. The basic position is that the tariff can be effective under fixed rates although, as was noted above, the extent will be affected by the impact on money supply and the general price level changes.[24] But tariffs will be ineffective and possibly perverse under floating rates.

Britain left the gold standard in September 1931 and shortly thereafter implemented protectionist policies. It was at this stage that Keynes gave up his advocacy of the tariff. On leaving the gold standard, Britain did not, however, permit completely free floating. It was at this time that the Exchange Equalization Account was established and the exchange rate entered a period of dirty floating. Under fixed exchange rates, a tariff diverts demand to home goods, and domestic output can thus be encouraged and incomes raised. But, under a floating rate, there is ultimately no change. Within a simple macroeconomic framework with floating rates, the tariff would bring about a rightward shift in the IS curve and a rise in interest rates. That would induce a capital inflow and so lead to an appreciation in the exchange rate. This then diverts demand from home goods back to imports and that process continues until interest rates are back at their initial point. Therefore, there should be no expectation of protection contributing to economic growth. In fact, Mundell went further than this in showing that under floating rates a new tariff was likely to be contractionary – it would actually reduce national output and income.[25]

Eichengreen has argued that the tariff was implemented not as an anti-unemployment policy but, 'rather as an attempt to strengthen the trade balance and prevent the exchange rate from depreciating excessively'.[26] Further, there was little faith in the power of floating rates to correct the current account deficit that had appeared. Eichengreen's view is that, because of the experiences of several countries, notably Germany, in the 1920s, the fear at the time was of dramatic exchange-rate depreciation and consequent hyperinflation. The policymakers, he argues, imposed the tariff in the knowledge that it may exacerbate unemployment and this was a price to be paid for exchange-rate and price stability. This line of reasoning is

---

[24] Brunner, 'Fisherian Framework' in *Inflation in the World Economy* (1976).

[25] R. A. Mundell, *Man and Economics* (New York, 1968).

[26] B. Eichengreen, *Sterling and the Tariff* (Princeton, 1981).

surely ahistorical for the British economy at this time. Even in the 1920s prices were falling in Britain. They fell more steeply in the world recession. Business people and policymakers craved price rises in 1931. Anything that could be done to raise prices was done. It was deflation that they feared, and felt was damaging.

Kitson and Solomou have recently attempted to estimate the impact of the tariff in Britain in the 1930s.[27] Their main contribution has been the estimation of a model purporting to explain manufacturing imports to provide a means of distinguishing between different policies, but particularly those of the exchange rate and protection. There are serious difficulties with their procedure, although they conclude favourably on protection, if without much precision. The strongest statement they make is: 'An overview of the natural influences on the recovery suggest[s] that it is the *interaction* of a changed trade policy with the "natural" influences that explain why Britain performed well in the 1930s . . .'.

The principal aspect that is not taken account of by these writers is the impact British protectionism had on the rest of the world. The impact of the world economy has already been alluded to above. Britain was still the major trading country in the world economy and, when it took the measures it did take, there were all manner of responses around the world. To isolate the domestic impact of tariffs in Britain is to ignore this and the ramifications that it had for world trade. The reverberations that undoubtedly swept around the globe and back to Britain can only have damaged British external trade and hence economic growth.

Conclusion

In looking at the experience in this period when the world economy can be said to have emerged and then torn itself apart the main conclusion must be that protectionism had a deleterious impact. There is a weak relationship between the extent of protection and economic performance in any one country, but the deterioration in international relations that spread in periods of protection must be judged to have damaged international trade, and overall performance. If we look beyond 1950, we see a period of rapidly improving trade liberalization (and other factors) accompanying rapidly improving economic performance.

[27] Kitson et al. *Protectionism and Economic Revival* (1990).

Appendix

Table 5.5 Destination of United Kingdom Exports (including re-exports) (Percentage of values at current prices)

	Industrial countries		Developing countries					Agricultural countries			
	Industrial Europe	United States	Dominions	Scandinavia and Russia	Argentina	India	Other Asia	Southern Europe, Middle East, and North Africa	Other Africa (excluding North and South Africa)	Central, & South America (excluding Argentina)	TOTAL
	[1]	[2]	[3]	[4]	[5]	[6]	[7]	[8]	[9]	[10]	[11]
1855–1864	31.0	12.4	11.7	4.5	0.8	10.2	4.3	13.1	1.5	9.7	100
1865–1874	34.8	12.1	9.5	5.6	1.1	8.2	5.9	12.1	1.1	9.3	100
1875–1884	32.7	10.3	13.4	6.1	1.1	10.1	6.3	10.3	1.3	8.0	100
1885–1894	28.2	13.7	13.7	5.8	2.2	11.0	6.2	9.8	1.3	8.1	100
1895–1804	26.7	11.6	15.7	8.1	2.1	9.8	6.9	9.7	2.1	8.1	100
1905–1913	24.9	10.9	15.3	7.4	3.7	10.2	8.0	9.4	2.6	6.8	100

Note: Components may not add to totals because of rounding.

[1] Includes Germany, Belgium, France, the Netherlands, Switzerland and Austria-Hungary.

[3] Canada, Australia, New Zealand and South Africa (excluding the Transvaal and Orange Free State until 1904).

[8] Includes, Italy, Greece, Spain, Portugal, Persia and Turkey.

[9] The Transvaal and Orange Free State are included until 1904.

[10] Including the West Indies.

Source: B. R. Mitchell, *British Historical Statistics*, (Cambridge, 1988) pp. 500–15.

References

Capie, Forrest, 'Effective Protection and Economic Recovery in Britain, 1932–37', *Economic History Review* (1991).

Cmnd, 'Reports on Tariff Wars Between Certain European States' (1938).

Eichengreen, B., 'The Eternal Fiscal Question' in Capie, Forrest (ed.), *Protectionism in the World Economy*, Edward Elgar, 1992).

Falkus, M., *The Industrialisation of Russia, 1700–1914* (MacMillan, 1972).

Findlay, R., 'Free Trade and Protection' in *The New Palgrave: A Dictionary of Economics* (MacMillan, 1987).

Imlah, A. H., *Economic Elements of the Pax Brittanica* (1958).

Isaacs, A., *International Trade: Tariffs & Commercial Policy* (Chicago, 1948).

Kitson, M., Solomou, S. and Weale, M., 'Effective Protection and Economic Recovery in the U.K. during the 1930s', *Economic History Review* (1991).

Krugman, Paul (ed.), *Strategic Trade Policy and the New International Economic* (MIT, 1986).

Krugman, Paul, 'Is Free Trade *Passé?*', *Journal of Economic Perspectives* (1987).

McCloskey, D., 'Magnanimous Albion: Free Trade and Britain's National Income, 1841–1881', *Explorations in Economic History*, vol. 17 (1980).

Nye, John Vincent, 'The Myth of Free-Trade Britain and Fortress France: Tariffs and Trade in the Nineteenth Century', *Journal of Economic History*, vol. 51, no. 1 (1991).

Pollard, S., *Peaceful Conquest* (Oxford, 1981).

Rogowski, R., *Commerce and Coalitions: How Trade Affects Domestic Political Alignments* (Princeton, 1989).

Snyder, R. C., 'Commercial Policy as Reflected in Treaties from 1931–1939', *American Economic Review*, V, 30, no. 4 (1940).

Snyder, R. K., *The Tariff Problem in Great Britain, 1918–23* (1944).

Sudararajan, V., 'The Impact of the Tariff on Some Selected Products of the U.S. Iron and Steel Industry', *Quarterly Journal of Economics*, vol. 84 (1970).

Webb, S. B., 'Tariff Protection for the Iron Industry, Cotton Textiles and Agriculture in Germany 1879–1914', *Jahrubucher fur Natiionalokonomik und Statistik*, vol. 183, (1977).

6

British Trade with Latin America (1870–1950)[1]

Rory Miller

Introduction

'British relations with Latin America have fallen badly into disrepair', a Royal Institute of International Affairs study group concluded in 1988. 'Since 1945', Victor Bulmer-Thomas, the convenor, remarked, 'Britain has followed a policy towards Latin America which has emphasised commercial relations to the exclusion of almost everything else; yet, ironically, our share of Latin American trade has gone steadily down'.[2] The decline, of course, predates 1945, and the figures relate a sad, if familiar, story. In 1913 Britain had supplied about a quarter of the Latin American countries' demand for imports but, by 1938, its share had fallen to 13 per cent. The decline continued after the inevitable losses caused by World War II: from about 7 per cent in 1950 to less than 3 per cent during the 1980s.[3] The United States

[1] I am grateful to Jonathan Barton, Douglas Farnie, Henry Finch, Robert Greenhill, John Knape, and Andy Marrison for comments on an earlier draft of this paper. They made many excellent suggestions for improvements, but are not, of course, responsible for the final result. Some of the research embodied in this paper was financed by the Nuffield Foundation and by the Research Development Fund of Liverpool University.
[2] Victor Bulmer-Thomas (ed.), *Britain and Latin America: a Changing Relationship* (Cambridge, 1989), pp. ix and 206.
[3] Rosemary Thorp, 'Economy, 1914–1929', in Leslie Bethell (ed.), *Latin America: Economy and Society, 1870–1930*, (Cambridge, 1989), p. 66; D. M. Joslin, *A Century of Banking in Latin America*, (London, 1963), p. 286; David Atkinson, 'Trade and Investment since 1950', in Bulmer-Thomas (ed.), *Britain and Latin America*, p. 104.

replaced Britain as the leading exporter to South America at the beginning of World War I, having already surpassed it in Mexico, Central America, and the Caribbean some years before. Germany overtook Britain briefly in the late 1930s and then permanently during the 1950s. Japan and France also surpassed Britain's trade in the next two decades. While such an erosion of Britain's commercial dominance occurred everywhere, the collapse was most rapid and most complete in Latin America.

The RIIA study group's deliberations were merely the latest expression of concern about trade with Latin America. Official anxiety dates back at least to the 1886 Royal Commission on the Depression of Trade and Industry. At periodic intervals during the following 60 years, the British government made further attempts to investigate the decline and discover measures which might reverse it. A Special Commissioner, Thomas Worthington, visited Argentina, Brazil, Chile and Uruguay in 1898; the Milne Mission went to Colombia, Venezuela, and Central America in 1912–13; Maurice de Bunsen toured most of the region in 1918; Viscount D'Abernon led a mission to Argentina, Brazil, and Uruguay in 1929 (following a goodwill tour by the Prince of Wales a few years earlier); and, in 1941, Lord Willingdon went first to Washington and then around South America to promote British commerce. Attempts to revive trade continued after 1945; these included the expansion of Latin American studies in British universities and the formation of the Latin American Trade Advisory Group in the mid-1960s, and successive 'export drives' targeted particularly on Argentina, Brazil, Mexico, and Venezuela. In 1992, for the first time, a British Prime Minister visited the region in an attempt to wave the commercial flag.

Many of the criticisms of British business which appear in the reports produced by these missions have found an echo among historians seeking explanations for Britain's diminishing share of world trade, especially in comparison with the success of Germany and the United States. S. B. Saul, who argued that, before 1914, South America was 'the most competitive area of all', and thus central to historical analysis, criticized Britain's 'inability or unwillingness to strike out into new lines or master new skills' in industries such as chemicals, motor vehicles, or electrical machinery. While recognizing that Britain had retained a fair proportion of the region's trade, especially in the decade preceding 1914, he commented that 'this was due to a large extent to her long-standing superiority in textiles and also to her large and growing trade in coal, neither of which were to prove very sound assets in the long run'.[4] David Joslin, writing about the 1920s, complained that 'British manufacturers were offering wares at prices or on credit terms that were barely competitive', and quotes at length from the D'Abernon Mission's

---

[4] S. B. Saul, *Studies in British Overseas Trade, 1870–1914*, (Liverpool, 1960), pp. 38–40.

indictment of British business methods.[5] Interpretations such as these suggest several areas in which British firms failed to compete: the development of appropriate new products; the adaptation of existing goods to changing tastes and expectations; price; marketing and sales methods; poor after-sales service; insufficient credit facilities; and the lack of competent and sympathetic government support for business initiatives.

Other historians have taken a different approach. Stephen Nicholas, for example, attempted to rehabilitate British exporters' marketing methods, arguing that, for many standard products like textiles or hardware, the merchant-house system, which both D'Abernon and subsequent historians have criticized as ineffective due to the inability of a single merchant to promote numerous products successfully, must have reduced transaction costs in small markets. As trade became more complex, he continued, merchants adapted by specializing, for example, in certain engineering products, while manufacturers began to establish their own sales offices overseas.[6] The most comprehensive reappraisal of the British trading experience in Latin America came, however, from D. C. M. Platt in 1972. For him, the diminishing interest which British exporters appear to have shown in Latin America represented a rational and deliberate refining of effort to take advantage of better prospects in the domestic and imperial markets. Far from being 'truly competitive', as Saul had suggested, Latin America was, Platt claimed, a risky market where working conditions were poor. It was thus hardly surprising that manufacturers concentrated their efforts elsewhere.[7]

In many respects, the historiography of British trade in Latin America seems to have advanced very little since then. There were some obvious shortcomings in Platt's work: his distrust of statistical data, his failure to use business archives, and his dependence on traditional qualitative sources such as travellers' accounts and consular reports. Subsequent research in British business history stimulated further doubts about Platt's perception of Latin American markets as relatively insignificant. D.A. Farnie, for example, claimed in his study of the cotton textile trade that 'Lancashire survived the growth of competition with its yarn and grey cloth in the markets of Asia by the more intense exploitation of the markets of South America'. For him, Latin America was the most important of all neutral markets in the nineteenth century.[8] The historians of companies such as Pilkington or ICI

---

[5] Joslin, *A Century of Banking*, p. 222.

[6] Stephen J. Nicholas, 'The Overseas Marketing Performance of British Industry, 1870–1914', *Econ. Hist. Rev.* 37: 4 (1984), 497–503.

[7] D. C. M. Platt, *Latin America and British Trade, 1806–1914*, (London, 1972), pp. 305–311.

[8] D. A. Farnie, *The English Cotton Industry and the World Market, 1815–1896*, (Oxford, 1979), pp. 93–6.

underlined the importance of the major South American markets to these firms in the inter-war period.[9] Such insights were not really incorporated into the literature on British trade with Latin America, however. A further problem was that many historians continued simply to halt their analysis in 1914, without considering the performance of British exports thereafter. Thus, they did not assess the extent to which Britain's trade after World War I was helped or hindered by the commercial and financial relationships that it had developed with the region in the late nineteenth century.

British Exports to Latin America before 1914

Certain features of Britain's trading links with Latin America in the nineteenth century need underlining before analysing export performance in more depth. First, Latin America was never a single undifferentiated market. Conditions ranged from the small and poor populations of Central American republics, such as Guatemala and Honduras, to wealthier markets such as Argentina (which imported more goods per inhabitant in 1913 than any other nation), Brazil, Chile and Uruguay. Thus, the success of the United States in displacing Britain as the leading source of imports in Central America and the Hispanic Caribbean in the late nineteenth century hardly represented a serious blow to British trade, except perhaps in Mexico and Cuba. As Platt argues, most of these markets were not worth special efforts. The assessment of British trading performance hinges on the larger (Argentine and Brazilian) and intermediate (Chilean, Uruguayan, Peruvian, Colombian, Venezuelan) markets in South America. In all of these, Britain lost its lead to the United States at some point between 1910 and 1916. Although it regained its primacy in a few years between the wars in Argentina, Brazil, and Uruguay, the loss of dominance in the west-coast republics, which had just preceded the outbreak of the conflict in Europe, proved to be permanent.

Second, commercial relationships were multilateral. Before the introduction of exchange controls in Latin America (in the 1930s), British sales to a particular country did not depend on a corresponding flow of exports to Britain. Brazilian coffee went primarily to the United States and Germany; Argentine wool and Chilean nitrate to continental Europe. Nor did British trade always rely on the presence of British merchants. Colombia and Venezuela, for example, to which Britain exported goods valued at £2.5 million in 1913, 60 per cent of them cotton textiles, possessed not one

[9] T. C. Barker, *The Glassmakers: Pilkington, the Rise of an International Company, 1826–1976*, (London, 1977), pp. 210 and 379; W. J. Reader, *Imperial Chemical Industries, a History. Vol. II: the first quarter-century, 1926–1952*, (London, 1975), pp. 219–30.

British house between them.[10] What bound the system together was the ubiquitousness of the 90-day bill of exchange drawn in sterling on a merchant house in London or Liverpool as a means of payment. Latin Americans could thus export to the United States or Europe, be paid in sterling bills by the merchant house handling their trade, and exchange them for local currency at a bank. These bills could then be purchased by importers, for those drawn on a 'first-class' British merchant house provided an acceptable means of payment whatever the source of the imports.

Third, the history of Britain's commercial relationship with Latin America was not one of a gradual but sustained erosion. Trends were much more complex, through time and across countries. In 1880 Latin America certainly did appear to be losing its significance for Britain. It then supplied only 4.5 per cent of Britain's imports and took 8.1 per cent of its exports. By 1913, however, these figures had risen to 9.9 and 10.5 per cent respectively, and, even in 1930, they remained at 9.3 per cent and 9.7 per cent. To a large extent, though, this was due to developments in two or three countries, in particular in the River Plate, where Britain's significance as a market for Argentina and Uruguay increased substantially in the first 30 years of the twentieth century. This experience in the Plate contrasted with fluctuations in the importance of the British market to Brazil and a steady decline in its significance for other countries.

Figure 6.1 shows the value of British exports to Latin America, in current prices, between 1870 and 1913.

At first glance, the rising trend, especially after the turn of the century, would suggest a quite positive interpretation of Britain's export performance. Nevertheless, contemporary observers and later historians have questioned some of its underlying features. At the time, officials worried about the competition offered by Germany in the major markets, raising questions about Britain's ability to compete in new products, such as chemicals and electrical equipment, or to satisfy Latin American tastes in older lines such as hardware. They expressed concern about the absence of British merchant houses and sales persons from large parts of the region and the ineffectiveness of those that remained, as well as the support given to German firms both by the German overseas banks and the Berlin government. In all these

[10] Unless otherwise stated all British export statistics are taken from the *Annual Statements of Trade and Navigation*, which appeared in the *Parliamentary Papers* until 1920, and thereafter as separate volumes published by the Board of Customs and Excise. An accessible source for Latin American statistics is B. R. Mitchell, *International Historical Statistics: the Americas and Australasia*, (London, 1983). The reliability of both British and Latin American sources can be questioned, especially for particular products and for short-term changes: *see* D. C. M. Platt, 'Problems in the Interpretation of Foreign Trade Statistics before 1914', *Jnl. Lat. Am. Studs.* 3 (1971), pp. 119–30.

British exports to Latin America 1870–1913

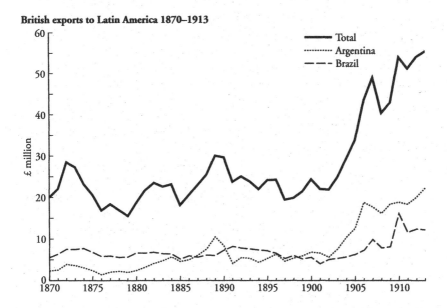

areas, by comparison, the British appeared negligent. For their part, historians agree that the apparent health of British exports before 1914 was due
to special factors: the expansion of the Argentine market as a result of
Argentina's own startling success in increasing exports and attracting foreign
investment, and Britain's continued competitiveness in a fairly narrow range
of goods, in particular coal, textiles, and certain engineering products. Where
they differ is whether this changing pattern of trade should be interpreted,
following Platt, as a rational decision to focus on the wealthiest markets and
those products where Britain retained a competitive edge, or whether the
concentration on Argentina and on technologically unsophisticated goods
indicates neglect and weakness on the part of British businesses. Thus, there
has been debate about the *concentration* and about the *composition* of Britain's
exports, and the extent to which they met the competition from other
industrializing nations.

The degree to which British exports were becoming dependent on
particular markets was obvious. Argentina had replaced Brazil as Britain's
leading market in South America briefly in the late 1880s. It did so
permanently after 1899. By 1913, Argentina alone purchased 40 per cent of
Britain's exports to Latin America, while just three other countries, Brazil,
Chile, and Uruguay, accounted for a further 40 per cent. Britain's success in
Argentina was hardly surprising, especially in view of the rapid increase in
British investment there (the precise figures are open to question, but Irving

Stone estimates it to have risen from £190.9 million in 1895 to £479.8 million in 1913). The critical case in the debate should be Brazil, however. Here, as Figure 6.1 shows, Britain's exports tended to stagnate until the decade immediately before World War I. This occurred despite Brazil's own successful export growth (an annual rate of 4.5 per cent between 1883 and 1913), and its appetite for British investment, which Stone estimates to have increased from £93 million in 1895 to £254.8 million in 1913.[11]

The literature on Anglo-Brazilian economic relations is relatively poor compared with that on Argentina, but two points may help to explain Britain's more disappointing performance in Brazil. British investment there tended to be portfolio (in government bonds) rather than direct (through companies which might have a preference for British products). In addition, the increase in demand created by rising exports in the 1880s and 1890s may have been channelled towards domestic sources of consumer goods, as a result of dvaluation and of higher import tariffs, rather than towards imports. Certainly industry in Brazil developed earlier and more extensively than in Argentina, providing British exporters with much more competition in products such as cotton textiles.[12] The British share of the Brazilian market for imports was already below 30 per cent in 1901 (compared with 35 per cent in Argentina). While it did not fall substantially between then and 1914, the German share continued to grow quickly (from 9 per cent to 16 per cent), and this suggests at least a partial failure of British suppliers to compete as Brazil's import profile changed.

If selecting the countries on which to concentrate is the first major problem in evaluating British export performance before 1914, assessing the significance of different products is the second. The composition of British exports to Latin America changed considerably in the half-century before 1914. Textiles declined from over 70 per cent of exports to about a third. Nevertheless, in cotton goods, British manufacturers do seem to have remained highly competitive with other exporters in a very segmented and difficult market.[13] The threat came principally from local factories protected by tariff barriers, especially in Mexico and Brazil. Even then, the loss of trade was concentrated on the lower and less valuable end of the market: in 1913

[11] Irving Stone, 'British Direct and Portfolio Investment in Latin America before 1914', *Jnl. Econ. Hist.* 37 (1977), 695. Brazil's export figures are from Bill Albert with Paul Henderson, *South America and the First World War: the Impact of War on Brazil, Argentina, Peru and Chile*, (Cambridge, 1988), p. 18.

[12] Warren Dean, *The Industrialization of São Paulo, 1880–1945*, (Austin, 1969); Stanley J. Stein, *The Brazilian Cotton Manufacture: Textile Enterprise in an Underdeveloped Area, 1850–1950*, (Harvard, 1957).

[13] A. J. Marrison, 'Great Britain and her Rivals in the Latin American Cotton Piece Goods Market, 1880–1914', in Barrie M. Ratcliffe (ed.), *Great Britain and her World,*

Brazil still purchased cotton textiles worth £2.3 million, though the level of its imports had fallen steadily since the early 1890s (*see* Table 6.1). Platt also draws attention to the woollen manufacturers' successful recapture of markets in South America, especially in the River Plate, after temporary problems in the 1880s. A further area of great success was the coal trade, which accounted for almost 12 per cent of Britain's exports to Latin America in 1913, to meet the demand for fuel from railways, steamships, and gasworks.

Table 6.1 Principal British exports to Argentina, Brazil, and Chile in 1913

(£000)	Argentina	Brazil	Chile
Cotton textiles	3809.4	2310.9	1185.0
Woollen textiles	1712.1	400.9	696.6
Linen textiles	334.4	240.3	47.9
Jute goods and yarn	179.1	299.1	29.7
China and earthenware	348.3	284.2	61.8
Food and drink	436.8	305.1	151.7
Coal and coke	3191.9	1900.9	644.4
Chemicals	398.0	203.1	63.9
Iron and steel manufactures	4196.5	1465.4	861.6
Machinery	2013.5	1462.8	643.1
Railway carriages	746.4	346.9	87.4
Ships and boats	354.4	211.9	34.6
Implements and tools	120.4	356.9	49.0
Electrical goods	386.1	259.5	77.6
Others	4413.8	2417.1	1376.2
Total	22640.9	12465.1	6010.5

Source: Annual Statement of Trade and Navigation, 1913.

Table 6.1, which shows the composition of Britain's exports to its three largest markets in Latin America in 1913, suggests that, in these wealthier countries, Britain was indeed selling considerable quantities of the capital goods and industrial inputs such as fuel and chemicals that the major Latin American economies increasingly required. But did they adequately meet the competition in these products? The literature on specific export sectors regarding trade with Latin America is patchy, but some points are fairly clear. In chemicals, the British alkali manufacturers dominated the market for

1750–1914: Essays in Honour of W. O. Henderson, (Manchester, 1975), pp. 309–48, is one of the few sectoral studies concentrating specifically on Latin America, and shows how official reports and the trade press can be imaginatively used for such an analysis.

caustic soda and soda ash, but fell behind in more advanced products. British suppliers of machinery for textile manufacturing, sugar and coffee processing, and flour milling remained successful, but other countries· tended to provide agricultural, mining, and oil equipment. The Germans, unsurprisingly, led in sales of electrical machinery to countries such as Argentina and Brazil. The question of railway equipment is more difficult to analyse, because of the problem of weighting the significance of particular items (rails, locomotives, rolling stock, construction materials) and of isolating the purchases of state railway companies, which might be expected to offer a more competitive market in which orders were determined by price and quality, from those of foreign firms. United States' officials certainly believed that Britain dominated markets because of the scale of its investments, quoting several examples of ways in which the British companies' consulting engineers in London supposedly favoured British suppliers. In 1913, they estimated, 75 per cent of the locomotives and 57 per cent of the passenger and freight cars imported into Argentina came from the United Kingdom. Yet, for both S. B. Saul and Roger Gravil, who calculate Britain's share of the Argentine market for railway equipment between 1908 and 1913 at 48–49 per cent, the performance seems poor, given the weight of British investments.[14]

Research of this kind, which tends to rely almost exclusively on British government reports and trade statistics, does not permit a conclusive answer to questions about the overall 'success' or 'failure' of British exports to Latin America before 1914. By attaching a greater or lesser significance to different products or markets, historians can construct either an 'optimistic' or a 'pessimistic' case. The biases and preconceptions of the officials who compiled the reports are frequently ignored, and there is too great a tendency, among contemporary commentators and among historians, to compare figures on a year-by-year basis rather than investigating long-term trends. To sustain a debate in these terms and at this level is not only inherently unsatisfactory, it ignores deeper questions about the foundations on which British trade with Latin America actually rested before 1914. These need explaining, because they are crucial to the analysis of the subsequent decline.

First, trade was based on the assumption that currencies would be freely convertible. This permitted British exporters to make sales even when Britain

[14] United States, Federal Trade Commission, *Report on Cooperation in American Export Trade*, (2 vols., Washington, 1916), I, 175–176; Saul, *Studies in British Overseas Trade*, pp. 78–9; Roger Gravil, *The Anglo-Argentine Connection 1900–1939*, (Boulder & London, 1985), pp. 100–2. Despite the importance of the sector, Platt devotes only a couple of pages, almost entirely based on consular reports, in *Latin America and British Trade* to the question of railway equipment. A fuller study using business archives and covering the inter-war period as well, is badly needed.

did not purchase Latin American products. The bilateral trade balances with individual countries did not matter. While Britain was running a considerable deficit on its visible trade with Argentina in 1913, to the tune of £18.3 million, it had a surplus of £7.9 million with Brazil and £1.7 million with Chile. No-one paid any attention to the problems that might arise from such imbalances in the future.[15] Second, a considerable, if unquantifiable, proportion of trade depended on the existing large stock of profitable direct investments, such as railways and public utility companies, which Britain had built up in Latin America, and on a continued flow of new ventures disposed to favour British suppliers (*see* Table 6.2).[16] By 1916 a total of 390 British companies were said to be operating in the region, providing a significant market for British goods.[17]

Table 6.2 Quoted British investments in Latin America, 1865–1913

(*£ million*)	1865	1875	1885	1895	1905	1913
Total	80.9	174.6	250.5	552.5	688.5	1179.9
(Percentages)						
Government loans	76	74	64	47	45	38
Other portfolio investment	2	2	4	11	8	16
Direct investment	21	24	32	42	48	46

* Note that there are problems with all existing calculations of investment. Lance Davis and Robert A. Huttenback, 'The Export of British Finance, 1865–1914', *Journal of Imperial and Commonwealth History* 13 (1985), pp. 28–76, estimate capital calls on the London market for *South* America and imply a total figure somewhat less than these. Svedberg's recalculation of direct/portfolio investment in Latin America was based on an earlier paper by Stone, but is in line with these figures: Peter E. Svedberg, 'The Portfolio-Direct Composition of Private Foreign Investment in 1914 Revisited', *Economic Journal* 88 (1978), pp. 768–77.
Source: Stone, 'British Direct and Portfolio Investment in Latin America before 1914'. *Journal of Economic History* 37 (1977) 698–701.

[15] This estimate excludes those imports (especially from Brazil) which were subsequently re-exported from the United Kingdom. Payments for invisibles like shipping, insurance, bankers' and merchants' commissions, interest and dividend payments, would have made Britain's current account surplus with Brazil and Chile much larger, while considerably reducing the deficit with Argentina.

[16] The relationship between investment and exports has not been particularly well specified, partly because of the difficulties of identifying investment flows, partly because economic historians have found anecdotal evidence much easier to handle.

[17] US, Federal Trade Commission, *Report on Cooperation*, II, 537–74.

Third, bulk exports, such as coal or cement, depended on the availability of shipping willing to offer cheap outward freights for cargoes to South America and therefore on the size and competitiveness of British merchant fleets operating in the region. Finally, particular groups of intermediaries played a significant role in directing orders towards Britain: the merchant houses which provided credit to local exporters in Peru and Chile; the technicians who established cotton mills in Brazil and Mexico; the consulting engineers of the railway and public utility companies operating in these countries and in the River Plate.

Before 1914, officials and business people in Britain seem scarcely to have considered the possibility that the foundations of their trade in Latin America might be quickly eroded. They generally took for granted the continued flow of investment and the dominance of British shipping, banking, and commercial credit. Rivals, such as the United States and Germany, in contrast, identified these very factors – investments, banking, and shipping – as the bases of Britain's superiority and attempted to replicate them. In addition, Germany tried to encourage emigration to southern Brazil and Chile, and military missions to Argentina and Chile to reinforce the market for German products.[18] Just before the war broke out, the United States government had also begun to encourage the expansion of US investment and banking in Latin America, as well as establishing a network of commercial attachés and special agents to report to the new Bureau of Foreign and Domestic Commerce on particular economic opportunities. The British government, on the other hand, seemed content with the collection of general information about economic trends and the occasional special mission. Yet, at a superficial level, British trade with Latin America appeared reasonably resilient. Some erosion had been inevitable because of industrial growth in the United States and Germany, but the British still retained a considerable share of the largest South American markets, and officials of other countries worried about their inability to make more than a marginal impression on Britain's commercial supremacy (*see* Table 6.3).

In fact, the resilience of British exports was an illusion, magnified by the economic boom which occurred in Latin America in the decade before 1913. The rapid expansion of exports to Argentina had been due to the country's spectacular, but unsustainable growth rates; Britain's share of its import trade had actually fallen by a few points since the turn of the century. There and

[18] The actual link between German military missions and arms sales is unclear: *see* Holger H. Herwig, *Germany's Vision of Empire in Venezuela, 1871–1914*, (Princeton, 1986), Chapter 4. On German relations with South America generally *see* Ian L. D. Forbes, 'German Informal Imperialism in South America before 1914', *Econ. Hist. Rev.* 31 (1978), 384–98.

Table 6.3 UK, US and German shares of Latin American import markets

(percentages)	United Kingdom	United States	Germany
Argentina			
1901–04	34	13	14
1910–13	30	14	17
1926–29	19	25	11
1935–38	22	16	10
1947–50	12	30	1
1961–64	9	26	13
Brazil			
1901–04	28	12	11
1910–13	27	15	17
1926–29	20	29	12
1935–38	12	23	24
1947–50	11	48	1
1961–64	3	33	9
Chile			
1901–04	37	10	26
1910–13	32	14	26
1926–29	18	32	14
1935–38	13	28	25
1947–50	8	47	1
1961–64	7	37	10
Peru			
1901–04	36	17	16
1910–13	30	25	18
1926–29	16	43	10
1935–38	12	34	19
1947–50	12	59	1
1961–64	7	41	12

Sources: Calculated from B.K. Mitchell, *International Historical Statistics; the Americas 1750–1988* (London) 1993, pp. 435–440 and 470–487; United Nations, *Yearbook of International Trade Statistics* (annual) passim.

in Brazil, the United States and Germany had taken greater advantage of the pre-war boom. Generally, too, British exporters had performed better in the older products than in those which would become central to trade after the war. Exports relied heavily on traditional industrial technologies: textiles, railways, and energy sources such as coal and gas. These were vulnerable to substitution by domestic manufacturers, by road vehicles, and by petroleum and electrical power. Britain's capacity to compete in these expanding sectors of international trade was much more open to question. Thus, there were already signs, for those who cared to read them, that Britain might find it difficult to preserve its commercial primacy in Latin America. Those who did show some concern about the future, however, like many subsequent historians, tended to formulate the problem largely in terms of the ability of British industry to compete with the United States and Germany, rather than considering whether the deeper foundations upon which British trade in the region rested might require greater attention and protection.

The Collapse of British Exports, 1914–50

It is fairly straightforward to outline the decline in Britain's trading position in Latin America which occurred over the following 35 years. It is clear from the figures for British exports which, in terms of volume, did not regain their 1913 level at any time during the inter-war period, and from the decline in Britain's share of the major Latin American markets which is evident in Figure 6.2.[19]

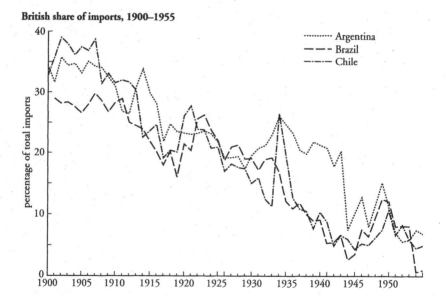

British share of imports, 1900–1955

.... Argentina
— — Brazil
—·—·— Chile

[19] Rory Miller, *Britain and Latin America in the Nineteenth and Twentieth Centuries*, (London, 1993), p. 185.

The outbreak of World War I resulted in an immediate fall in Britain's exports and in its share of Latin American markets, in the short term because of the disruption caused by the suspension of normal credit, shipping, and marketing facilities, and then because the United States partially filled the gap left by the withdrawal of British and German suppliers. Additional reasons for the decline were the uneven growth of industrial production within South America, especially in Brazil, and the export licensing arrangements instituted by the British government, which favoured the Dominions and aroused protests from British interests in Latin America.

The revival of British trade immediately after the war, however, was disappointing. By 1922 the volume of exports to Latin America had reached no more than 48 per cent of the 1913 figure, compared with a figure of 69 per cent for British exports as a whole. While they did recover more ground during the 1920s, at their peak in 1928–9, they still amounted to little more than 80 per cent of the 1913 level. As regards competition, concentration and composition, the pre-war patterns persisted. German exporters had recovered fairly quickly, and the United States, which briefly lost its lead to Britain in Argentina and in Brazil in the early 1920s, again seemed to have established its dominance by the end of the decade (*see* Table 6.3). Argentina continued to provide Britain with its principal market in Latin America, taking 43 per cent of its exports to the region in 1928, while Brazil accounted for 22 per cent. Besides the continuation of US and German rivalry and the concentration on the two major markets, there was also little change in the composition of Britain's exports. The share of textiles actually rose. In 1928 cotton goods accounted for 25.1 per cent of the total, and woollens and other textiles a further 15.4 per cent. The role of coal receded, to 5.8 per cent of the total but, in products such as chemicals (3.3 per cent), electrical goods (3.3 per cent) and motor vehicles (0.6 per cent), Britain remained a relatively insignificant supplier in comparison with the other industrial countries.[20]

The collapse of trade during the maelstrom of the early 1930s was inevitable in the short term. By the middle of the decade, however, many Latin American economies had begun to experience quite strong growth, especially in manufacturing, and this established a renewed demand for imports of machinery and other capital and intermediate goods. Yet British exports never regained more than two-thirds of their 1929 volume in any

---

[20] It is difficult to determine the precise figures for exports of such products from the *Annual Statements of Trade*, especially for the smaller countries. These figures have been reworked so that 'electrical goods' includes items such as insulators and electrical machinery, which the Board of Trade placed in other categories. 'Motor vehicles' includes chassis as well as complete vehicles, but not tyres or components.

year during the decade. The geographical concentration of exports became even more marked, as Britain became particularly dependent on a privileged position in Argentina which, in 1938, accounted for 52 per cent of all Britain's sales to Latin America.[21] The volume of exports to Brazil, in contrast, dropped to just over a quarter of the 1913 level, as US and German penetration of the market increased rapidly. Figure 6.2 clearly shows the extent to which the British lost their position in countries other than Argentina once the recovery from the Depression began.

The advent of World War II further undermined Britain's influence. The demands of the conflict inevitably reduced Britain's ability to supply Latin American markets with anything but essential goods such as tinplate and coal, without which Britain's own wartime need for foodstuffs could not have been fulfilled. By the time the Willingdon Mission departed for Latin America late in 1940, it had become little more than a cosmetic public relations exercise. By the end of the war the position was even grimmer. In 1946 Britain's exports to Latin America totalled £55.6 million, in real terms only one-third of the 1913 level. In Brazil the United Kingdom retained less than 5 per cent of the market for imports, and, although it still supplied over 10 per cent of Argentina's, this was in part due to the strained relations between the government in Buenos Aires and the US administration, which had led Washington to impose a trade embargo. A brief recovery in Britain's trade did occur at the end of the 1940s, when exporters managed to take advantage of a boom in Latin American demand, the slower industrial recovery of their European competitors, and the benefits resulting from the devaluation of sterling in 1949, but thereafter Britain's share of Latin American markets slipped behind that of the other major industrial powers (*see* Table 6.3).

Explaining the decline after 1914

Certain interpretations of Britain's trading performance in Latin America would suggest that the decline was almost inevitable once the rapid growth of the US economy at the end of the nineteenth century forced its government and entrepreneurs to seek outlets for its industrial exports and for its foreign investment. The implication of Platt's argument, for example, is that, faced with increasing competition in a region which was largely marginal to its own imperial interests, the British government and business élite deliberately concentrated on domestic and colonial markets, leaving Latin America to the United States, to Germany, and to local manufacturers. The apparent complacency on the part of British industrial and commercial

---

[21] The anomalous position of Argentina is also very obvious in Figure 6.2.

interests, which more critical historians have identified, can therefore be justified as a rational path to follow. Certain developments in the inter- war period might provide some support for such reasoning. International cartels in the 1930s tended to divide markets, in chemicals, submarines, or tyres, for example, in such a way that British companies negotiated preferential access to imperial markets in return for either open competition or US privileges in Latin America. This could be interpreted as a deliberate refining of effort. In such an interpretation, too, Britain's declining share of the Brazilian market might be ascribed simply to Nazi Germany's eagerness to develop a trade which British business did not consider worthwhile.

Just as for the period before 1914, however, there are problems with any interpretation which suggests that British industrialists deliberately and voluntarily concentrated their efforts in such a coherent and rational manner. Such a policy was certainly not apparent to their rivals. It is clear that, even during World War II, US business people and officials still saw British interests as the principal obstacle to the establishment of their own economic hegemony in South America, especially in view of the apparent success of the British in displacing US trade in Argentina during the 1930s. For their part, British officials continually made it clear after 1919 that they believed it necessary to safeguard Britain's economic interests in Latin America as far as possible. A Department of Overseas Trade paper commented in the early 1920s, for example: 'We must expand our overseas markets if we are to continue to pay our way; and apart from India and the Dominions South America is at present perhaps the quarter of the Globe to which we can most hopefully look to fill the gap'.[22]

In March 1939 a further official memorandum on German competition began with the statement that Latin America was 'an expanding market', and complained that Britain was not obtaining its proper share of the trade, especially in view of the immensity of its investments.[23] A growing body of evidence from business historians also suggests that, during the inter-war period, Latin America, particularly Argentina and Brazil, played a significant role in the global strategy of many British manufacturing companies, among them Gourock Ropes, J. & P. Coats, British American Tobacco, Reckitt & Colman, Pilkington, Lever Brothers, Bryant & May, Glaxo, Dorman Long, and ICI. The deliberate restrictions on trade which the government event- ually imposed during World War II were forced upon Britain by short-term exigencies, much to the regret of economic policymakers who recognized

[22] Department of Overseas Trade, 'British Naval, Military and Air Representation in South America' Paper 102 (no date: late 1922 or early 1923?), BT 90/19, PRO.

[23] 'Memorandum on German Competition in South and Central America', 21 March 1939, F18151/018/1, T 160/1160, PRO.

that in the post-war world Latin America would be a key area for trade and particularly for Britain's ability to earn dollars.[24] By then, however, the damage had been done. The crucial decades were the 1920s and 1930s, and the tone of the 1939 memorandum is telling in its grim recognition that by then serious problems existed in Britain's commercial relations with much of South America.

It became clear between the wars that there was a growing disjuncture between Latin American demand and the ability of many British manufacturers to supply it. The most important report of these years, that of the D'Abernon Mission, was scathing in its condemnation of the products of British industry ahd of the methods that firms employed to market and sell them:

> In new departments of trade we have been completely outdistanced. . . . We have excelled in railroad construction and shipbuilding; others have taken the place that should have been ours in aviation, road construction, and motor transport. . . . Our methods of production, representation, advertisement, marketing, and sale require thorough revision. . . . British firms too often manufacture and try to sell what they think the customer ought to have rather than what he likes. . . . A considerable volume of British trade is lost owing to adherence to old methods and inadequate representation.[25]

Regarding Britain's trade with Argentina, its most important market, D'Abernon stated: 'The large Argetine demand is for new commodities of commerce and we do not supply them. Either we do not make them or we do not market them. . . . The average Argentine household thinks more now in terms of motor cars, gramophones, or radio sets than of Irish linen, Sheffield cutlery and English china and glass'.[26] Such comments have formed the basis for the more critical interpretations of Britain's commercial decline in Latin America advanced by historians such as David Joslin or Roger Gravil.

It is important to recognize, however, that this condemnation of Britain's industrialists and traders contains several distinct elements. First, there was a failure of British enterprise in new products and, significantly, in sectors which were not dominated by international cartels. Electrical equipment was one such case. Here, British manufacturers found it difficult to compete on large contracts with German rivals, such as Siemens and AEG, who had established a network of sales offices and had access to much better credit

---

[24] Keynes called the abandonment of British trade 'imprudent': R. A. Humphreys, *Latin America and the Second World War* (2 vols., London 1981 & 1982), I, 53–4.

[25] United Kingdom, Department of Overseas Trade, *Report of the British Economic Mission to Argentina, Brazil, and Uruguay*, (London, 1930), pp. 6, 45–6.

[26] Department of Overseas Trade, *Report of the British Economic Mission*, pp. 18–19.

facilities. In aviation, Britain had possessed a high reputation in 1918, but then failed to take advantage of it, partly due to a lack of effective representation, in the following decade. Sales of aircraft to Latin America between 1926 and 1930 averaged little more than £150,000 a year. In motor vehicles, including components and spares, the British record was appalling. In the second half of the decade, sales to the whole region averaged less than £1 million annually, at a time when the market for such products was expanding rapidly. The United States supplied over 90 per cent of the Argentine market, one of the largest in the world: in the second quarter of 1925 Argentina imported 11,250 cars, of which just 8 came from Britain.[27] In Brazil North American automobile and road construction interests undertook a co-ordinated campaign in favour of motor transport, with the result that, by 1928, US companies supplied 99 per cent of Brazil's motor vehicles, many of them from local assembly plants.[28] Evidence from Argentina and other countries provides examples of British merchant houses which expanded their specialized interests in the importation of motor vehicles and machinery, but were forced to turn to US manufacturers because of the inability of British firms to supply, finance, and service the right products for the Latin American market.

Second, manufacturers of older products fell behind on price, quality, and styling. For members of the British Chamber of Commerce in Buenos Aires, Paul Goodwin states, 'the crucial issue that overshadowed all others [in explaining Britain's declining competitiveness] was price'.[29] The rise in the value of sterling against the dollar during the first half of the 1920s contributed to this. But there were other problems, too. Sheffield tool-making firms, for example, had lost markets in South America as American patterns, which they did not manufacture, became standard. Their candid admission of their failure to make proper business tours or establish local agency arrangements explains their inability to acquire accurate information about changing tastes.[30]

In both the newer and older branches of trade, then, similar criticisms can be found. British manufacturers did not make what Latin Americans wanted to buy, and their prices were unattractive; they did not have sufficient

---

[27] Raúl García Heras, *Automotores norteamericanos, caminos, y modernización urbana en la Argentina, 1918–1939,* (Buenos Aires, 1985), pp. 17 and 120–22. Sales of complete motor cars to Argentina averaged 102 per annum between 1926 and 1930.

[28] Richard Downes, 'Autos over Rails: How US Business Supplanted the British in Brazil, 1910–1928', *Jnl. Lat. Amer. Studs.* 24 (1992), 551–83.

[29] Paul B. Goodwin, 'Anglo-Argentine Commercial Relations: a Private Sector View, 1922–1943', *Hisp. Amer. Hist. Rev.* 61 (1981), 33.

[30] United Kingdom, Overseas Trade Development Council, *Report of the Sheffield Industrial Mission to South America, August–November 1930,* (London, 1931), p. 14.

representation, with the result that they did not monitor or canvass demand properly; they were unable to provide the finance, marketing skills (especially in advertising), and the after-sales facilities that successful penetration of the changing markets of countries such as Argentina and Brazil demanded.

Although the balance of the evidence therefore tends towards a rather critical interpretation of British export performance between the wars, difficulties remain with an analysis that concentrates solely on the shortcomings of British industrialists and their production and marketing techniques. The qualitative data on which it depends are complex and frequently contradictory, presenting the historian with the problem, just as for the pre-1914 period, of determining how significant and typical particular pieces of information are. Few historians have made much use of business archives to study industrialists' perceptions of trade with Latin America in detail. There is little explanation of why, with the possible exception of Argentina, the British position in Latin America should decline so rapidly, in comparison with other areas of the world where similar criticisms of British commercial methods were also commonplace. One superficially attractive explanation for this might be to argue that Britain could never have withstood the rivalry of the United States in an area so close to its own frontiers, adding perhaps a Plattian gloss to the effect that business people recognized this, even if officials did not, and wisely allocated resources elsewhere. North American historians have certainly viewed Latin America, along with eastern Asia, as the prime area for US economic expansion in the early twentieth century.[31] But again, for the major markets such as Argentina and Brazil, there are problems with such an argument. These two countries were equidistant from the United States and Europe. The evidence that British business interests and officials there feared the US advance and attempted to resist it is overwhelming. An alternative approach would be to return to an analysis of the bases upon which the expansion of British exports in the boom period before 1914 had rested. This might help to explain why, in the end, Britain was unable to withstand the establishment of US commercial hegemony south of Panama.

In fact, World War I and the Depression of the early 1930s shattered the structural foundations of Britain's pre-1914 trading relationship with South America. In the first place, the war had a serious effect on Britain's position in services and investment, accelerating the erosion which had begun to occur as a result of other countries' advances in shipping, banking, and

---

[31] *See*, for example, Joseph S. Tulchin, *The Aftermath of War: World War I and U.S. Policy toward Latin America*, (New York, 1971), and Jeffry A. Frieden, 'The Economics of Intervention: American Overseas Investments and Relations with Underdeveloped Areas, 1890–1950', *Comparative Studs. in Society and History* 31 (1989), 55–80.

lending. By 1919, aided by the war's impact on its European rivals, the United States had established the beginnings of a commercial banking network in Latin America, and instituted direct and regular shipping services with the west coast via the Panama Canal. A growing proportion of trade was conducted in US dollars rather than in sterling bills, thus reducing the role of British intermediaries. More importantly, Britain could no longer export capital on the pre-war scale, a fact that contemporaries took some time to realize. One Foreign Office official had rather complacently remarked in 1917: 'Brazil will always need the London market for the flotation of its loans and trade will necessarily follow'.[32] In practice, however, the New York capital market became much more important than London for Latin America during the following decade: US investment increased particularly quickly between 1924 and 1928. The British government, in contrast, had barred almost all new Latin American loans during the first half of the 1920s so as to protect sterling and return to the Gold Standard. While some lending to governments did revive after 1926, there was very little new direct investment from Britain (except for the oil companies), even though the principal enterprises that had been established before 1914 generally remained profitable. Moreover, at the end of the decade, British capitalists began to sell public utility companies in Argentina and Chile to US interests, to the alarm of other business people and officials who feared that British industry would lose orders as a consequence.

The Depression was the second blow for British exporters, and further undermined the foundations of their trade although, again, it took some time for this to become clear, because US exports to Latin America were much more income-elastic and thus fell more sharply in the early years of the crisis. The flow of British loans, which had begun again in the second half of the 1920s, now stopped entirely; more seriously, the profitability of the railways and some of the public utility companies collapsed. The railway companies in Argentina, which also faced intense competition from road transport as well as the recession, largely ceased to pay dividends and to place orders for anything but the most essential new equipment. This had a devastating effect on British trade. On one estimate, the railways' purchases, which covered a wide range of products, had accounted for about a quarter of Argentina's imports from Britain in the 1920s.[33] The Depression also destroyed the free market in foreign exchange which had made multilateral trade possible.

[32] Quoted in Emily S. Rosenberg, 'Anglo-American Economic Rivalry in Brazil during World War I', *Diplomatic History* 2 (1978), 131.
[33] Pedro Skupch, 'El deterioro y fin de la hegemonía británica sobre la economía argentina, 1914–1947', in Marta Panaia, Ricardo Lesser and Pedro Skupch (eds.), *Estudios sobre los orígenes del peronismo*, (Buenos Aires, 1973), II, 19.

Faced with a desperate shortage of hard currency because of the collapse of commodity prices, almost every Latin American country established exchange controls and import quotas, defaulted on its foreign debt, and began to seek bilateral trade agreements to safeguard markets for its exports. For the first time, therefore, the British government, which was itself moving towards a system of Imperial Preference, culminating in the Ottawa Agreements of 1932, found itself forced to consider its priorities in Latin America. In effect, this meant answering two questions. With which countries should Britain attempt to negotiate reciprocal concessions? And should investors or exporters have priority in the allocation of the foreign exchange made available by Latin American countries to British creditors?

The response was to protect existing patterns of trade and investment as far as possible, to maximize short-term returns, but with devastating consequences for British interests in the longer term. With the introduction of Imperial Preference, Britain could exert its greatest leverage over those countries whose élites depended on the British market and which faced competitive threats from within the Empire. Certain Latin American producers had faced problems in marketing their exports in the late 1920s and early 1930s due to embargoes, protection for farmers and minerals producers (especially in the United States), and the spread of preferential trade agreements, which circumscribed the free markets for products such as sugar. Utilizing the influence these problems gave it, Britain thus negotiated reciprocal trade and payments agreements with Uruguay (1935), Peru (1936, though never formally ratified), and, most importantly, with Argentina. Under this agreement, the Roca-Runciman Pact, which was negotiated in 1933 and then revised in 1936, Argentina obtained guaranteed access to the British market for most of its meat exports in return for concessions which included a list of duty-free imports and the promise that most of the foreign exchange arising from sales to the United Kingdom would be made available to British creditors.

The consequence for Britain, however, was the loss of position in countries where it did not possess similar leverage and where, after Roca-Runciman, it could hardly object to the negotiation of reciprocal concessions with other industrialized nations. The principal damage occurred in Brazil, which signed its first commercial agreement with Nazi Germany in 1934. There Britain's share of imports fell from 20 per cent in 1933 to around 12 per cent in 1936–8. A further element in this decline, at least until the Vargas Government defaulted completely on its foreign debt in 1937, was that, in allocating the foreign exchange which Brazil made available, the British government gave priority to investors in the public debt and to the large British companies in Brazil which needed to make remittances, rather than to manufacturers and exporters. The Department of Overseas Trade's gloomy 1939 report on German competition found that, throughout Latin America but especially in Brazil, Chile, Colombia and Uruguay, British industrial companies had to wait months for payment whereas, under the compensation trade system, their German competitors received funds immediately. The choice Britain confronted in deciding between the conflicting claims of investors and exporters for the limited foreign exchange available was not one which faced Germany, whose own investments in Latin America had been largely relinquished during World War I, or the United States, where the scandals over the loans made to Latin America in the 1920s had undermined political support for such investors.

World War II further hastened the collapse of British trade. The United States strongly opposed the continuation of Britain's bilateral arrangements with Argentina beyond those necessary to fulfil its demands for food, especially as Washington viewed successive administrations in Buenos Aires as pro-Axis. Under pressure from US manufacturers, the Roosevelt administration also used the Lend-Lease arrangements to limit Britain's trade with Latin America. Alan Dobson writes that there was 'considerable sympathy in the State Department for American exporters who wished to break the hold Britain had on a number of Latin American markets, and fair and reasonable export restrictions imposed on Britain because of Lend-Lease were seen as legitimate contributions to the achievement of that goal'.[34] Much more important than the opposition of the United States, however, in cutting Britain's wartime exports was the desperate financial position the government faced after the fall of France, which forced it to limit imports from Latin America (and thus the supply of sterling to purchase British goods). At the same time, British industry was totally directed towards the war effort; export licensing became highly restrictive. One official confessed in February 1941 that 'there can no longer be any question ... of increasing our trade or even of retaining markets against postwar years'.[35] A few months later a Board of Trade official admitted to the United States:

> We have abandoned, for the time being, almost the whole of our pre-war objectives. It is now entirely a question of securing indispensable imports, if necessary by sacrificing our investments and even our post-war prospects. ...
> Our principle is to pay with invisibles as far as possible and only to stimulate

[34] Alan P. Dobson, 'The Export White Paper, 10 September 1941', *Econ. Hist. Rev.* 39 (1986), 64. This comment also supports the argument above that, in the eyes of contemporary US observers, Britain's commercial position in Latin America still did not appear to have declined irredeemably. They could not detect the signs of deliberate withdrawal which Platt supposes.

[35] Foreign Office telegram to Santiago, Lima, Bogotá, and Rio de Janeiro, 16 February 1941, OV 6/17, Bank of England archive.

exports when there is a balance which cannot be made up otherwise. . . . *It is perhaps even true to say that we shall require U.S. help to hold or recover markets in South America and to maintain our capital investments.*[36]

As the war proceeded, Britain's demand for imports from Latin America increased and it ran up considerable debts with the major South American countries, which had to accept payment in the form of sterling credits accumulated in blocked Special Accounts in London.[37] The restrictions on exports and the growth of these Special Accounts, the essential features of wartime economic policy, thus reinforced the priority already given to investors rather than to exporters in the 1930s. Britain actively attempted to persuade countries such as Argentina, Brazil, Uruguay, and Peru to use Special Account sterling to pay interest on debts rather than placing further strains on its export capacity. After 1943 Special Accounts were used to liquidate British investments (at quite favourable prices in view of the deterioration of assets that had occurred) at a time when British industry was still largely unable to supply the capital goods which Latin American countries required. This process of disinvestment led Victor Perowne, the Head of the South American Department of the Foreign Office, and one of the most astute analysts of Britain's changing relationship with Latin America, eventually to remark in 1947 that the future emphasis in Britain's policy should be 'on trade, rather than, as hitherto, on safeguarding our historical position as owners of invested capital'.[38] The problem, as Keynes and other officials had foreseen, was that little basis remained on which to rebuild trade in a region now dominated economically and politically by the United States. The final irony came when the Argentine economy, on which British exports had depended so much since the turn of the century, entered into a prolonged recession in the early 1950s.

The exogenous shocks, therefore, of the two wars and the Depression accelerated the disintegration of Britain's commercial relationship with Latin America, because they undermined the bases on which trade had depended

[36] 'U.K. Trade Policy in Latin America', memorandum by R. Fraser, May 1941, OV 6/17, Bank of England archive. My italics: this sentence shows a remarkable misunderstanding of US attitudes and policy towards Britain's economic role in Latin America.

[37] On the Special Accounts *see* Jorge Fodor, 'The Origins of Argentina's Sterling Balances, 1939–1943', in Guido di Tella and D. C. M. Platt (eds), *The Political Economy of Argentina, 1880–1946*, (London, 1986), pp. 154–82, and Marcelo de Paiva Abreu, 'Brazil as a Creditor: Sterling Balances, 1940–1952', *Econ. Hist. Rev.* 43 (1990), 450–69.

[38] Quoted in C. A. MacDonald, 'The United States, Britain, and Argentina in the Years immediately after the Second World War', in di Tella & Platt (eds), *The Political Economy of Argentina*, p. 185.

before 1914: the dominance of British shipping; the free convertibility of currencies; the role of sterling as the principal medium of international trade; multilateral settlements rather than bilateral trade agreements; and Britain's stock of overseas investments and continued ability to export capital. These developments took officials and business people by surprise. It would certainly be ahistorical to criticize them for not foreseeing the detailed pattern of events that cumulatively weakened the British position, just as it would be to charge them with short-sightedness in not realizing that Brazil, which they largely neglected throughout the 1930s and 1940s, would replace Argentina as the leading economy in South America. But should such an interpretation completely exonerate British governments and business people from blame for the decline of British trade? Was it totally the result of factors beyond their control? Or should they have noticed the trends earlier and acted more positively?

There is considerable evidence to suggest that the private sector and government officials in Britain were slow to recognize and respond to these changes, and that they remained intellectually locked into the structures and institutions established in the 'golden years' immediately before 1914. For the inter-war period, as noted earlier, there is strong evidence that British manufacturers were unable to supply products, such as motor vehicles, for which demand in Latin America was expanding rapidly, and that British marketing and sales methods remained relatively old-fashioned. The flow of new ventures which British entrepreneurs had founded in Latin America before 1914 largely ceased thereafter, with the exception of Royal Dutch-Shell in Venezuela and those manufacturing companies that established subsidiaries in Argentina or Brazil. Commercial banking, in which Britain had traditionally led and which was fundamental to its export trade, also appears to have lost its enterprise and dynamism. Indeed, in Geoffrey Jones's words, 'It is plausible that without the backing of Lloyds [which purchased the London and River Plate Bank in 1918 and the London and Brazilian Bank in 1923] ... British overseas banking would have been eliminated from Latin America'; even with this support the British banks struggled through a series of crises in the 1920s and 1930s.[39] Moreover, as exports became more sophisticated, the British financial system proved unable to offer the medium-term credit facilities that purchasers of electrical equipment, for example, required. This was only belatedly recognized when the Export Credits Guarantee Department began to expand its medium-term business

[39] Geoffrey Jones, 'Competitive Advantage in British Multinational Banking since 1890', in Geoffrey Jones (ed.), *Banks as Multinationals*, (London, 1990), p. 48. *See* also Geoffrey Jones, *British Multinational Banking, 1830–1990*, (Oxford, 1993), pp. 141–5 and 159–62.

after the Depression, but it was too late and on too small a scale to help to sustain British trade with Latin America. British financial institutions never played the role either of the German commercial banks, which had a much closer relationship with manufacturers and exporters, or of the Export-Import Bank, which actively supported US trade in Latin America from the later 1930s.

It is difficult also to find examples where the actions of the British government positively stimulated exports. There was plenty of diagnosis of the reasons for decline, but little attempt to remedy it, largely due to the commitment of resources that this would have necessitated, and also perhaps to the government's reluctance to play a more interventionist role and its unwillingness particularly to undertake a sustained campaign to persuade British firms of the need for remedial action. In fact, the government's short-term fiscal problems frequently had the effect of further undermining trade. Thus, the plans for establishing a network of commercial attachés in Latin America after World War I, as the United States had done in 1914–15, were quickly cut to just two posts, in Buenos Aires and Rio, while the service attachés, who were vital in channelling orders for British shipyards and arms manufacturers, were completely withdrawn.[40] The officials in the British embassies and legations in Latin America, most of whom had been trained in the *laissez-faire* ideals of the pre-1914 world, often remained reluctant to take an active role when faced with the need to support British firms against aggressive US or German commercial diplomacy. And when the British government did have to make some positive decisions, over the allocation of foreign exchange in the 1930s, it became clear that the interests of the City of London, rather than the needs of exporters for prompt payment, were its priority. In Brazil, particularly, this had a damaging impact on trade, one which was all to little effect once the Brazilians suspended payments on their foreign debt. The frustration among all sectors of British business in Brazil, the importers who had suffered from foreign exchange restrictions earlier in the decade and the investors who now lost remittances, became acute. 'What are we, the British, doing?' demanded Rothschilds's representative in Rio in 1939. 'Nothing! Just sitting back with inertia allowing our prestige and past performance in all affairs here to fade away.'[41]

[40] Department of Overseas Trade, 'Measures for Promoting British Trade', Paper 88, BT 90/18; 'British Naval, Military, and Air Representation in South America', Paper 102, BT 90/19, PRO.

[41] Quoted in Stanley E. Hilton, *Brazil and the Great Powers, 1930–1939: the Politics of Trade Rivalry*, (Austin, 1975), p. 215.

Concluding Comments

The collapse of Britain's commercial position in Latin America in the first half of the twentieth century was so rapid that, as the events after 1950 showed, it became irreversible. Broadly speaking, there are four possible sets of interpretations. First, as Platt proposed, the diminishing interest of British exporters in the region might represent a deliberate refining of effort. Second, the decline might be due to an accumulation of factors outside Britain's control: the effects of the wars and the Depression; the desire of the United States to create its own 'informal empire' in Latin America; the economic policies of the Latin American countries themselves. Third, the rapidity of the decline might reflect a collective failure of British government and business to compete with more aggressive rivals in meeting Latin American countries' demands for imports. Fourth, the structures of British business in Latin America, which had developed before 1914, may have become unsuitable foundations for the maintenance of trade thereafter. These explanations are not mutually exclusive: they may overlap or apply to some markets or industrial sectors more than to others.

Platt's interpretation may have some validity for the smaller economies, but it lacks evidence from business archives, and there is little sign of a deliberate retreat from the major countries of South America, either by the government or by business interests, until the critical decisions of the mid-1930s at the very earliest. Even then, it was largely a response, not to overwhelming US pressure, but to short-term economic considerations which most hoped would be temporary. Moreover, the reaction of several leading manufacturers was not to withdraw but to invest. Argentina and Brazil were significant markets, for many companies the most important outside the developed world, the Dominions and India; on the margin, the intermediate markets of Peru, Chile, Uruguay, Colombia, and Venezuela could also merit attention. The decline in British trade with these more important countries was due much more to the way in which the changes that occurred in the international economy in the first half of the twentieth century disrupted the foundations on which Britain's unique financial and commercial relationship with Latin America had been based, and to the failures of British government and a substantial part of British business. The continuing poor performance of British trade with Latin America since 1950, even after the removal of the dead weight which the investments made before 1914 had become, and despite sporadic official attempts to revive the relationship, suggests that the decline has been rather more than the result of uncontrollable events or the irresistible expansion of US influence. The evidence from Latin America would suggest a fair degree of short-sightedness, arrogance, and institutional and intellectual inflexibility among business people, officials, and politicians.

The history of Britain's trading relationship with Latin America in the first half of the twentieth century thus raises broader questions. The preference shown for the Empire and Commonwealth between the 1930s and 1960s, to the detriment of Britain's relations with other areas of the world, may not have been worth it in the long term. Industrial exporters may have suffered from a gulf in understanding between themselves and government, and thus a lack of sympathetic officials and supportive policies. And the City of London's role in the economy and in influencing economic policy not only seems to have done little to halt Britain's decline in its Latin American markets after World War 1, but may actually have accelerated it. The evidence from Latin America would tend to support interpretations of Britain's industrial decline which emphasize the problems resulting from the divergent priorities of government, finance, and industry, and from the frequent need to take short-term measures of economic and business management at the cost of the long-term strategies required to overcome more fundamental problems.

References

Abreu, Marcelo de Paiva, 'Anglo-Brazilian Economic Relations and the Consolidation of American Pre-Eminence in Brazil, 1930–1945', in Christopher Abel and Colin Lewis (eds), *Latin America, Economic Imperialism and the State: the Political Economy of the External Connexion from Independence to the Present*, (London, 1985), pp. 379–93.

Albert, Bill, *South America and the World Economy from Independence to 1930*, (London, 1983).

Albert, Bill, with Henderson, Paul, *South America and the First World War: the Impact of War on Brazil, Argentina, Chile and Peru*, (Cambridge, 1988).

Downes, Richard, 'Autos over Rails: How US Business Supplanted the British in Brazil, 1910–1928', *Jnl. Lat. Amer. Studs.* 24 (1992), 551–83.

Goodwin, Paul B., 'Anglo-Argentine Commercial Relations: a Private Sector View, 1922–1943', *Hispanic Amer. Hist. Rev.* 61 (1981), 29–51.

Gravil, Roger, *The Anglo-Argentine Connection, 1900–1939*, (Boulder & London, 1985).

Hilton, Stanley E., *Brazil and the Great Powers, 1900–1939: the Politics of Trade Rivalry*, (Austin, 1975).

Miller, Rory, *Britain and Latin America in the Nineteenth and Twentieth Centuries*, (London, 1993).

Platt, D. C. M., 'Problems in the Interpretation of Foreign Trade Statistics before 1914', *Jnl. Lat. Amer. Studs.* 3 (1971), 119–130.

Platt, D. C. M., *Latin America and British Trade, 1806–1914*, (London, 1972).

Rosenberg, Emily S., 'Anglo-American Economic Rivalry in Brazil during World War I', *Diplomatic History* 2 (1978), 131–52.

di Tella, Guido and Platt, D. C. M. (eds), *The Political Economy of Argentina, 1880–1946*, (London, 1986).

Thorp Rosemary, (ed.), *Latin America in the 1930s: the Role of the Periphery in World Crisis*, (London, 1984).

Tulchin, Joseph S., 'Decolonizing an Informal Empire: Argentina, Great Britain and the United States, 1930–1943', *International Interactions* 1 (1974), 123–40.

United Kingdom, Department of Overseas Trade, *Report of the British Economic Mission to Argentina, Brazil, and Uruguay*, (London, 1930).

7

Imperial Power and Foreign Trade: Britain and India (1900–1970)

B. R. Tomlinson

One of the great clichés of British imperial history is that 'trade followed the flag'. Debate about the connection between British economic growth and overseas expansion runs through the historiography of the eighteenth, nineteenth and twentieth centuries, being most recently revived through the concept of 'gentlemanly capitalism'. The classic issues are still those of imperial acquisition, although arguments about the retention and adaption of the Empire in the first half of the twentieth century are now frequently discussed in these terms as well. Recent reworkings of these themes have identified the importance of mercantilism – the assumption that national power and national wealth are the dual goals of nation-states competing in the international system – as the basis for understanding the foreign and imperial economic policies of all the major trading nations throughout the twentieth century.[1]

Such revisionist views do make us rethink broad arguments about the success and failure of individual national economies, and of the international institutional arrangements for trade, investment and growth. Few bilateral

---

[1] For introductory accounts of British imperial and international history in the twentieth century along these lines, *see* Paul Kennedy, *The Rise and Fall of Great Powers: Economic Change and Military Conflict from 1500 to 2000* (London, 1988), chapters 6–7; Correlli Barnett, *The Collapse of British Power* (Gloucester 1984) and John Darwin, *Britain and Decolonisation: the Retreat from Empire in the Post-war World* (Basingstoke, 1988). There is also an extensive literature on the costs and benefits of British imperialism in the nineteenth century – *see* for example, P. K. O'Brien, 'The Costs and Benefits of British Imperialism, 1846–1914', *Past and Present*, 120 (1988) pp. 163–200 and

trading relationships, however, have been subjected to the detailed scrutiny needed to identify and test with any precision the links between national power and foreign trade. The aim of this chapter is to examine the relationship between political control and British trading competitiveness in south Asia, one of the largest and most important parts of the Empire/Commonwealth, and one with which Britain retained close ties after independence. The chief countries of the south Asian mainland – India, Pakistan and Bangladesh – were ruled as the British Indian Empire until 1947. For the next 26 years West and East Pakistan formed a single state, until the creation of Bangladesh in 1971.

The Start of Britain's Decline in India

At the beginning of the twentieth century, India was Britain's most important imperial possession, and provided the largest single export market for its goods, including most of the great staple industries of the Edwardian age. In the years before World War I, British rule in India was secure; India had an important place in the imperial system as a market for British exports (visible and invisible), and as a source of foreign currency earnings that enabled London to meet part of its deficit with other trading partners. In the 1920s and 1930s the imperial polity was steadily eroded, and, in 1947, India and Pakistan became sovereign states within the Commonwealth and the Sterling Area. In the inter-war period, and after independence, the economic connections between Britain and south Asia were also weakening, with domestic industrialization and competition from trading rivals undermining Britain's dominant position.

It was inevitable that Britain's export competitiveness in India would decline as her political control and influence weakened through the twentieth century. The pattern of interconnection was complex, however, and its rises and falls in intensity cannot be related simply to a map of the changing content of formal political connections or policymaking. The subtleties of the relationship can properly be shown only by statistical analysis. What we need are consistent estimates of Britain's market shares in south Asian imports of manufactures, that can be compared with similar estimates for other areas of the world. By this means, we can then isolate the periods in which British exports to India and Pakistan performed significantly better,

---

Avner Offer, 'The British Empire, 1870–1914: a Waste of Money?', *Economic History Review*, XLVI, 2 (1993) pp. 215–38. On the concept of 'gentlemanly capitalism', *see* P. J. Cain and A. G. Hopkins, *British Imperialism: Innovation and Expansion, 1688–1914* and *British Imperialism: Crisis and Deconstruction, 1914–1990* (Harlow, 1993).

or worse, than the average of British exports to the world as a whole, or to other regions at a similar stage of economic development and political evolution.

The analysis of this chapter is based on the figures for British exports of manufactures provided in two, linked, studies of trade and growth – Alfred Maizels, *Industrial Growth and World Trade* (Cambridge, 1963), which covers the period from 1899 to 1957, and R. A. Batchelor, R. L. Major and A. D. Morgan, *Industrialisation and the Basis for Trade* (Cambridge, 1980), which covers the period from 1950 to 1971. These two sources calculate the value of world trade in manufactures at the peaks of cyclical waves in the international economy, in constant prices and in terms of a single currency (US dollars at 1955 exchange rates). One of the regions separated out is mainland south Asia, designated as 'India' from 1899 to 1937, and 'India and Pakistan' from 1950 onwards.

There is a number of problems with using these data for a study of Indo-British trading relations. Firstly, the inclusion of Pakistan with India after 1950 makes it more difficult to assign change due to government policy unambiguously, because the Government of Pakistan followed rather different import policies to those of its larger neighbour. For practical purposes, the particularism of Pakistani policy has been ignored in this chapter, which considers only the relationship between Britain and India after 1950. Secondly, the totals for 1899 to 1937 include British imports into Burma, which was administered as part of the Indian Empire up to that date, and exclude it thereafter. It has not been possible to correct for this distortion, which is not likely to have been very large. Finally, the selection of the peak years of the global trading cycle may not correspond exactly to conditions in south Asia. Again, it has not been possible to correct any distortions this may have caused.

Despite these difficulties the Maizels/Batchelor estimates are an invaluable source from which to calculate the relative performance of British exports in the Indian market over the twentieth century. Our concern is chiefly with the competitiveness of British exports there, compared to their performance in the world as a whole. The best straightforward indicator is that of market share, which can be calculated without much difficulty. Table 7.1(a) gives the market shares of British manufactured exports in south Asia compared to their performance in the world as a whole, and in the 'Southern Dominions' of South Africa, Australia and New Zealand, whose economic and political relationship to Britain was in some ways comparable to that of India. To compare changes in British competitiveness, Table 7.1(b) plots the rate of change in Britain's market share in exports to India, the 'Southern Dominions' and the world between the successive trade cycle peaks. This table does not capture a rate of change because it is based simply on the

Table 7.1(a) Market shares of exports of British manufactures as imports to India, southern dominions and world 1899–1971 (%)

	India*	Southern Dominions**	World
1899	85	78	36
1913	80	71	30
1929	53	54	20
1929	58	57	22
1937	40	54	20
1950	52	71	26
1955	38	59	19
1950	53	72	27
1955	38	60	20
1959	42	51	17
1963	24	43	15
1963	25	45	15
1967	19	33	12
1971	23	29	11

Table 7.1(b) Market shares of British manufactures as imports to India, southern dominions, and world 1899–1971 (% change)

	India*	Southern Dominions**	World
1899–1913	−6	−9	−16
1913–1929	−34	−24	−32
1929–1937	−31	−5	−7
1937–1950	+30	+31	+30
1950–1955	−28	−17	−27
1955–1959	+10	−15	−14
1959–1963	−43	−16	−14
1963–1967	−24	−27	−24
1967–1971	+21	−12	−8

Note: Percentage change figures calculated from unrounded totals.

* India = British India 1899–1937; India and Pakistan (not Burma) 1950–1971.

** Southern Dominions = Australia, New Zealand, South Africa.

Percentages are based on the totals in Maizels and Batchelor; these are in US$ at 1955 exchange rates in constant prices. 1899–1929 at 1913 prices; 1929–1950 and 1950–1963 at 1955 prices; 1963–1971 at 1967 prices.

Source: Alfred Maizels, *Industrial Growth and World Trade* (NIESR, Cambridge University Press, Cambridge, 1963)

comparison of fixed points; it does allow us in a rough and ready way, however, to identify the periods in which British competitiveness in India improved relative to its global performance, and in which periods it deteriorated.

Table 7.1(b) provides a crude but effective index of the competitiveness of British goods in India compared to their performance in the world as a whole, as measured by market shares of world exports of manufactures. British exports increased their market share (that is, became more competitive) in India than in the world as a whole between 1899 and 1913, between 1955 and 1959, and between 1967 and 1971. Perhaps the most striking performances were in 1955–9 and 1967–71 when British goods improved their market share in India while losing it in the world as a whole. In four time periods – 1913–29, 1937–50, 1950–5 and 1963–7 – the competitiveness of British goods in India was about the same as globally, while the worst periods for British competitiveness in India were clearly between 1929 and 1937 and between 1959 and 1963 when British goods lost more market share in India than they did in the world as a whole. As Table 7.2 shows, British goods were under attack from Japanese exports in the earlier period and from American goods in the later one.

These estimates of competitiveness based on market shares for imports tell us nothing directly about competition between imported goods and domestically produced manufactures. Such competition was clearly important for consumer goods in the 1920s and 1930s, and for a range of intermediate and capital goods in the 1950s. Indian production of cotton goods, for example, competed more directly with British exports by the 1920s than did the imports from the other major overseas supplier – Japan. The growth of the Indian cotton industry in the late-colonial period was certainly striking: in 1900, 63 per cent of cotton textile consumption in India was provided by imports (almost all of them British), 13 per cent was supplied by domestic mills, and 24 per cent by handicrafts. By 1936 these proportions had been reversed, with handlooms supplying 25 per cent, domestic mills 63 per cent and imports 12 per cent (of which about one-third came from Britain).[2] Maizels provides some further calculations, which are set out in Table 7.3.

Of Britain's global loss of markets due to import substitution in semi-industrial countries, Indian competition accounted for 39 per cent between 1913 and 1929, and 47 per cent between 1929 and 1937.[3] Overall, British goods faced more severe competition from import substitution in India than in the Southern Dominions, at least until the 1950s, and lost their market

---

[2] N. S. R. Sastry, *A Statistical Study of India's Industrial Development*, Bombay, 1947), page 88.

[3] Maizels, *Industrial Growth and World Trade*, pages 230–1.

Table 7.2 Market shares of major exporters of manufactures to India*, 1899–1971 (%)

	United Kingdom	Western Europe	United States	Japan	Index of world exports to India
1899	85	13	1	0	100
1913	80	16	2	1	174
1929	53	21	9	14	179
1929	58	21	8	12	100
1937	40	22	8	29	64
1950	52	17	16	9	77
1955	38	32	15	12	92
1950	53	17	17	9	100
1955	38	31	15	12	121
1959	42	37	11	8	137
1963	24	25	33	14	184
1963	25	26	35	11	100
1967	19	33	30	14	94
1971	23	30	25	18	84

Note: Column 5 gives an indicator of the expansion or contraction of the Indian market for global imports of manufactures.
* India = British India 1899–1937; India and Pakistan (not Burma) 1950–1971.
Source: R. A. Batchelor, R. L. Major and A. D. Morgan, *Industrialization and the Basis for Trade* (NTESR, Cambridge University Press, 1980).

Table 7.3 Britain's loss of exports to semi-industrial countries, $mil at 1955 prices

	1913–29		1929–37		1937–50		1950–59	
	A	B	A	B	A	B	A	B
India/Pakistan	250	231	390	134	52	–112	206	124
Southern Dominions	102	262	290	50	356	–352	890	453

A = effect of import substitution
B = effect of Britain's share of imports
A minus sign indicates an increase in British sales

share to local competitors even more before independence (1929–37) than after (1950–9). Furthermore, in the 1920s and 1930s almost all of the local competition to British imports was genuinely local – it was the result of the activities of indigenous industrialists, not of multinational corporations (MNCs). In the 1950s, MNCs (many of them British) and the Indian public sector played a larger role in replacing imports.

Changing Links in the Indo-British Economy

Even with the simplified versions of the statistics of British competitiveness presented in these tables, it is clear that there is a number of important features in each main time period that require further exploration and explanation. These can best be examined in chronological order. The analysis is based around the changing institutional links that bound the Indo-British economy together. They took two forms – public policy and private business. The role of government action should have been important in cementing any imperial connection that boosted British trade with India. Private business links were important because, with the exception of cotton textiles, so much of India's imports consisted of intermediate and capital goods. Thus, India's capacity to import was linked closely to capital formation, a large part of which (in the colonial period at any rate) consisted of foreign investment or the use of capital controlled by expatriate firms. Thus, the business history of colonial south Asia must form an important part of any explanation of the relationship there between imperial power and the success of British trade.

Between 1899 and 1913 British exports in India exhibited a classic imperial relationship. While Britain's market share of Indian imports fell very slightly – from 85 per cent in 1899 to 80 per cent in 1913 – this was a good deal less than the fall in Britain's market share in the world as a whole. In other words, British goods retained their competitiveness in India better than they did overall. Using Maizels's full set of tables, it is possible to break down the aggregate figures into individual commodities. These data make it clear that the slight weakening in Britain's position in India was due largely to the poor performance of exports of metal manufactures; other staples such as machinery, textiles and transport equipment held their market share while that of chemicals increased. All categories of exports, however, did significantly better (or less badly in the case of metals which suffered a severe fall in their share of the global market) in India than in the world as a whole.

In the years before World War I British domestic and expatriate capital dominated the Indian investment market. Figures for capital flows that match those available for British exports cannot be provided. For the period 1900–14, however, we do have some recent thoroughly researched estimates for capital called up in London on behalf of the Indian government and of companies operating in south Asia presented in Lance E. Davis and Robert A. Huttenback, *Mammon and the Pursuit of Empire: the Political Economy of British Imperialism* (Cambridge, 1986). These confirm the established picture of British investment in colonial India weighted heavily towards government debt, and towards transport – especially the railways.[4] Davis and Huttenback's minimum estimate of £43.21 millions for British investment in India in this period represents about 13 per cent of total private British investment in the Empire, and just over 4 per cent of total investment overseas. Of private capital called up by companies operating in India between 1900 and 1914, 73 per cent was for the transport sector; about three-quarters of government debt in that period was also concerned with railway finance. Estimates of capital stock suggest that about 40 per cent of total British investment in India in 1914 was in the private sector, and 60 per cent in government bonds. Davis and Huttenback's figures suggest that about 45 per cent of the capital called up in London for south Asia between 1900 and 1914 went to the private sector. Within India, British and expatriate companies dominated most sectors of industry, with the partial exceptions of cotton textiles and iron and steel. Even here, however, most capital equipment, training and industrial organization was British in origin and inspiration.

Between 1913 and 1929, much of the 'normal' imperial relationship in trade and finance was undermined. In the 1920s, British exports lost competitiveness in the world as a whole quite sharply but they lost their edge to a slightly greater extent in India than globally. Just over half of Britain's loss of exports was the result of import substitution; among foreign manufacturers, the chief gainer from Britain's decline was Japan, although the United States and continental Europe also increased their market shares. In commodity terms, the problem was particularly acute for metal manufactures and textiles, which lost a greater percentage of market share in India than globally. No other commodity group did particularly well in India in the 1920s, although transport equipment and machinery exports lost significantly less of their market share in India than globally.

There is a number of reasons for the changed fortunes of British exporters in India in the 1920s. In the first place, our figures may be distorted because 1929 was not the peak year in the Indian trade cycle; the severe local recession that turned into the Great Depression had begun there in 1928.

---

[4] Davis and Huttenback, *Mammon and the Pursuit of Empire*, Table 2.6. For a convenient presentation of capital stock estimates for British public and private capital investment in India from 1900 to 1939, *see* A. K. Banerji, *India's Balance of Payments: Estimates of Current and Capital Accounts from 1921–22 to 1938–39* (Bombay, 1963) and *Aspects of Indo-British Economic Relations, 1858–98* (Delhi, 1982).

Lancashire cotton goods were badly affected by the political boycott that accompanied nationalist agitation against imperial rule, and textiles made up only 41 per cent of the value of British exports to India in 1929, compared to 62 per cent in 1913. Even without the political complications, however, British textile exports were running into severe price competition from Japan as well as from Indian mills. For metals, machinery and transport equipment, changes in government policy, resulting from nationalist pressure and financial stringency, damaged significantly Britain's hold on the market for stores for the state-controlled railway system. The new stores purchase rules of the 1920s required tenders to be lodged in New Delhi, not London, and favoured goods of adequate, rather than best, quality. The result was to boost sales of European products over British ones, especially of Belgian steel sections and rails.

The years between 1929 and 1937 were catastrophic for British exports to India, and they more than halved in value. About three-quarters of these losses resulted from domestic competition. Most of this was in textiles, but a wide range of consumer and intermediate goods was affected to some extent. High tariff levels, balance of payments difficulties and the growth of domestic investment in infrastructure and industry all boosted import substitution. In cotton goods, declining consumer incomes, as a result of the agricultural depression, damaged sales of higher-quality Lancashire cloth, and the rise of domestic competition from Ahmedabad and elsewhere increased the pressure. Textiles were also the weakest sector of British competitiveness in the market for imports to India, but all major commodities lost a larger market share in India than globally in this period. Japan was the chief beneficiary of Britain's decline, and took over the position of dominant supplier of imported cotton goods. Again, it was changes in the structure of the market, rather than direct price competition between British and Japanese producers, that caused this.

Overall, during the 1930s, Britain's position declined more in India than in the world as a whole. This was particularly striking in comparison with the Southern Dominions of Australia, New Zealand and South Africa, which had formal political independence but retained close institutional economic links, public and private, with the United Kingdom. Here, Britain's market share of imports declined by only 5 per cent, compared to 31 per cent in India, although her total export loss was greater than this because of import substitution. It is noteworthy that India took part, as the Southern Dominions did, in the discussions surrounding the creation of schemes for Imperial Preference in trade, at the Ottawa Conference of 1932 and elsewhere. Despite India's much more complete formal constitutional subordination to the British Government, however, these arrangements seem to have had a far smaller effect in reinforcing inter-imperial economic ties than in the case of the colonies of settlement. By contrast to the difficulties of the 1930s, the early post-war years were a boom time for British exports, although the domestic economy of the United Kingdom was still under-stocked and undercapitalized until the early 1950s. The absence of pre-war rivals in export markets is shown by the fact that, between 1937 and 1950, all the major classes of British exports increased their market shares in the world as a whole, the only time that this has happened in the twentieth century. In India (now the independent government of India and Pakistan), with the exception of metals and chemicals, most British exports increased their market shares as well. Only textiles and miscellaneous goods grew more competitive in India than elsewhere, however; overall, British exports recaptured less of their old markets in India than in the world as a whole. Import substitution continued to erode the British position in south Asia, although intermediate and producer goods now made up the bulk of Britain's exports. The British share of imports increased at the expense of Japan and continental Europe (especially Germany); the United States' share of the Indian market increased substantially, but from a very low base.

The chequered fortunes of British exporters in the Indian market in the inter-war years were matched by instabilities in business relationships. Expatriate firms made high profits during World War I, but remitted most of these during the post-war boom, at a time of an unusually favourable exchange rate between the rupee and sterling. British investment, public and private, peaked in the early 1920s, but declined sharply thereafter. The Indian economy failed to grow rapidly over the course of the 1920s, which limited the incentive for fresh capital investment from Britain. In the public sector, furthermore, financial stringency and budgetary constraints led to cut-backs in public works and in the development of infrastructure.

During the 1920s and 1930s, the Indian industrial economy underwent a considerable structural change in ways that did not benefit British capital very directly. Industrial growth and diversification took place partly as a result of public policy changes which encouraged import substitution, partly because of shifts in the terms of trade between agriculture and the rest of the economy, and partly in response to the emergence of new business organizations with their roots in the indigenous trading economy. The established British expatriate managing agency houses remained quite closely tied to their old staple activities in jute, coal and tea, and lagged behind indigenous entrepreneurs in the boom industries of the 1930s, such as paper, sugar and cement. The only exception to this pattern of stunted growth was the role of subsidiaries of British multinational manufacturing firms, which began to enter the Indian market seriously in the inter-war period and, by 1939, had come to dominate the market for a wide range of consumer goods, such as processed food, tobacco, toiletries, and pharmaceuticals, as well as for electrical equipment and some sectors of chemicals and metal manufactures. The volume of such investment was limited, however, and the amount of capital goods imports that it generated remained quite small.

As a consequence of these changes, as well as of the increased political lobbying power of Indian business people, the ability of British firms to command the capital goods import sector declined sharply in the inter-war years. In some sectors, notably public utilities such as electricity supply, Indian firms now dominated the market, and took care to purchase non-British capital equipment for political, as well as economic, reasons. The public sector also weakened its reliance on British supplies, as the new stores purchase rules took effect. By the 1940s, the institutional links that had previously bound the Indian economy tightly to British exports of capital, equipment and expertise, had been severely weakened. The reduced competitiveness of British goods in India was one clear result.

The two post-independence decades from 1950 to 1971 can be dealt with more briefly. Overall, this was a period of steady decline in the competitiveness of British exports to south Asia and to the world as a whole although, in terms of value, British exports to south Asia peaked in 1957. This overall decline masks some considerable fluctuations. The years from 1950 to 1955 and from 1959 to 1967 were periods of clear-cut decline of British competitiveness in India – British exports to India performed less well than British exports to the rest of the world, or than world exports to India. The nadir of Britain's trading relations with south Asia came in 1959–63 when, in the face of strong competition from the United States, British exports performed worse there relative to their overall performance than in any other period of the twentieth century. In 1950–5 and 1963–7, the British performance in south Asia was rather less bad, and Britain's loss of export competitiveness was no worse than in the world as a whole. The periods 1955–9 and 1967–71 saw some improvements in Britain's competitive position in India, with values of exports and market shares rising. More significantly, in these periods, British exports performed a good deal better in south Asia than globally, increasing market shares there at a time when their global market shares were falling. Ironically, as Table 7.1(b) makes clear, British goods were able to increase their market shares most decisively in south Asia after the ending of colonial rule.

One important omission from these figures refers to sales of arms and military equipment, which formed a significant component of south Asian imports after independence.[5] Complete estimates of arms sales cannot be

[5] The following account is based on data in Stockholm International Peace Research Institute, *The Arms Trade with the Third World* (Stockholm, 1971), chapters 5 and 16, and Michael Lipton and John Firn, *The Erosion of a Relationship: India and Britain since 1960*, (London, 1975), chapter 11.

compiled; the data we have suggest that Britain dominated the market for Indian arms imports in the 1950s, but that it lost ground significantly in the late 1960s, especially to the USSR. For Pakistan, by contrast, the United States has always been the largest supplier. Imports of arms into south Asia amounted to about 10 per cent by value of total imports during the late 1960s, the peak period for Indian restocking after the 1965 war with Pakistan. The highest annual figure of all was in 1958 at over $300 million (in 1968 prices). About one-half of arms imports from Britain were recorded in the official trade figures, with the other half disguised under special government expenditure accounts. On this basis, we can estimate that the totals of British exports to south Asia may need to be revised upwards by about 5 per cent to take account of unlisted trade in armaments and military equipment.

In the 1950s and 1960s, the south Asian subcontinent was a major market for world arms sales, taking 12–15 per cent of world exports. India was Britain's largest single Third World market for arms between 1950 and 1961, taking over 40 per cent of such exports in this decade. By the late 1960s, however, Britain supplied only about 10 per cent of south Asian arms imports. The reasons for this decline were similar to that in the civilian economy; training and equipment links weakened at a time when other suppliers were prepared to offer greater incentives. For India, new ties with the Soviet Union became particularly important after the 1965 war; the USSR supplied two-thirds of south Asian imports of major weapons (all of them to India) between 1965 and 1969, having supplied only one-fifth in 1960–4. The British share, by contrast, dropped from 64 per cent in 1955–9, to 34 per cent in 1960–4, to 13 per cent in 1965–9. New foreign policy interests were partly responsible for this shift, but the chief reason was financial. Britain did provide significant amounts of general military aid to India between 1963 and 1967, as well as a loan of $13.2 million for a naval dockyard and the purchase of three frigates in 1964. The Soviets generally offered better terms by the mid-1960s, however, were prepared to accept payment in rupees and to allow eventual local manufacture, and provided a cheaper and apparently more effective product in many areas.

After independence, even more than before, India's imports consisted of investment goods, and so the fortunes of her trading partners depended heavily on their exports of capital as well as of goods. Although British investment had come under challenge from domestic entrepreneurs before 1945, Britain was still the dominant foreign investor in India at independence (in the following discussion of capital flows and aid, 'India' means the Republic of India alone, excluding Pakistan, for which comparable data are not available). In 1948 Britain had supplied 80 per cent of all outstanding foreign private investment in India. By the end of the 1960s, however,

Britain's relative importance as a source of private capital had declined quite sharply from her earlier dominance. By 1960, the British figure was 68 per cent of the total, compared with 14 per cent from the United States, and 18 per cent from other countries; by 1968 the British total had fallen to 35 per cent, the US total had risen to 20 per cent, and that of other countries to 45 per cent. The amount of British private investment in India rose by just under a half during the 1960s, while that of the United States doubled and that of other countries tripled.[6] A very approximate general estimate suggests that about 6 per cent of Indian private fixed investment was owned by foreigners in 1948, rising to 7 per cent in 1957 and 8 per cent in 1971, with the British share of this falling sharply from over four-fifths in 1948, to under two-thirds in 1957, and to less than half by 1971. Between 1968 and 1971 the total value of British companies in India increased slightly, from £277.2 million to £289.8 million, although this represented a small fall in India's holdings of total British private investment, from 4.96 per cent to 4.35 per cent.

The reasons for the decline in the dominance of British private investment in India after 1947 are well established.[7] In the 1950s British firms were heavily involved in a narrow range of activities in the Indian economy, operating predominantly by means of wholly owned subsidiary companies set up through direct investment. Most of the increases in British-owned capital stock in the 1960s came from reinvestment in established activities. From the late 1960s on, however, such companies were subject to increasing government restriction, and a new growth area for foreign investment was opened up for portfolio investment in the service sector, mostly in the form of loan capital for construction and utilities, often in partnership with public-sector firms. By the early 1970s, investment in services made up a quarter of foreign private investment, while direct investment in manufacturing represented less than half of the total. This trend, which was continued through the decade, gave less scope to British firms, and hence less demand for British imports, than to their rivals from the United States and West Germany. While Britain remained by far the largest single source of direct foreign investment in Indian manufacturing throughout the 1970s, she had

[6] Estimates of British private investment to India after 1947 are available in Lipton & Firn, *Erosion of a Relationship* chapter 6.

[7] See Ibid., B. R. Tomlinson, 'Continuities and Discontinuities in Indo-British Economic Relations: British Multinational Corporations in India, 1920–1970', in Wolfgang J. Mommsen and Jurgan Osterhammel (eds), *Imperialism and After: Continuities and Discontinuities* (London, 1986) and 'British Business in India, 1860–1970', in R. P. T. Davenport-Hines and Geoffrey Jones (eds), *British Business in Asia since 1860* (Cambridge, 1989).

been replaced in 1976 by the United States as the largest national owner of all business investment.

Since 1947, official transfers of capital through aid programmes have been much more important than private capital flows as a source of foreign investment in India. For the first decade of independence, the most important source of public capital inflow was the sterling balances that India and Pakistan had accumulated in London as a result of the Indian Empire's military expenditure on Britain's behalf between 1939 and 1945. Between 1947 and 1956 India bought capital goods, and financed balance-of-payments deficits, by drawing on these assets; during the late 1940s, the hard-currency ration was very limited, and so exports of British goods were probably increased artificially. This brought little joy to the British government, however, which wanted to use Britain's scarce export production to earn dollars for the metropolitan economy.[8] The last of India's wartime balances were spent in the foreign exchange crisis of 1956–7. Since this date, bilateral aid on a government-to-government basis has provided the chief means for channelling financial resources into south Asia. The annual flow of bilateral aid to the subcontinent averaged $1,314.1 millions during the 1960s. Britain remained a significant aid donor to south Asia, but it was now by no means the only one. Between 1960 and 1971 the United States sent an annual average of $885.2 million to India and Pakistan combined, while the United Kingdom sent $96.6 million, West Germany $96.1 million, Canada $82.2 million and Japan $56.1 million.[9]

It is not clear how aid contributed directly to capital formation in India, but more aid certainly meant more public investment and more imports of manufactured goods. Aid covered as much as 40 per cent of India's import bill in the late 1960s, although most of it was tied in ways that limited considerably its value to the Indian authorities. For donor countries, however, the connection is much clearer, with the surge of US exports to India in the early 1960s closely linked to major aid programmes of those years. To a lesser extent, the same is true of continental Europe in the late 1950s, backed by the 'Aid to India' consortium set up in 1957, of which West Germany was a prominent member. Overall, between 1957 and 1971, the 'aid-trade ratio' for major donors (that is, utilized aid as a percentage of India's imports from major donors) rose from 21 per cent in 1956/7–1960/1 to over 50 per cent in 1966/7–1970/1, with the British ratio hitting a peak

---

[8] On the getting and spending of India's sterling balances, and their implications for Indo-British economic relations, *see* B. R. Tomlinson, 'Indo-British Relations in the Post-Colonial Era: the Sterling Balances Negotiations, 1947–49', in A. N. Porter and R. F. Holland (eds), *Money, Finance and Empire 1790–1960* (London, 1985).

[9] For data on aid flows and totals, *see* Lipton and Firn, *Erosion of a Relationship*, chapter 7.

of 81 per cent in 1969–70. For Britain, the sharp rise in competitiveness between 1967 and 1971 was helped by an increase in the amount of aid allocated to India and to new rules that led to the tying of that aid to British exports more effectively, as well as to the effects of the sterling devaluation of 1967 and large arms sales.

Conclusion

The most obvious conclusion that can be drawn from this analysis is that public policy and formal political ties cannot entirely explain the fluctuations in the intensity of the Indo-British economic relationship. The years in which the British government had something approaching a positive imperial economic policy – 1929–37, 1937–50 and 1950–5– were not the years in which British competitiveness in India increased. Imperial preference was clearly either a disaster or an irrelevance; the existence of the sterling balances, and controls over their expenditure, did not boost British sales to India more than to the world as a whole, despite the fact that India and Pakistan were the largest holders of such balances after 1945. There may be special reasons that can explain this apparent paradox. Imperial preference was powerless against Japanese competition because the devaluation of the yen in the 1930s overcame the high tariff barriers on non-British exports to India. Much British effort was expended in the late 1940s to ensure that the sterling balances were managed in such a way as to prevent India from using her assets in London to buy up the capital goods that were needed for domestic reconstruction, or to earn dollars elsewhere in the world. Even if we take these factors into account, however, it is clear that something other than simple policy prescriptions are needed to explain the history of British competitiveness in India in the 1930s, 1940s and early 1950s.

For the rest of our period the message is the same. There are no clear initiatives in policy or changes in India's formal political relationship with Britain that can easily explain why the relative competitiveness of British goods against other imports into India should have been better than their global record after 1950. The improvement in Britain's competitiveness in the late 1950s and late 1960s may in part have been the result of executive action. The formation of the Aid to India consortium after the foreign-exchange crisis of 1956–7 probably increased India's official disposable sterling resources faster than those of other currencies. The renewed Indian foreign exchange problems of the late 1960s, the devaluation of sterling in 1967, and a new hardening of British aid conditions (especially the more rigorous double-tying) probably increased India's propensity to buy British goods in 1967–71.

As we have already seen, private institutional links through foreign firms and capital investment provide another context in which to explain the fluctuating fortunes of British manufactured exports to south Asia. Although private capital flow figures and measures of expatriate and multinational business activity cannot be analysed with any great precision, there is some evidence that, to an important extent, they were correlated with the pattern of British competitiveness.

The decade or so before World War I was a boom period that saw substantially increased British private investment in India, partly as a result of the establishment of the rupee on the Gold Standard with a fixed exchange rate. After 1913, private capital inflows continued but at a diminished rate, while public capital imports (mostly for railways) hit new peaks in the early 1920s but failed to grow substantially thereafter. There was some small net disinvestment in public capital in the 1930s; for private capital, the evidence is much less clear-cut, but Indians certainly came to control a larger percentage of the private capital stock in the secondary and tertiary sectors by 1945. The years from 1929 to 1950 were consistently difficult ones for many established British companies in India. From the early 1920s onwards, and especially in the 1930s and 1940s, the British-owned managing agency partnerships that had traditionally dominated the Indian manufacturing and import/export sectors were operating under severe constraints, caused by economic difficulties rather than by political problems. In the post-colonial era, British private capital exports to India peaked in the late 1950s and slumped markedly in the 1960s. A high proportion of this capital went to finance the expansion of subsidiary companies of multinational enterprises. One significant boost to capital imports was the policy of the Indian government, in the foreign-exchange crises of the late 1950s and late 1960s, of relaxing its rules about foreign participation, to allow parent companies to increase their capital stake by importing capital goods for their subsidiaries. The difficulties that British-based MNCs have had in adapting to changed opportunities in the Indian economy, however, have limited their participation in the business sector substantially since 1967.

The rise and fall of business institutions clearly had an important effect on the bilateral economic relationship between Britain and India, and on the competitiveness of British manufactured exports to south Asia. Overall, the nature of business links seems to have had little to do with political ties or policy prescriptions. Even the exercise of formal British imperial control gave little direct favouritism to British firms in India, except in a few areas seen as especially important to the security of the state, such as shipping, stores and defence supplies. Similarly, after 1947, British companies faced little effective official discrimination; their decline in the latter half of the twentieth century, like their rise 100 years before, had more to do with economic circumstances than with political conditions.

These conclusions make it difficult to identify a close correlation between the exercise of political power and trading competitiveness in Britain's dealings with south Asia before and after independence. Indeed, this study suggests that the Indo-British economy was little different to any of Britain's other bilateral relationships even before 1947. The pattern of economic interchange between south Asia and the United Kingdom, as measured through the performance of exports of manufactured goods, can best be explained by such general factors as broad patterns of demand and supply, flows of public and private capital, and the operations of international firms. Compared to their global performance, British exports were at their most competitive in south Asia in 1959–63 and 1967–71, and were at their least competitive in 1959–63 and 1929–37. In these circumstances it is worth asking whether an analytically separate entity that we can call the 'British imperial economy' can be said to have existed at all.

To question the existence of an imperial economy in this way is not to claim that the British Empire was an illusion, nor to deny that British rule in India enriched the United Kingdom significantly at India's expense. We must accept, however, that in this instance colonial control, and post-colonial political and economic influence, were no guarantee of British export competitiveness. Thus, the Indo-British trade relationship in the twentieth century cannot be understood as primarily a mercantilist one or, if so, as remarkably ineffective. Over the last 100 years or so, one of the most consistent and pressing concerns that has faced the managers of the British economy has been how to counter the threat to national wealth and power caused by uncompetitive exports, and the low productivity of industrial labour and capital. Despite all the power, pomp and glory of the British raj, political control and influence in south Asia did little to provide a solution.

Notes on Contributors

Forest Capie, after a doctorate at the London School of Economics, taught at the Universities of Warwick and Leeds. He is currently Professor of Economic History in the Department of Banking and Finance at City University Business School. He has authored or co-authored or edited 16 books and over 100 articles on monetary, banking and trade topics. He is Editor of the *Economic History Review*.

P. N. Davies is Emeritus Professor of the Department of Economic and Social History at the University of Liverpool. He is the author of numerous books and articles on maritime affairs including (with Professor T. Chida) *The Japanese Shipping and Shipbuilding Industries: A History of their Modern Growth*, (Athlone Press, London and New Jersey, 1990). He is currently president of the International Maritime Economic History Association and Vice-president of the International Commission on Maritime History. At present he is completing a history of the British fruit trade and is working on the correspondence of Cornes and Company (London–Yokohama: 1864–1912).

Charles Feinstein is currently Chichele Professor of Economic History, University of Oxford and Fellow of All Souls College, Oxford. Publications include (with R. C. O. Matthews and J. C. Odling-Smee) *British Economic Growth, 1856–1973* (Oxford, 1982); *Studies in Capital Formation in the United Kingdom, 1750–1920* (Oxford, 1988); and *Banking, Currency and Finance in Europe between the Wars* (ed.) (Oxford, 1995).

Rory Miller is Senior Lecturer in the Economic History of Latin America at the University of Liverpool. He is the author of *Britain and Latin America in the Nineteenth and Twentieth Centuries* (Longman, 1993), and several articles on British business relations with Latin America. His current research focuses on the Latin American operations of British multinational companies since World War I.

Kenneth Morgan is Principal Lecturer in History at Brunel University College. He is the author of *An American Quaker in the British Isles: The Travel Journals of Jabez Maud Fisher, 1775–1779* (Oxford, 1992) and *Bristol and the Atlantic Trade in the Eighteenth Century* (Cambridge, 1993)

Sidney Pollard is Emeritus Professor of Economic History at the University of Bielefeld and Honorary Senior Fellow in the Department of History at the University of Sheffield. Recent publications include: *Typology of Industrialization Processes in the Nineteenth Century* (Chur/London: Harwood, 1990), *Wealth and Poverty:* An Economic History of the 20th Century (London: Harrap, 1990), (edited, and contributions), and with Karl Ditt (ed.), *Von der Heimarbeit in die Fabrik* (Schöning: Paderborn, 1992).

B. R. Tomlinson is Professor of Economic History in the Department of History, University of Strathclyde. He has published widely on the economic and political history of India and the British Empire, notably in *The Indian National Congress and the Raj, 1929–42* (1976), *The Political Economy of the Raj, 1914–47* (1979) and *The Economy of Modern India, 1860–1970*, in *New Cambridge History of India*, vol. III. 3 (1993).

Index

Printed and bound by CPI Group (UK) Ltd, Croydon, CR0 4YY

23/04/2025

14660945-0005